Gene Kassebaum

DELINQUENCY and SOCIAL POLICY

prentice-hall, inc.
englewood cliffs, new jersey

Library of Congress Cataloging in Publication Data

KASSEBAUM, GENE
Delinquency and social policy.

Bibliography: p.
1. Juvenile delinquency. 2. Corrections. 3. Social policy. I. Title.
HV9069.K36 364.36 73-22274
ISBN 0-13-197970-1
ISBN 0-13-197954-X (pbk.)

PRENTICE-HALL SERIES IN SOCIAL POLICY

Howard E. Freeman, Editor

10 9 8 7 6 5 4 3 2 1

Printed in the United States of America.

Prentice-Hall International, Inc., London
Prentice-Hall of Australia, Pty. Ltd., Sydney
Prentice-Hall of Canada, Ltd., Toronto
Prentice-Hall of India Private Limited, New Delhi
Prentice-Hall of Japan, Inc., Tokyo

CONTENTS

ACKNOWLEDGMENTS

I wish to express my appreciation to the authors and publishers whose works are quoted in this book. I have also profited from informal conversations with personnel and former inmates of delinquency control programs.

I am grateful (if that is the word) for a devastating review by Susan Chandler of an earlier draft of this manuscript, which helped in the revision. I also wish to thank series editor Howard E. Freeman and the two other reviewers, who provided me with numerous specific criticisms. The review of correctional program effectiveness has been influenced by my long friendship and sometime association with David A. Ward. I have been helped by and am grateful for the support services generously provided by the Social Science Research Institute of the University of Hawaii and, in particular, the assistance of Freda Hellinger, who supervised the typing of the manuscript. I was also helped in many ways, including the typing of other drafts and last minute changes, by Jesse Ohta, Janet Tanahara, and Phyllis Kawabata of the Department of Sociology, University of Hawaii. Meda Chesney-Lind, also of the University of Hawaii, was kind enough to locate some references urgently needed while I was far from my files and library. Since a book is a joint effort, it is usually not necessary for an author to thank the publisher for getting the book out. But my location in India (1973–74) imposed additional difficulties while the book was going to press, and I must mention with thanks the editorial help of Shirley Stone of Prentice-Hall during this period.

Gene Kassebaum
Professor of Sociology
University of Hawaii

Chapter 1

INTRODUCTION

In this short book I shall attempt a sociological approach to the phenomena of juvenile delinquency and the policies of control that confront it. The elements of this discussion may be forecast as follows:

1. It will be the view presented in this book that "juvenile delinquency" is too imprecise a term to convey clear meaning. It is a label for many different acts and conditions. Children commit offenses of many different types. Some of these are thefts and assaults, which, if an adult is convicted of doing them, are felonies or misdemeanors entailing criminal penalties. In other cases children are held to be in need of corrective intervention when their conduct or condition contravenes special rules for children, although such acts are not regarded as offenses for adults. Still other children are brought before the courts (and have even been adjudicated as delinquents) only because they have been victims of or in flight from guardians, families, or civic agencies.
2. Much of what is labeled delinquency is conduct that arises out of the conflict of children with older persons, when that conduct is subject to the labeling and sanctioning of social agencies charged with its suppression.
3. Delinquency cannot be understood apart from the social conflicts of which it is a part. The most relevant conflicts are those rising along the lines of generation, sex, race, and class. The patterning of delinquency rates is crucially connected to both the legal institutions and rules that mediate efforts at crime and delinquency control, as well as to the in-

formal, subterranean, or illegal practices of police, courts, and correction agencies in handling youth.

4. Delinquency and organized delinquency control are inextricably intertwined. Social policies not only develop in response to perceived delinquency, but delinquency develops in response to social policies. The effect of some policies has been the extension of legal protection to minors, and the effect of other policies has been the creation of categories of delinquency that did not previously exist. Juvenile delinquency cannot be understood apart from a consideration of the peculiar legal institutions that have been set up to deal with youth separately from the ordinary criminal justice processes for adults. The process by which an allegation is proven and the way in which an offending child is sanctioned or treated differs from adult criminal procedures chiefly in being more informal and offering to the accused fewer protections against abuse by authority.
5. Delinquency control programs typically embody contradictory mandates that inhibit the accomplishment of any particular objective. Current delinquency control programs are ineffective in reducing delinquency rates and are escalating the scope, scale, and cost of intergenerational conflict.
6. The remedies of delinquency can come from a more honest adjudication of this conflict, restoration of civil rights to young persons, and the promotion of the integration of young persons into the wider community. The reduction of delinquency requires the achievement of basic changes in the civil rights of children and youth and the winning of increased political and social power for minorities and communities with high crime and delinquency rates.

The appearance of one more book in a long list of publications on crime and delinquency needs some extended justification. This volume is intended to provide materials for a critical perspective on juvenile crime prevention and control programs. The emphasis is on programs: what thinking the program is based on, who is included, how it operates, and its measurable effects. In one sense—and in a special sense—problems addressed by this book are the problems of program and policy evaluation.

Social psychological research on crime has recently emerged from a century of nearly exclusive preoccupation with the study of the characteristics of the offender and has at last turned to a study of the agencies of law enforcement, criminal justice, and correction for a better understanding of the social phenomena we call crime and delinquency. The legacy of that long period of positivist research for some differentiating feature of the delinquent or the criminal that would reveal the cause of criminal behavior is still with us, despite the surprisingly meager results of a century of work. In all the years since Lombroso we have very few empirical studies that convincingly and clearly distinguish the offender from the nonoffender, and even these few studies admit of more than one interpretation. The clearest difference between criminal and noncriminal is that the criminal is a person who has been found to have violated the law and has been dealt with as such. In fact, the earlier that finding is officially made, and the longer the offender is involved with police, courts, and corrections, the more clearly a differentiated criminal or delinquent that person becomes. So it is understandable that sociological attention began to focus on the important and complex legal and social institutions that are assigned the work of defining, apprehending, and sanctioning delinquent and criminal conduct. That research began to pick up in the late 1950s, and accelerated through the '60s and '70s to the present.

The Evaluation of Social Control Programs

The shift from a concentration on the characteristics of the offender to a concentration on the processes by which persons come to be defined as offenders, and the manner in which they are dealt with after that determination, has greatly expanded the range of problems addressed by the sociologist. This range is now quite wide and includes what may be called evaluation of *crime reduction* programs, *crime control* programs, and *criminal justice* programs.

Crime reduction means the aim of decreasing the probability of a criminal law violation. Such efforts include reforms in the substantive criminal statutes themselves, removing what many think is inappropriate use of criminal sanctions to handle many questions involving morals, demeanor, or social and political policy. For example, in many jurisdictions we have already stopped cycling and recycling chronic drunks through the police station, jail, and municipal court; we have come some way toward changing the legal vulnerability of adult homosexuals; and in some states, Hawaii and New York for example, old laws making abortion criminal have been repealed. Here also is included removal of precipitating conditions of delinquent behavior, so far as these are known in the community (poverty and racial discrimination being two prime examples). And included here should be programs of reducing post-conviction offenses.

Crime control includes programs designed to increase the difficulty of committing a crime, the effort to increase the probability of detection and apprehension of the offender, and the employment of effective deterrents to crime. Technical devices to lock up or safeguard or trace property, and technical and administrative means of increasing the effectiveness of law enforcement will be discussed below. The question of the optimum allocation of the finite resources of law enforcement is receiving more rational review lately as studies of the problems of law enforcement accumulate.

Programs within criminal justice endeavor to improve the equity and accuracy of the administration of justice in juvenile and adult agencies. Equity is most sensitive to class, race, and sex differences and their relation to the manner in which an accused person is treated; accuracy is the extent to which any given procedure in justice distinguishes between the guilty and the innocent. Research on the exercise of legal discretion in invoking the law, the nature of police-community relations, recent studies of the functioning of the courts, particularly the juvenile courts, and a series of studies evaluating correctional programs and their effects on prisoners and parolees have greatly accelerated in the past decade.

Virtually all these areas are the object of research in the social sciences, some to a trivial extent at present and others to a major degree. Our concern will be to draw conclusions from some of this experience to anticipate difficulties that may arise in the research we are about to see in the next few years. Of particular interest is the question of what agencies do with the results once a study is completed.

When someone proposes an empirical evaluation, they should be asked what they expect the payoff to be from such an endeavor. How long a time before the study will produce data of use to the problem that actuates the evaluation? Can the problem be solved or programming guided by measurement of the variables chosen, or are there other questions, too sensitive to be safely pursued, which everyone knows lie beneath the surface? Are the criteria of evaluation germane to the problem? It may be rather useful to begin any conference about starting some evaluation research project in an agency by asking the following question: What would the agency staff do if handed the results of the study in an envelope right now? What would they be prepared to do after opening the envelope and reading the conclusions of the study? For example, are they prepared to use the results to affect programming? Are they hoping merely for results to use in arguing for more money from the legislature? But, for example, if a program is evaluated and no difference is found between the program and a control group, are they prepared to discontinue the program? Or is a program unlikely to be directly affected in any way; is it felt merely to be "useful" to get some data to advance basic understanding of an area? In this case, is an evaluation of program effects the most intelligent approach to the question?

Unless there is some specification of what decisions would be made about a program when the results of the evaluation are known, it may be an empty exercise.[1] A committee may take a vote on an issue, but it must specify rules for taking action after counting yeas and nays, or the matter will be as unsettled as before. This is a simple-minded idea and need not be stressed, except that it is amazing how many evaluations of programs have been undertaken without any clear-decision rule being adopted in the beginning, which may account for the fact that so few evaluations, after they have been done, have had immediate effects on the program.

Program evaluation proceeds, in more cases than not, from a combination of external funding for the project and a willingness for it to be studied (or inability to evade it) by the agency in question. In this case the agency may not be so closely involved with the project that it will commit itself to say what it would do in each of several possible outcomes of the study. The question then becomes what *will* happen once the data are in? What usually happens is that the results are published, often commercially, and are available to the field in general and to interested parties in political disputes in particular. It then becomes important to understand the political context of program evaluation if we are to anticipate to any degree what difference it will make just what is discovered about the program.

In the decade just past, major research was done on programs in juvenile and adult criminal justice and corrections. Correctional effectiveness studies investigated one variant or another of vocational or academic instruction or counseling, guided group interaction or other forms of client, peer, or group-centered discussions, and various forms of post-release supervision of ex-inmates. Many of these studies were done in prisons or youth correctional institutions, but some included probation,

[1]Thinking this out in the beginning leads to a consideration of what objectives are regarded as sufficiently important that some group in the government or community will be unhappy if they do not appear to be reached. In corrections, and in criminal justice agencies in general, the problem of selecting criteria—sensible criteria that is—for evaluation is bedeviled by the existence of several different and sometimes contradictory objectives that the community or the government hold for criminal justice and correction systems. Criminal justice agencies (police, courts, probation, prison, parole) are supposed to accomplish several different objectives:

a. to protect the community by detecting crime and delinquency, apprehending and confining law violators.

b. to impose punishment that expresses social indignation (makes person pay for his crime).

c. to deter people from violating the law by making them fear consequences.

d. to bring about rehabilitation of convicted offenders.

Sometimes interchangeable sanctions are provided that relate to different kinds of objectives (for example, where law provides for fine *or* jail). Rehabilitation in criminal justice is widely expected to accomplish the long-run aim of lowering the recidivism rate, but it has not really displaced the other aims, all of which are demanded by various groups in the public. Indeed, there are many who believe that we have overloaded our criminal justice and correctional systems with contradictory multiple responsibilities.

parole, or community halfway houses, and other forms of diversion from institutional controls and custody.[2]

The results do not support the expectations that programs conducted in reformatory settings produce reduced post-release parole violation or subsequent criminality. Most studies that used experimental designs found no difference between treatment and control groups; studies that were not experimental did not find program effects that stood up after statistically controlling for differences in parole risk in the samples. Some differences were found to reflect differential processing of misconduct of treatment and control subjects by agencies or personnel consciously or unconsciously anxious to vindicate a new program.

What was the impact of these negative results that accumulated through the 1960s? Did the host departments discontinue the programs found to be nonproductive of specific effects compared with other prisoners who were not exposed to them? The answer is interesting. The agencies did not discontinue the programs for the most part but interpreted the results in such a way as to argue for more funds for program expansion; or they rejected the results outright. But other interested parties found these results of some use in developing arguments for reallocating resources or in pressing the suit of a client seeking release from "treatment." One state has made a massive effort to close all its youth reformatories; legislatures of other states and attorneys for youthful plaintiffs are pressing for an end to long indeterminate sentences for purposes of "rehabilitation" when in fact so little rehabilitation is in evidence.[3] Even Presidential fact-finding commissions serve a role in this indirect sense. It is well known and has often been commented upon in both moods of despair and fury by unsatisfied critics that commissions may be merely devices of various national and local governments to respond to calls for action by creating safe blue ribbon panels who merely document the obvious and buy time in crisis. In fact however, some of the better and certainly more complete data that exist have been produced by these commissions. The Kerner Commission, The Violence Commission, and The New York State Commission on Attica were, for the period of their existence, in command of far larger staffs, more political clout, and had greater access to agency files, witnesses, and other information than any academic research project. Their immediate sponsors do not necessarily

[2]For one such study, and a review of other research on correctional program evaluation, see Gene Kassebaum, David A. Ward, and Daniel M. Wilner, *Prison Treatment and Parole Survival: An Empirical Assessment* (New York: John Wiley & Sons, 1971).

[3]James Robeson with Carol Sanders & Suellen Stalder, *The California Prison Parole & Probation System*, Technical Supplement No. 3, A Special Report to the Assembly Ways & Means Committee: Subcommittee on Criminal Justice (Sacramento, California, December 1968). See also James Robeson and Gerald Smith, "The Effectiveness of Correctional Programs," *Crime and Delinquency* 17:1 (January 1971).

carry out the commission recommendations, and the commissions themselves may have no power to enact, but the information they uncover is drawn upon in subsequent skirmishes and litigation and may contribute to change after the commission has disbanded and faded.

The point is that change in programming does not necessarily come from on top or from within the agency. There are a number of interested parties in the prevailing national dialogue over crime and corrections, law and order, civil rights, justice and injustice. Putting data and conclusions into public print may be among the more useful things the sociologist can do.

Program evaluation will be called for by various clients with various programs they wish to put forward. As the politization of law enforcement, court, and correctional problems continues, program evaluation studies will increasingly, one may surmise, differentiate into two types: a rather tightly trimmed operation research carried out in many cases by the agency itself, which takes the agency's objectives as given and asks how close the program comes to reaching them; and a second type of evaluation that will be supported from outside and will possibly take the agency's goals themselves as problematic. Such studies will likely focus on the side effects of the program, will seek to establish latent functions of programs, and will be sensitive to political questions of equity as much as with effectiveness. Indeed, the evaluation of criminal justice programs, and the analysis of equity or inequity of the implementation of the law, may assume as much importance, for a variety of clients, as the correctional effectiveness research of the 1960s. Whatever the type, the political contexts in which the results will be interpreted will continue to exert a major influence on whether evaluation results lead to program change. This book is directed to the persons in law enforcement, criminal justice, juvenile court, education, or welfare, as well as to the citizen at large or the prisoner within, who have the interest and energy —and courage—for this demanding critical dialogue.

Chapter **2**

CHILDHOOD'S CRIMES

> On entering the first yard, we were shewn 49 reputed thieves, under 16 years of age.
>
> . . . casting my eye from countenance to countenance, as they turned themselves round to examine their visitors from their elevated situation on the Treadmill, I could not select one from amongst them who had the appearance of being a novice. . . .
>
> They were all upon the Treadmill, the power of which is applied to no useful purpose. . . .
>
> Just as I was leaving the yard, a boy was brought to the gate, six years of age. He was dressed from head to foot in a new prison suit, and as he was endeavouring fruitlessly to roll up his trousers, which were much too long for him, he joined in the mirth which his appearance occasioned. . . . (Edward P. Brenton, [*Report of the*] *Society for the Supression of Juvenile Vagrancy* (c. 1832), in Sanders, 1970, p. 139)

2.1 Introduction

This book is concerned with how youths come to be defined as delinquent, with the manner in which laws and the official agencies of local government deal with batches of young people defined as delinquent, and with what effect. In the statistics on these dealings and their consequences, the voices of the actors themselves will be blurred into a collective chorus. The research quoted will concentrate on their delinquent behavior, their roles as accused, as probationer, prisoner, parolee. Their "record" will be cited. It will be easy to lose sight of the ordinary aspects of their lives as children, as youth, as kids.

In a sense this disparity between the labeled delinquent and the ordinary kid marks the focus of much of the book: on the manner in which distinctions between law abiding and unlawful are made, and the consequences of those distinctions for the kids and for the community and society in which they live. At the outset it will be useful to get a perspective on the social process by which juveniles are arrested, adjudicated, supervised, and instructed.

A description of the varieties of delinquent behavior or rule-violating behavior is impossible to assemble from even a detailed enumeration of official rates such as crimes known to the police, arrests on various charges, or convictions or juvenile court dispositions. One reason is that discretion in informal handling by many police contacts, bargaining about the charge in connection with pleas of guilt, and the exercise of judgement by the police and the court, make it impossible to reconstruct actual behavior from official decisions made, even fairly, by social control agencies. The basic data do not exist. The fact is that the social character of delinquent acts has not been taken sufficiently seriously by social scientists who study crime and delinquency. There are gaps in even simple information about criminal offense behavior because all the components of the social act have not been described.

An offense requires two roles to be enacted; one is the offender whose behavior is regarded by a second, an enforcer, as in violation of the law. In the more serious breaches of the criminal law a third role is involved, that of a victim. The victim may be an individual person or group of persons or it may be a corporate entity. If the crime is one involving the invasion or damage of premises, or the stealing of property or valuables, usually some persons or group can be identified—the owners, the management, the public authorities—as the victim. Of course an important and exceedingly large set of offenses have no victim that can be specified.

Each of the roles—the offender, the enforcer and the victim—can be thought of as oriented to each of the other roles, and to involve as well a self-conception or set of values or conceptions regarding that role held by the incumbent. We can be said to have an adequate description of a criminal incident when we have described the way in which the three roles are played. The gross possibilities that should be taken into account may be expressed in a schematic such as in the paradigm below.

Not many studies answer all the questions posed by the paradigm. The best community studies produce an understanding of the interaction among the roles of offender, victim, and enforcer because the scene of

TABLE 2.1

Actor Orientations to Other in Delinquent or Criminal Offenses

		Role as Object		
		Offender	*Victim*	*Enforcer*
	Offender	self-concept perceived opportunities commitment to values and groups	contact with victim perception of victim interaction with victim or with group of which victim is member	view of enforcer as legitimate crooked, ineffective, likely to intervene, etc. Prior experience with suspended sentence, previous commitments, assessment of cost of conviction
Role as Actor	*Victim*	knowledge or acquaintance with offender interaction with offender	definition of incident as crime	view of law enforcement as effective, helpful, approachable; decision to invoke authorities
	Enforcer	policy toward categories of possible offenders information about tactics toward particular accused person police version of offender	value of victim as complainant or witness view of public expectation re: law enforcement police version of offense	view of job; role conception; group support in agency; assessment of political implications; resources at disposal; training

action is under observation, rather than one or another of the roles. (For example, Suttles, 1968.) Frequently, however, the community study is not explicitly concerned with the tabulation, recording, and measurement of delinquent acts, patterns of acts, consistencies within individuals or groups, patterns of law enforcement, victim behavior, and so on. Hence the community study gives broad categories within which observation would be possible but seldom gives precise descriptions of the volume and patterning of delinquent or criminal offenses.

The probability that a violation will take place, that it will be defined by the victim as a crime and will be designated by law enforcement as a delinquent or criminal act, and that some person will be arrested, charged, and convicted and that the accused will be sanctioned, are questions answerable to the extent that the orientations and conduct of the incumbents of the roles of offender, victim, and enforcer are described and understood. A complete description of an act of forcible rape, or car theft, or assault, would entail information stipulated in Table 2.1. Only where the probability of a given action or perception is very high can the possibilities be reduced to an assumption that such an event will always be seen as a delinquency, or that an incident will routinely be reported as a crime, and so on. The circumstances surrounding offenses, and the contingencies affecting the likelihood that it will be labeled an offense of a given type simply have not been sufficiently well studied to date, and for most major offense patterns there are serious gaps in our knowledge. Sociologists attempt to overcome this by having recourse to official records, to anecdotes, or to occasional observation of persons cast in the role of offender or probable offender. But the study reasonably begins with a consideration of the rules defining misconduct.

2.2 Offense Codes for Minors

So broad are the powers of the public agencies with respect to youth, so limited are the legal rights of children, and so diffuse are the specific laws dealing with juvenile dependency, delinquency, and youth crimes, that it is impossible to set forth the statutes defining offenses of youth in any simple list. It is fundamental to Western criminal doctrine that adult citizens should be subject to criminal sanctions *only* for behavior. The law holds that the behavior must be specifically proscribed prior to a specific prosecution, and that the definition of offenses, accusation, and punishment of offenders is to be strictly limited to certain legitimately denoted agencies and no others. It further provides many procedural standards that constrain the accusatorial and coercive power of the State and safeguards the civil rights of the accused and the convicted. By comparison, the theory and practice of the law in regard to youth is a good deal less orderly. Many children are subjected to police and court attention because of a suspected violation of a statute defining an act that also would be a misdemeanor or felony if committed by an adult. But a larger number of children are before the court because of laws couched in language far more diffuse than would be tolerated in adult criminal procedure. Indeed, the definition of juvenile delinquency is not limited to statute offenses, it merely *starts* there. Delinquency goes on to include a myriad of other actions, conditions, and statutes. Elements of present or past definitions of delinquency include:

Violation of any law or ordinance
Immoral or indecent conduct
Immoral conduct around school
Engages in illegal occupation
(Knowingly) associates with vicious or immoral persons
Grows up in idleness or crime

(Knowingly) enters, visits house of ill repute
Patronizes, visits policy shop or gaming place
Patronizes saloon or dram house where intoxicating liquor is sold
Patronizes public poolroom or bucket shops
Wanders in streets at night, not on lawful business (curfew)
(Habitually) wanders about railroad yards or tracks
Jumps train or enters car or engine without authority
Habitually truant from school
Incorrigible
(Habitually) uses vile, obscene, or vulgar language (in public place)
Absents self from home without consent
Loiters, sleeps in alleys
Refuses to obey parent, guardian
Uses intoxicating liquors
Is found in place for permitting which adult may be punished
Reports self so as to injure self or others
Smokes cigarettes (around public place)
In occupation or situation dangerous to self or others
Begs or receives alms (or in street for purpose of)
(Rubin, reprinted in Teele, 1970, p. 5)

For example, the state of California has the following omnibus provisions in its statutes.

600. Any person under the age of 21 years who comes within any of the following descriptions is within the jurisdiction of the juvenile court which may adjudge the person to be a dependent child of the court:

a. Who is in need of proper and effective parental care or control and has no parent or guardian, or has no parent or guardian willing to exercise or capable of exercising such care or control, or has no parent actually exercising such care or control.

b. Who is destitute, or who is not provided with the necessities of life, or who is not provided with a home or suitable place of abode, or whose home is an unfit place for him by reason of neglect, cruelty, or depravity of either of his parents, or of his parents, or of his guardian or other person in whose custody or care he is.

c. Who is physically dangerous to the public because of a mental or physical deficiency, disorder or abnormality.

601. Any person under the age of 21 years who persistently or habitually refuses to obey the reasonable and proper orders or directions of his parents, guardian, custodian or school authorities, or who is beyond the control of such person, or any person who is a habitual truant from school within the meaning of any law of this State, or who from any cause is in danger of leading an idle, dissolute, lewd, or immoral life, is within the jurisdiction of the juvenile court which may adjudge such person to be a ward of the court.

602. Any person under the age of 21 who violates any law of this State or of the United States or any ordinance of any city or county of this State defining crime or who, after having been found by the juvenile court to

> be a person described by Section 601, fails to obey the lawful order of the juvenile court, which may adjudge such person to be a ward of the court.

The problem of reaching a general description of childhood crimes by aggregating the standards of separate criminal justice agencies across the country is further complicated by variation from district to district. The age criteria of childhood vary, and may differ for males and females. The types of cases over which courts have jurisdiction may likewise vary in state law. The large number of different community agencies, public and private, other than juvenile court, which may adjust or refer cases, makes difficult the precise determination of how children may be designated as "troublesome." Since the juvenile court supplies social services (such as child placement) in addition to punishment for crime (in fact if not in theory), it is necessary to disentangle these functions. This is not always easy because of the inclination toward euphemisms in juvenile court records. Also, community conventions about youth behavior vary greatly, and the unofficial and illegal kinds of regulation and harassment to which youth may be subject by agencies will thereby vary from place to place.

Despite this variation, the juvenile courts are of paramount importance. It is on the mandates of the courts and the records that we must focus to grasp the legal basis of delinquency. The reach of these courts extends to and includes childhood delinquency, neglect, and dependency. These terms may be defined as follows:

> *Delinquency* comprises cases of children alleged to have committed an offense that if committed by an adult would be a crime. It also comprises cases of children alledged to have violated specific ordinances or regulatory laws that apply only to children, such as curfew regulations, school attendance laws, restrictions on use of alcohol and tobacco; and children variously designated as being beyond control, ungovernable, incorrigible, runaway, or in need of supervision . . . according to national juvenile court statistics, the latter two groups account for over 25 percent of the total number of delinquent children appearing before children's courts and between 25 and 30 percent of the population of State institutions for delinquent children. (President's Commission: Task Force Report on Juvenile Delinquency and Youth Crime, 1967, p. 4)

The distinction between neglect and dependency seems to pivot on whether the child's condition, services, or supervision are provided by a present guardian or parent, even though inadequate in the eyes of the court (neglect), or whether there is a complete or virtual absence of parent or guardian (dependence). Even this distinction is a matter of judgement, and until very recent times many courts applied terms such as "dependent" to include family conditions felt to be deficient by the court even though a parent was present, particularly if the parent repudiated the child.

The President's Commission on Law Enforcement and the Administration of Justice recommends that "dependency should be eliminated from the jurisdiction of the juvenile court" (President's Commission: Juvenile Delinquency and Youth Crime, 1967, p. 27). The Commission goes on to caution that even for neglect cases, the court staff's opinions about children should not be imposed on a family willy-nilly. Some juvenile court laws provide a sponge term that asserts the State's claim to intervene but to stop short of alleging crime or delinquency. A "Person In Need of Supervision" is defined in the following very broad terms:

> Those otherwise in need of supervision include (a) any minor under 18 years of age who is beyond the control of his parents, guardian or other custodian; and (b) any minor subject to compulsory school attendance who is habitually truant from school.
>
> The New York Family Court Act (1963) calls a non-criminal misbehavior a "person in need of supervision" (PINS):
>
> > (a) "Juvenile delinquent" means a person over 7 and less than 16 years of age who does any act which, if done by an adult, would constitute a crime.
> >
> > (b) "Person in need of supervision" means a male less than 16 years of age and a female less than 18 years of age who is an habitual truant or who is incorrigible, ungovernable or habitually disobedient and beyond the lawful control of parent or other lawful authority.
>
> The category of "neglected minor" includes, besides the usual case of parental inattention or abandonment, "any minor under 18 years of age . . . (b) whose environment is injurious to his welfare or whose behavior is injurious to his own welfare or that of others." (President's Commission: Juvenile Delinquency and Youth Crime, 1967, p. 26)

In an effort to extend the flexibility of juvenile court proceedings to youthful offenders about the age of juvenile court jurisdictions, certain laws have come into use. The President's Commission comments:

> (e) Wayward Minor Proceedings—Wayward minor procedures seek to extend definitions of misbehavior, disobedience, incorrigibility from juveniles to older minors, usually 16 to 21. The condition of waywardness is more a legal status attached to the individual than an offense. It is sometimes termed a civil offense. The conduct subject to complaint generally includes truancy; habitual running away from home; failure to obey lawful commands of parents or guardians; habitual association with thieves, pimps, procurers, dissolute persons; being found in a house of prostitution, or deporting oneself as to willfully injure or endanger personal morals or health; being morally depraved or in danger of becoming so.
>
> In some jurisdictions, such as New York, the wayward minor is tried in adult court but given special correctional treatment including preadjudication investigation, not necessarily with a requirement of his consent (as parents are usually the complainants). In Michigan wayward minor petitions limited to ages 17 to 19 are generally heard in juvenile court. The New York Wayward Minor Act of 1923, limited to magistrates courts,

> applies to youths 16 to 21 whose conduct may lead to crime. Some persons so adjudicated are committable to the State department of correction reception center. Wayward minor proceedings may be substituted for criminal (misdemeanor or less) charges for youths who have no prior record and who do not deny the criminal charge, but this is a practice sanctioned by the courts as a means of avoiding full criminal treatment, not a legislative provision. (President's Commission: Juvenile Delinquency and Youth Crime, 1967, p. 123)

The avowed intention of the category of wayward minor is stated to be the avoidance of long-term stigma resulting from early conviction for felony. As such it somewhat resembles the argument for juvenile courts 80 years ago. But it is a two-edged blade, because it can result in liabilities for the youth without corresponding defenses.

Although in many cases the juvenile offense is a close analogy of adult misdemeanor or felony, often the criteria for admissible evidence or for judging whether an offense took place are distinctive of the informality of the juvenile court and the severely limited civil rights of the child. Until recently, for instance, the minor's security against self-incrimination and his right to counsel were not recognized in juvenile court. In addition to procedural differences, data not related to a question of the specific charge are often as important as or even more important than the establishment of the guilt or innocence of the child.

The proliferation of regulations, and the diffuse power of the court to intervene in youthful conduct, has created a number of noncriminal offenses, for the correction of which the youth can be found to be a "person in need of supervision," or otherwise dealt with through the sentencing and supervisory powers of the court. Curiously, the law is as severe or even somewhat more severe on the noncriminal offenders, as shown in a survey reported by Paul Lerman. Table 2.2 shows disposition of juvenile cases at three stages of processing in 1965.

Once in detention, many children have difficulty getting out, since release depends in part on the availability and receptivity of a home to which to be released. Since "juvenile status" offenses frequently arise out of a conflict between child and family, these children may have greater problems in securing release and spend longer terms in detention than children charged with felony and misdemeanor type offenses. Lerman did a study of Manhattan in 1963, noting the range and average length of sentence of boys incarcerated. In comparing delinquent with male PINS (Persons in Need of Supervision, the noncriminal designation in New York) he reports:

> The range of institutional stay was two to 28 months for delinquents and four to 48 months for PINS boys; the median was nine months for delinquents and 13 months for PINS; and the average length of stay was 10.7

TABLE 2.2

Disposition of Juvenile Cases at Three Stages in the Judicial Process—19 of the 30 Largest Cities, 1965.

	Part I (Most Serious Adult Offenses)	Part II (All Other Adult Offenses)	Juvenile Status Offenses
% Court Petition after complaint	57% N=(37,420)	33% (52,862)	42% (33,046)
% Convicted — if brought into court	92% N=(21,386)	90% (17,319)	94% (13,857)
% Placed or Committed— if convicted	23% N=(19,667)	18% (15,524)	26% (12,989)

Source: Lerman, 1971, p. 38.

months for delinquents and 16.3 months for PINS. Regardless of the mode of measurement, it is apparent that institutionalization was proportionately longer for boys convicted and sentenced for juvenile status offenses than for juveniles convicted for criminal-type offenses.

These results on length of stay do not include the detention period, the stage of correctional processing prior to placement in an institution. Analyses of recent detention figures for all five boroughs of New York City revealed the following patterns: (1) PINS boys and girls are more likely to be detained than are delinquents (54 to 31 percent): and (2) once PINS youth are detained they are twice as likely to be detained for more than 30 days than are regular delinquents (50 to 25 percent). It is apparent that juvenile status offenders who receive the special label "persons in need of supervision" tend to receive more time in custodial facilities at all stages of their correctional experience than do delinquents. (Lerman, 1971, pp. 38–39)

At least one ruling has called into question the practice of authorizing PINS petition for males only up to age 16, but authorizing them for females up to age 18. Judge Pilato in Rochester, New York, heard a case involving a PINS petition filed by the mother of a girl accused of having left home at age 17 to live with a man. Her defense counsel (court appointed) claimed sex discrimination. The judge ruled in favor, stating:

> The specialized handling of 16 and 17 year old females from their male counterparts in truancy and disobedience cases . . . is not based on any established unique characteristics of 16 and 17 year old females. (*National Newsletter*, Children's Division, American Humane Association, Vol. 1, No. 5 (February-March 1972): p. 4)

The effect of decades of development of a court system and law enforcement agencies with broad discretionary powers has been the proliferation of definitions of offenses only minors may commit.

Even within the category of conduct that corresponds to statutorily defined misdemeanors and felonies for adults, the great latitude of the court for imposing sanctions alters the practical meaning of acts such as vandalism, simple assault or petty theft, any of which might and do result in a minor being committed to a youth correctional institution from his teens to age 21; an adult, if convicted of similar acts, could be merely fined or placed in jail up to 30 days. It is thus very important to distinguish among several kinds of activities of the juvenile court.

The most commonly observed legal distinctions seek to separate the clearer criminal offenses from either conduct in violation of special standards for children, or states of neglect or dependency. The former are termed juvenile delinquents (a minor who has been convicted of an act that would be a crime if done by an adult); the latter termed persons in need of supervision, or officially regarded as "beyond the control of parents" or guardians, or habitually truant, and so on.

Sometimes the state has proceeded against a minor in adult criminal court by waiving the jurisdiction of the juvenile court. Since the case of Kent v. the United States however, it has been established that waiver itself requires a hearing in which the juvenile is represented by an attorney to determine if waiver abridges his rights.

2.3 The Offenses of Youth: Rationales for the Intervention of the Juvenile Court

Juvenile justice operates partly within the regular criminal justice and law enforcement agencies, and partly outside of it, as a differentiated system. The police deal directly with children, as they do with adults. Some children are detained in jails. Some so-called youthful offenders are adjudicated in the criminal courts and punished in the corrections departments. The juvenile court, as we have seen, developed out of the criminal justice system to become a separate agency. In its wake developed a separate juvenile correction and parole agency pattern.

The overall range of criminal law enforcement and justice consists of the police activities of detection of crime and identification of perpetrator, taking suspect into custody (arrest), charging, determination of guilt or innocence, sentencing, post-sentence punishment, custody, treatment, and post-release parole control, and where it occurs, revocation of parole to return the parolee to custody. The system is theoretically and formally an adversary process. The most important procedures underscore the legitimacy of a defense by the accused and explicitly call for a contest between prosecution and defense, in front of a third party (judge, jury) whose decision is supposed to be impartial. But the system, in many ways, does not operate as adversary proceeding. The great bulk of the work is done because of the waiver of certain rights by the accused, the submission of pleas of guilt, and the negotiation of charges and recommendations for punishment in consideration for certain conveniences rendered to the prosecution by the accused. The police or the court may decide, formally or informally (or even secretly), not to proceed against an accused, or to proceed less severely, or to proceed to the fullest extent provided by law, or even to exceed the limits provided by law. (Allen, 1965; Bayley and Mendelsohn, 1969; La Fave, 1965; Newman, 1966; Packer, 1968; Remington *et al.*, 1969; Skolnick, 1966.)

The police operate in terms of public mandate and pressures, their own occupational-professional conception of the job, and certain covert influences from other levels of government, or from improper sources, such as bribery or collusion with criminal activities.

The actual implementation of the criminal law by police is influenced by a number of factors: the allocation of available police resources among a variety of activities, including criminal law enforcement, peace keeping, traffic, surveillance for noncriminal purposes, and other work the police are called upon to carry out; the perceived seriousness of a particular offense; the status, reputation, and behavior of the victim; the status, reputation and demeanor of the suspect; pressure from citizen groups; police perception of the potential for solution in any given case, and their concern (or lack of it) with negative impact of a given policy of law enforcement in a particular instance. There is no consistent policy governing the actions of law enforcement agencies in different areas toward juvenile or adult offenders or citizens as a whole. Behavior that in one police jurisdiction might be the cause of a booking and petition will in another jurisdiction be more commonly dealt with in an entirely informal fashion. In general it seems warranted to state that where the status of the accused is debased, the volume of police contacts is high but actual law enforcement may be selective. Statistics show a high rate of contacts subsequently unfounded (or charges dropped) among minorities (blacks, Puerto Ricans, Chicanos).

2.4 Juvenile Delinquency as an Indication of Community Conflict

The law itself, and the work organization of law enforcement, combine in defining conduct as delinquent. There is another source, prior to and sustaining the law and the agencies of control. This third force is the result of diverse conflicts in the community life conditions in which delinquent conduct takes place. The inner-city ghetto and the delinquent gang have been studied in efforts to understand this force in delinquency.

Bernard Cohen (1969), in research on juvenile delinquency in Philadelphia, distinguishes between the gang (as a large highly developed aggregate with elaborate terminology of member-positions, usually a gang name, and a local territory) and the delinquent group (a small clique who come together from time to time, having little or no structure, no name, no territory as a group). The shaping influence of the gang is clearly demonstrated in Cohen's data. Gang and nongang offense seriousness is approximately the same up through age 14 and begins to diverge from then on, as mutually assaultive gang activities begin to draw police charges. There are no discernible differences in age at first arrest between gang and nongang members. Gangs were scored higher on offense activity than groups (Cohen, 1969, p. 79); more often used weapons, had younger victims, were almost entirely intra-racial in conflict, and were understood as part of what Cohen calls "internecine subculture of violence." Internecine subculture is described as a set of meanings in which youth of roughly comparable age, sex, and class background are potential aggressors and potential victims, two roles in which players can and must alternate.

> The social structure of the internecine subculture consists then of at least two primary roles: offenders and victims. Actual role participation or selectivity of which members of the subculture will assume the role of offender or victim depends upon the particular exigencies that arise, always however offenders are potential victims and victims potential offenders. (Cohen, 1969, p. 103)

The gang is seen as oriented to territory claims and defense of territory in the urban ghetto where private living space is highly contested and insecure and where public space is under patrol by police and welfare workers. This in turn is related to the ecological and social segregation of lower-class black youth by white-controlled society. Hence aggregate statistics of delinquent behavior in this type of situation is a reflection of an overall ecological pattern, a pattern in which youths are both victim and offender.

The President's Commission on Crime amassed descriptions of slum life that are consistent with Cohen's interpretation.

> What the inner-city child calls home is often a set of rooms shared by a shifting group of relatives and acquaintances—furniture shabby and sparse, many children in one bed, plumbing failing, plaster falling, roaches in the corners and sometimes rats, hallways dark or dimly lighted, stairways littered, air dank and foul. Inadequate, unsanitary facilities complicate keeping clean. Disrepair discourages neatness. Insufficient heating, multiple use of bathrooms and kitchens, crowded sleeping arrangements spread and

> multiply respiratory infections and communicable diseases. Rickety, shadowy stairways and bad electrical connections take their accidental toll. Rat bites are not infrequent and sometimes, especially for infants, fatal. Care of one's own and respect for others' possessions can hardly be inculcated in such surroundings. More important, home has little holding power for the child—it is not physically pleasant or attractive; it is not a place to bring his friends; it is not even very much the reassuring gathering place of his own family. The loss of parental control and diminishing adult supervision that occur so early in the slum child's life must thus be laid at least partly at the door of his home. (President's Commission: Juvenile Delinquency and Youth Crime, 1967, p. 45)

Few studies utilize direct observation of the behavior of youth to determine the variety and amount of unlawful conduct characteristic of such persons. One such study by Short and Strodtbeck reports observations made of 598 members of 16 delinquent boys' gangs in Chicago. The observations were made by Youth Board workers attached to the gangs or the area in which the gangs were living. Such workers were known to be in close touch with these gangs, and much of the behavior rated occurred in public or accessible settings, or could be directly inferred from other contacts.

The youth workers were provided a list of 69 categories, and were asked to indicate whether each boy had "engaged in a particular type of behavior only a few times or many times" (Short and Strodtbeck, 1965, p. 81). (Or, as is apparent later, if he never engaged in such behavior.) These 69 items were then collapsed into a shorter list of 37 items "on the basis of similarity of item content." These latter items were then statistically analyzed to determine patterns of association among them. Correlations among the 37 measures varied in magnitude but were nearly all positive; that is to say, some items were very likely to be indulged in by the same boys, and other items were relatively independent of one another. These correlations were searched for patterns larger than pairwise associations by the technique of factor analysis. Five underlying factors were isolated. Each factor may be thought of as a basis of several of the items hanging together, suggesting that the separate items may be several measures of something more general that underlies them.

The first factor seems to measure *conflict.* Items associated along this factor were "individual fighting," "group fighting," "concealed weapons," and "assault." The second factor is located by such items as "sports," social activities, gambling, joy riding, suggesting group social activities, or as Short and Strodtbeck label it, *stable corner activities.* A third factor seems to be a measure of recreation and sexual experience, "sexual intercourse," "statutory rape" (ie., nonforcible sex relations with girl under 16 years), "petting." The fourth factor was associated with breaking away from gang activities in such ways as fathering an illegitimate child, common law marriage, homosexuality. The fifth factor extracted includes correlations with auto theft, driving without a license, public nuisance, use of alcohol, and running away from home. Such actions loosely indicating assumption of a nongang adult style Short and Strodtbeck call *authority protest.* (Discussion of the factors is found in Short and Strodtbeck, 1965, pp. 89–92; see also the secondary analysis of these data by Nutch and Bloombaum, 1968.)

It is clear that much of the focus of activity of gangs has nothing specifically to do with criminal statutes or with offenses that would be criminal if done by adults. In considering official data on delinquency, this underlying conflict must be kept in mind.

2.5 How Are Persons Labeled Delinquent?

Given the broad mandates, diffuse and vaguely defined laws, and informal procedures that characterize the juvenile justice agencies, it is hard to obtain the data on precisely what it is that children do to get them into the status of "juvenile delinquent." The records are difficult to interpret. The very language of the agencies is at times euphemistic, at other times starkly accusatory. A 14-year-old girl, whose coital precosity brings her to police or welfare attention, may be variously classified by the juvenile court as "immoral," a "person in need of supervision" (PINS), or as a "dependent ward of the court" or as having been in "an unfit home." Only a close reading of the girl's file would reveal the allegation of sexual impropriety that is at the basis of the court's displeasure. On the other hand, a child may be listed as committing larceny when in fact he is accused of stealing a comic book from a newsstand. Summary tabulations of statistics obscure the behavioral details.

There is growing awareness that the development of formal bureaucratic agencies to deal with social nonconformity is closely related to the production of official statistics that are difficult to relate back to a "real" world of a common experience. How many crimes "really" occur, how many children are "really" delinquent, are questions that can be precisely answered only if the concepts and the indicators of these words are clear. Yet in the human transactions that underlie them, these are often essentially problematic. Even if all persons involved would agree that in a given instance an offense took place, the operating characteristics of the agency itself necessitate reduction of a myriad of details to accounting categories. A recent monograph on Criminal Statistics comments:

> Little is known about the type and nature of information on offenders that influence the decisions made about them by police, courts, probation officers, and others. Little is placed on record, and the detailed records (case

> histories) often contain conflicting information. In few case papers is it possible to find out what the basis is for the information recorded. Much of it may be hearsay evidence, and no record is made of who may have said what and to whom. Yet many important decisions are made about offenders on the basis of such data. Obtaining better statistical data, therefore, is not merely a matter of extracting more information from the case histories or personal files, tabulating it, and publishing it. (NIMH, Criminal Statistics, p. 7)

An agency must define events as falling inside or outside its jurisdiction. Such a classification may or may not accord with popular usage, or even the viewpoints of those directly involved in the event. The criminal law itself provides, in theory at least, an adversary model. It is recognized that in both trial and appeals courts the basic questions must be disputed, but for record-keeping purposes investigators behave as though the categories were not in doubt. The record kept by the agencies obscures the negotiated nature of the decisions leading to the ultimate classification; it obscures differences in law enforcement policy, in quality of defense, in plea bargaining, and in popular readiness or reluctance to define and report to police events as criminal victimization. Surveys of samples of the general population reveal that the rate of citizen-recalled criminal victimization is much greater than would be deduced from the level of crimes known to police. Many events are recalled as crimes by the victim but were not reported by them to the police when they occurred. Some that were reported were not felt by the police to have been crimes. Using the victim survey data, one out of five households in the United States was victimized by crime or delinquency in the course of a year; this is nearly double the rate of crimes known to police (Hood and Sparks, 1970, pp. 23–37). This does not include victimless crimes, such as drug use, alcoholism, gambling, prostitution and certain prohibited sexual behavior, and cannot include offenses in which the respondent has been victimized but does not realize it. Some offenses are routinely handled in ways that do not provide input to official records. Private detective and security services, for example, may not report every case of apprehended shoplifting to the police.

Conversely, there are persons who suffer some effects of preventive, investigative, or regulatory treatment from law enforcement agencies without having actually victimized anyone. A large proportion of youth offenders are informally warned, counseled and released, put under surveillance, scolded, threatened or harassed by the police, all without a written record. Of the remainder, a large number of children are informally adjudicated by the court without a petition. Thus, official police and juvenile court data are gross underestimates of the volume and nature of offenses. Of the two sources, data on police contacts, and offenses known to the police, are more complete than the court data, but conventional categorization introduces serious problems in the police data.

The Standard Classification of Offenses, used since 1930 by law enforcement agencies that contribute to the Uniform Crime Reports, divide certain recorded offenses into 26 categories and records and counts offenses by rules peculiar to this classification scheme. Sellin and Wolfgang comment:

> . . . the use of the (Standard Classification of Offenses), based on legal labels, suppresses all but the most serious crime, when the incident comprises two or more separate offenses, and thus understates reality. By grouping together all offenses carrying the same legal labels, without taking into account differences between them, the classification makes it impossible to observe possible qualitative changes in any given class of criminality over time. By not segregating attempted from completed crimes, the actual tangible physical harm to persons or property cannot be measured. The hierarchy of crimes in the classification does not guarantee that all offenses of a given class are necessarily more injurious than some of those placed in a lower class. Finally, whether a criminal homicide or a motor vehicle theft, for example, is counted, each is given the same weight of one. (Sellin and Wolfgang, 1969, p. 3)

So poorly do present official records work even for the establishment that the President's Commission on Law Enforcement and the Administration of Justice was unable, after an 18-month study, to say whether the national crime rate *in fact* was increasing.

Other more specific criticisms of the Uniform Crime Reports are that the definitions of crimes themselves are misleading. Auto theft is listed as a major offense, yet nearly 9 out of 10 cars so listed are returned to their owners. The use of $50 as the cutting point for grand larceny is grossly out of line with the value of U.S. currency in the present period and inflates the apparent number of serious thefts.

2.6 How Many Children Are Labeled Delinquent?

The most extensive data on delinquency are available from a national survey of Juvenile Courts of the United States. The best overall data on dependency and neglect are taken from 1,648 courts directly reporting such cases. (Juvenile Court Statistics, 1971)

Somewhat more than 1,100,000 delinquency cases (not counting traffic cases) were adjudicated by the juvenile courts in 1971, or about 3.1 percent of all children age 10 through 17 in the U. S. (HEW's definition of delinquency includes criminal law violation, municipal ordinance violation, and conduct proscribed by laws applied only to children).

These data show the preponderance of males over females, and the great proportion of cases disposed of by court without a formal petition. In 1971, 845,500 boys' and 279,500 girls' cases of delinquency were disposed of officially by juvenile courts in the United States. Of these 58 percent were processed or informally "adjusted" without a petition formally invoking the court's jurisdiction.

These data show an increase of all types of delinquency cases in the courts in recent years. In 1940 the juvenile courts in the United States handled approximately 200,000 cases. The increase over succeeding years exceeds the growth of population in the ages subject to juvenile justice.

Female cases rose twice as rapidly, as a proportion of the court's dispositions, as did male cases. This narrowing of the difference in male and female rates has been noticeable since 1965. (From 1965 to 1970 juvenile female rates increased by 78 percent compared with 44 percent for males.) Nevertheless, although the increase in the female rate has been more rapid, the court is still mainly concerned with delinquencies alleged for boys. Boys are referred to juvenile court about three times as frequently as girls. The report also comments on increase in the rate of offenses of varying severity.

Types of Offenses

> Data are not available in the national juvenile court statistical reporting program on the types of offenses (nonstatus offenses that would be crimes if committed by adults and juvenile status offenses, such as truancy, ungovernable behavior, etc.) for which juveniles are referred to the courts. To examine these, one needs to rely on the data on police arrests of juveniles reported by the Federal Bureau of Investigation in its Uniform Crime Reports. Inasmuch as the police are the major source of referral of delinquency cases to juvenile courts, the offenses for which juveniles are arrested should pretty well represent the nonstatus offenses for which juveniles are referred to court.
>
> In the 1971 edition of Uniform Crime Reports, the Federal Bureau of Investigation reported that arrests of juveniles under 18 years of age, for all types of offenses combined, more than doubled between 1960 and 1971. For a group of serious offenses selected as being most reliably reported (criminal homicide, forcible rape, burglary, robbery, aggravated assault, larceny, and auto theft), the combined increase between 1960 and 1971 was 107 percent. When offenses against the person (homicide, forcible rape, aggravated assault, and robbery), generally accepted as being the most serious crimes, are selected from the reliably reported group, the increase between 1960 and 1971 was 193 percent.
>
> As determined from police arrest data, all types of offenses—serious as well as relatively minor—have been increasing with the most serious ones showing substantially greater proportionate increases. Serious offenses against

persons, however, still only represent about 3 percent of all arrests of juveniles. (Juvenile Court Statistics, 1971, p. 3)

The rate of delinquency actions before courts per 1000 children 10 through 17 years of age increased from 20.1 in 1960 to 34.3 in 1971. The rate is much higher in urban areas than in rural. Both increase over time, and differences between urban and rural may reflect differences in decisions to handle misconduct in the court.

The FBI's Uniform Crime Reports give several measures based on reports submitted by law enforcement agencies. For 1970, in a court of offenses known to police and cleared by arrest (not necessarily conviction), 34.8 percent, or some 955,812, were cleared by the arrest of someone under 18 years of age.

Of all arrests made in 1970 (including many that did not lead to charges of any kind), 9.2 percent were of persons under the age of 15, and 25.3 percent were under the age of 18.

The assaultive offenses of the list comprise a small proportion of the total volume of charges resulting in arrests; of violent crimes youth under age 18 commit less than one fourth. Several hundred thousand, on the other hand, are for age status-specific law violation (e.g., curfew, liquor laws, runaway) or general conduct (disorderly, vandalism). Of the property offenses, burglary is most prevalent among youth who are arrested.

Neither the court data nor the police data include children who were processed for dependency, neglect, or "special proceedings." Neglect and dependency cases that reached juvenile courts in 1971 totaled 130,900. The court data also exclude ordinary traffic violations except the most serious, where a charge of delinquency was lodged. Wolfgang, Figlio, and Sellin (1972), in an important longitudinal study, draw upon school and police data on the the experience of a cohort consisting of all males born in 1945 and residing in Philadelphia from age 10 through 18. Individuals in the cohort totaled 9,945, of whom 35 percent showed at least one recorded contact with the police at some time. This percentage was higher for nonwhite than for white boys: 50 percent of nonwhites and 29 percent of whites. Race and socioeconomic status are correlated of course, in Philadelphia as elsewhere in the U.S., and these rates reflect the disadvantaged class position of blacks as well as the special burdens imposed by racism. Of the 7,043 whites in the cohort, 30 percent were classified low socioeconomic class (SES)[1]; of the 2,902 *nonwhites* in the cohort, 84 percent are lower SES. Thus the overall differences by race reflect gross class and income differences. However, race differences continue to be

[1]Based on median family income of census tract in which he resides, 1960 census data. These data are highly correlated with occupation, housing quality, and overcrowding.

important even within income categories. Differences between whites and nonwhites are smaller among the higher SES youth than among lower SES youth. (See Table 2.3.)

The authors regard race and SES as most strongly related to probability of police contact, when compared with other factors such as type of school attended, intracity mobility, highest level of education attained, "intelligence" score, and measures of school achievement. Most of the variance of these latter correlates of delinquency are themselves largely accounted for by race and class. When the cohort is further divided into youth with no police contact, once-only, contact, and multiple contact cases, the latter are more likely to be lower-class nonwhites than are the other two categories. The relative seriousness of offenses[2] charged to lower SES nonwhites is greater than that of the offense record of other groups.

The differences between white and nonwhite youth are mainly due to a greater proportion of repeat offenders among lower SES nonwhite. The white and nonwhite rates per 1,000 cohort individuals are approximately the same among youth with one police contact only; for youth with multiple contacts ("recidivists"), the rates per 1,000 cohort individuals are approximately equal except for lower SES nonwhites, who have more than twice the role of recidivist youths.

Differences between the races on offense rate (the number of alleged delinquent *acts*) are greater than the differences in offender rate (the

TABLE 2.3

Differences by income class in percent youth with one or more police contacts		
Lower	.449	.185 difference
Higher	.264	
Differences by race in percent youth with one or more police contacts		
White	.286	.216 difference
Nonwhite	.502	
Differences between races, within income categories		
Lower SES youth		
White	.356	.173 difference
Nonwhite	.529	
Higher SES youth		
White	.255	.105 difference
Nonwhite	.360	

Source: Adapted from data in Chapter 4, Wolfgang, Figlio, and Sellin. © 1972 by the University of Chicago Press.

[2]Measured by the technique developed by Sellin and Wolfgang, 1957.

number of delinquent boys). The offense rate per 1,000 cohort boys for whites is 633, for nonwhites it is 1,983. For boys with only one recorded police contact, however, the races are more similar; for nonwhite low-income boys, 49.9, low income whites, 37.4; higher-income white boys show only half the offense rate of higher-income nonwhites. The rate of certain offenses is much greater than others, and the majority of offenses (disorderly conduct and "other," i.e., nonindex, offenses) do not involve injury, theft, or property damage.

The offense rates when weighted by the *seriousness* of each offense differ considerably between whites and nonwhites: 2,594.4 per 1,000 nonwhite cohort boys, 587.9 per 1,000 white cohort boys.

In all of the above, it is important to observe that only 30 percent of all offenses recorded are those classified by the Uniform Crime Reports as index offenses (crimes of injury, theft, and property damage). The remainder of the 70 percent are acts that are only offenses when alleged of minors.

Wolfgang and his colleagues classified boys with five or more alleged offenses as chronic offenders; these constituted 18 percent (627) of their total of 3,475 boys with police contacts but accounted for 51.9 percent of all offenses recorded. Nonwhite boys are more likely than white boys of being in the chronic category (14.4 percent as opposed to 3 percent).

The advantage of cohort data is that experience over time can be analyzed, and that the base of observations about delinquency is not a sample of persons known to court but a population at large, any of whom being a "potential" case known to the court. Looking at these longitudinal data, Wolfgang and his associates found 51 percent of all boys who committed a *non*index first offense (i.e., an act not involving injury, theft, or property damage and not criminal for adults) did not have further arrests; 43 percent of those whose first offense involved injury, 37 percent of theft first offenders, and 32 percent of combination (injury and theft) were seen no more. Overall 46 percent "desisted from further known delinquency after the first offense, 35 percent after the second and 20–30 percent at each remaining stem (Wolfgang, Figlio, and Sellin, 1972, p. 163).

More striking are the probabilities of subsequent offenses; after the second offense, the probability of a subsequent offense is nearly constant, as one proceeds from the third to the fifteenth offense. This contradicts a popular notion that the probabilities of recidivism climb with each succeeding offense. (This, however, is an impression apparently conveyed by the repeat appearances of those boys who do recidivate, and the nonappearance of those who, at any given stage, desist.) Moreover, the probability of violence does not increase over the number of offenses.

In these transitional probabilities from one offense to the succeeding

TABLE 2.4

Type of Offense by Race of Delinquents

Offense	Nonwhites N	%	*Rate per 1,000 Cohort Subjects*
Homicide	14	.24	4.8
Rape	38	.66	13.1
Robbery	173	3.01	59.6
Aggravated assault	181	3.14	62.4
Burglary	394	6.84	135.8
Larceny	802	13.93	276.4
Auto theft	187	3.25	64.4
Other assaults	365	6.34	125.8
Forgery and counterfeiting	4	.07	1.4
Fraud and embezzlement	1	.02	.3
Stolen property	23	.40	7.9
Weapons	212	3.68	73.1
Prostitution	1	.02	.3
Sex offenses	84	1.46	28.9
Narcotics	0	0	0
Liquor law violations	108	1.88	37.2
Drunkenness	117	2.03	40.3
Disorderly conduct	851	14.78	293.2
Vagrancy	15	.26	5.2
Gambling	49	.85	16.9
Road violations	0	0	0
Other traffic violations	12	.21	4.1
All other offenses	2,123	36.88	731.6
Hospital cases	0	0	0
Investigations	0	0	0
Minor disturbance	1	.02	.3
Missing persons	1	.02	.3
Reports affecting other city departments	0	0	0
Total	5,756	100.00	1,983.5

Source: Wolfgang, Figlio, and Sellin, pp. 68–69. © 1972 by the University of Chicago Press.

offense, race and social class differences are apparent; lower SES nonwhites have police contacts at an earlier age, with shorter intervals between contacts, are charged with more serious offenses, and are more likely to be arrested subsequently at each succeeding offense.

TABLE 2.4 (cont.)

Whites			Total		
N	%	*Rate per 1,000 Cohort Subjects*	*N*	%	*Rate per 1,000 Cohort Subjects*
0	0	0	14	.14	1.4
6	.13	.9	44	.43	4.4
20	.45	2.8	193	1.89	19.4
39	.87	5.5	220	2.15	22.1
248	5.56	35.2	642	6.29	64.6
387	8.68	54.9	1189	11.64	119.6
239	5.36	33.9	426	4.17	42.8
172	3.86	24.4	537	5.26	54.0
1	.02	.1	5	.05	.5
3	.07	.4	4	.04	.4
7	.16	1.0	30	.29	3.0
58	1.30	8.2	270	2.64	27.1
2	.04	.3	3	.03	.3
63	1.41	8.9	147	1.44	14.8
1	.02	.1	1	.01	.1
165	3.70	23.4	273	2.67	27.5
102	2.29	14.5	219	2.14	22.0
883	19.81	125.4	1,734	16.98	174.4
6	.13	.9	21	.21	2.1
40	.90	5.7	89	.87	8.9
4	.09	.6	4	.04	.4
25	.56	3.5	37	.36	3.7
1,974	44.28	280.3	4,097	40.11	412.0
1	.02	.1	1	.01	.1
9	.20	1.3	9	.09	.9
0	0	0	1	.01	.1
2	.04	.3	3	.03	.3
1	.02	.1	1	.01	.1
4,458	100.00	633.0	10,214	100.00	1,027.0

This longitudinal research of Wolfgang and his associates opens new insights into questions of the amount and frequency of recorded delinquency and, when extended as a subsequent study promises, the consequences of various policies of intervention and control.

Chapter 3

CONFORMITY AND RULE-BREAKING

Introduction

The previous chapter showed that in a mass society there are a large number of rules applying to childhood and youthful conduct, and a large number of agencies and officials to enforce those rules.

In the present chapter we will seek to account for conformity of conduct to expectations in social life, and to describe the rather extensive and pervasive rule-breaking that also prevails. We will show that among all types of youth there is a great deal of rule-violating behavior; we will describe the nature and extent of this behavior and distinguish it from and relate it to officially labeled delinquency.

3.1 Conceptions of Social Order and Disorder

Social order is a historical fact; so is social change. Scholars have differed in the importance they ascribe to each in explaining the organization of social life. One tradition in sociology takes social order and structure as a tendency of groups or social systems; it presumes persistence of patterns over time, congruence of expectations from one member of the group to another, the existence of common values uniting members of social systems, and a tendency for social systems to return to something like equilibrium when disturbed.

This tradition of social theory takes the fact of social order as evidence for the existence of *norms,* that is, common expectations to which social conduct is sensitive. A normative explanation of social order relies heavily on the hypothesis that socialization of the infant and the newcomer brings about learning and internalization of the standards of the group. Deviance, a motivated departure from norms, is countered by the nagging of internalized standards in the conscience of the deviant, by informal social control exerted by other persons in interaction with the deviant, or by the application of sanctions through the imposition of formal (authorized, official) social controls. While this way of defining conformity and deviance clearly specifies a difference between them, note that it implies that deviance is closely dependent on a *particular* order for its meaning. If the order itself were to shift, a particular action could lose its "deviant" significance.

But, claims another tradition of theory, order need *not* be taken as evidence of consensus. These theories regard a particular pattern of order as an arrested phase in the fundamental historical process of social change. This view questions the extent to which consensus really prevails, and it sees normative structures derived from the values of a dominant class or segment of the society that can effectively manipulate rewards and sanctions so as to maintain the system in a given state. This tradition assumes continuous change in states of social affairs, the problematic nature of norms and expectations in many situations, the existence of conflicts among groups, the instability of structured patterns, the conflict of expectations, and the use of coercion in maintaining certain forms of social order. For this view, coercive power is the ultimate resource on which authority rests. But coercive control consumes large amounts of social power. It is difficult to extend and maintain control throughout even a tightly regulated system in the face of sources of value differences and clashes of interest. Societies with bases for differentiated social solidarity (class, ethnicity, generation, sex, etc.) may become politicized or even polarized through conflict, and exhibit wholesale disaffection and departure from norms. Such a society exhibits a *plurality* of contending values rather than a normative order. (That is, instead of value consensus it has class conflict, black power movement, a generation gap, or women's liberation movement.) Where the norms themselves are called into question or come under attack, and where the locus of authority or power may be shifting, we more properly speak of social change rather than deviance. Efforts of some groups to stem such change are defenses of a particular way of life, defenses of an old order versus a new, rather than the maintenance of an equilibrated system that merely remains steady by modulation of deviance. In short, for the first tradition in sociology, consensus and complementarity of expectations are presumed to lie beneath the surface turmoil; for the second tradition, change is latent in the arrangements of any given period in the history of a society. (Damerath and Peterson, 1967; Dahrendorf, 1964; Gouldner, 1970; Parsons, 1937; 1951; Sprott, 1952; Zeitlin, 1968.)

Both those theories that assume a tendency to equilibrium and those theories that assume a tendency to conflict and change must distinguish between the *maintenance of order in the face of deviance* from the *defense of the status quo in the path of social change.* Social scientists have largely sidestepped the problem by developing two lines of theory and research: the study of deviance and the study of social change. While this provides a certain convenience, it is awkward because of the somewhat indiscriminant use of the concept of social control to refer both to the processes by which deviance is countered and the processes by which fundamental change in the system is resisted. But deviance implies the existence of common values, and change implies a breakup or transformation of hitherto common values. We must thus distinguish among two types of social control, or at least two styles of employment of social control. This has not been sufficiently studied to date, but is the hub of the "delinquency problem" in America: how to distinguish between the use of manipulation or control of young persons who offensively deviate from a commonly held norm, and the use of sanctions and power by one group (the older) to suppress another (the younger) for its own convenience.

3.2 Expectations

The degree of individual conformity to group patterns, and the extent to which one or more "patterns" predominate in a group, are both basically empirical questions. There exists fragmentary evidence only, and such data as do exist are indicative of the great variability of conformity depending on time, place, and circumstance. We have knowledge of some groups in which behavioral patterning is very closely followed by all participants. Rituals and ceremonies prescribe each step, and departures from these prescriptions are held to be serious errors. For example, rules for the recitation of the Holy Koran in classical Arabic stipulate even the pitch of the intonation, and the points at which breath should be taken; the performance of the medieval court music of Japan (gagaku) is striking in the uniformity of the player's movements in the slightest detail; likewise, military drill, court manners, rules concerning whom one may and may not marry, and permissible modes of dress for males and females have all been rigidly determined at some time and place. Erving Goffman has reminded sociologists of the value of examining published "etiquette" rules for determining idealizations of proper form in many groups. Hundreds of social situations and exchanges are discussed in these guides to proper conduct, which seek to provide models for the instruction of those not born to the highest circles whose traditions ostensibly set the pattern (Goffman, 1963).

Goffman has also pointed out many aspects of the situational proprieties that prevail in behavior in public places such as the avoidance of excessive self-involvement (for example, obviously staring at oneself in the mirror), how one sits or walks, how one regulates direct eye contact with other persons, and the physical distance maintained between persons who are interacting. This sociology of everyday life reveals the surprising degree to which many groups maintain standards of proper conduct and the sensitivity shown to departures from such conduct rules.

This is not to imply that expectations are so rigid that departures from pattern are inevitably met with countermeasures. On the contrary, observation confirms that groups often employ tactics to avoid the disruption imposed by both departure from rule and countermeasure to enforce compliance. Indeed, the commonest technique is for the group to ignore the violation but to cover in such a way that the violator is made to feel that covertly the participants are quite aware of an impropriety. For example, at more formal or conventional public dinner gatherings, inadvertent flatulence is regarded as a breach of etiquette. Seldom would this lapse be sharply called to the offender's attention, however; more likely the group, or the offender's companion, would quickly speak, introducing a topic of conversation that is to absorb everyone. In coarser company, merriment might ensue, marking a different pattern of proper behavior, which does not so much prohibit such actions as it does exact a price for them by making the perpetrator the object of jest and amusement. Only small children beyond the reach of such civilities are openly rebuked or instructed.

The means by which conformity to pattern is achieved are varied. Sociologists distinguish two main categories: internally programming people to know the expectation and to be desirous and able to conform to it (i.e., to motivate conformity), and providing external pressures and sanctions to be used in the event of threatened or actual noncompliance (i.e., to compel conformity). The first of these is generally referrd to as *socialization* (making a person social, that is, fitting him or her to behave properly in a group); the second of these is referred to as social *control* (exerting authority or force to increase the difficulty or cost of noncompliance). There are many forms of each, and there are some social processes that are mixtures of both.

3.3 Socialization: The Programming of Inner Controls

We may distinguish between *primary* socialization and *secondary* socialization. The former refers to the efforts of parents and others psychologically significant to the baby to include certain personal and interpersonal traits in the newborn. Primary socialization takes place because the baby is the object of action by others, chiefly the parents or others who care for it. In this early experience, not only is certain behavior rewarded and fostered and other behavior not rewarded and discouraged, but the child learns to take the cognitive, emotional, and evaluative perspective of others into account in assessing its own conduct. Learning to be a member of a group implies learning more or less accurately to look at one's own conduct from the standpoint of significant others with whom one interacts. This process of becoming a member of a particular group is advanced when the child begins to organize more generalized features of separate perspectives of individuals into a collective or group perspective, real or imagined, which is the beginning of internalized standards of approved and disapproved conduct. *To the extent that socialization is accomplished,* the individual knows what is expected of him, places a positive value on fulfilling these expectations, and steers his conduct so as to stay within limits of those expectations.

There is nothing in this idealized conception that presumes that all conduct would be thereby determined by socialization. For one thing, there are fewer and more restricted expectations than there are conduct possibilities; that is, the socializing "others" cannot prescribe all actions even in theory. More important, the socialization may be inadequate, inconsistent, or inappropriate (Bredemeier and Stephenson, 1965, especially Chapters 3 and 4). Inadequate socialization is a partial accomplishment of the intended process, where rewards, motivation, amount of interaction, or other interpersonal factors have not been of sufficient strength or duration to induce the learning of expectations and the acquisition of gratification-dispositions that motivate conduct in accordance with expectations.

Inconsistency in socialization occurs when more than one set of expectations applicable to the same conduct is learned and lead to different forms of action. Inconsistency is quite common, reflecting cleavages in the group to which the conduct is referred (that is, the group into which the person is being socialized.) In primary socialization this group is almost always a family or kinship unit, and inconsistency may be resolved only with considerable difficulty and with important consequences for personality development.[1]

Inappropriate socialization is said to have occurred when the subsequent situation in which an individual must act is wholly unforeseen in the socialization process. Unless learning can continue to take place for individuals living in changing situations, conduct becomes less adaptive as the individual grows older.

Subsequent learning of expectations does of course take place. This is what is meant by secondary socialization. After acquiring basic human social traits by early incorporation of the perspectives of salient family members, the growing person joins peer, school, and work groups as he advances in age and in scope of roles. Each important group imposes a learning task on the newcomer similar to the situation of the child entering the family. The more uniform or integrated the social system, the more overlap and transfer of learning is possible from one group to another; the more the society is composed of different social solidarities, the more likely that each subsequent socialization imposes distinctive problems.

A social system may be sufficiently pluralistic in value orientations, in role expectations, in language, culture, life style, rights, and powers of component groups that any particular individual is socialized primarily to be sensitive to the standards and expectations of a subset of the component groups in the system. He then more or less understands the other groups depending on the number and extent of cleavages among those groups in the society. Where those cleavages do not exist or are minimal, there may be considerable consensus on value orientations, and we speak of norms. Often values are in conflict, and the groups espousing various values contend in a struggle to determine whose values shall prevail. A value that wins out in this competition may be the norm. Where there are close competitors the assumption that common values or norms are recognized by the population may be unsupported, a problem to which we will return from time to time in this book.

The influence of the expectations of others in a group on individual conduct may be quite strongly evoked and documented even in simple situations. Illustrations may clarify the point to be made. Consider the well known "autokinetic" effect. It is a property of visual perception that if the eye is fixated on a small point of light in an otherwise darkened room, the light will appear to shift, even though in fact it is stationary. The extent to which it is perceived to move is variable among individuals. The experimental task in question is to present subjects with the light in

[1]The development of psychological defense mechanisms and anxiety are among the more important of these consequences.

a dark room and ask them to estimate how much the light moves. If persons are first tested individually, and then placed in a group where individual perceptions are announced audibly, the individual ranges of reported movement established in the first condition converge. If after the group condition individuals are again tested alone, the group mean persists in their estimates (Sherif, 1935). In another well-known experiment by Solomon Asch, a naive subject is asked to estimate which of three lines is equal to a criterion; the stimulus lines are grossly different in length, and the task produces few errors for individuals tested without manipulation. When experimenter's confederates posing as subjects precede the subjects in announcing a wrong perception, the number of errors for the naive subject dramatically increases (Asch, 1953). In a more elaborate demonstration of conformity, the psychologist Stanley Milgram set up a convincing situation in which a naive subject is led to believe he is taking part in a learning experiment that requires that he administer punishing electrical shocks to another "subject" in an adjoining room, who is the learner (Milgram, 1964). In fact the experiment is a hoax, and there is no shock, and no real learner. But the majority of the subjects persisted to the end of the trials, giving what they believed to be near-lethal jolts of electricity to the protesting fake subject, primarily because they were told they should do so by the "experimenter." Conformity in behavior is thus possible to demonstrate in very simple situations, using gross manipulation.

Note that we have considered two different orders of explanations of conformity to pattern, but two that are related. In socialization we have the learning of cognitive definitions, need dispositions, and evaluative standards, which dispose the individual to see things, like or dislike things, and value things more or less as others in the group do. In the structure of social relations we see that opinions and expectations of others in the situation of action exert a strong influence on the behavior of an individual who has been sensitized to those influences. The experimenter's confederates in the Asch and Milgram experiments were exerting an influence in the situation of action, but the readiness of subjects to respond to those purely social pressures was derived from socialization.

Socialization can be frustrated and truncated. Learnings of the novice (baby, newcomer) or unlearning and relearning of the experienced, are efforts that are not lightly evoked. Bredemeier and Stephenson postulate that persons will have

> an incentive to change if something happens to their situation that (1) reduces the rewards they are receiving from their present behavior . . . or (2) increases their estimate of the rewards they will receive from the new behavior, or both. (Bredemeier and Stephenson, 1965, p. 92)

This is often facilitated by separating an individual from reference groups that would reward old behavior, or from individuals who would reciprocate his old behavior, since informal subgroups often frustrate the goals of formal socialization attempts. For example, infants are initially rewarded for virtually any kind of babble that can be perceived by parents as attempts to talk. Later, childish babble does not earn approval, and grammatically orthodox verbal behavior is required before the child is rewarded. Ethnographers have provided accounts of *rites de passage* in which former statuses are ritually effaced and removed to symbolize the entrance of a person into a new age-set or other status. In formal organizations, the degradation of former statuses or groups is often deliberately promoted as part of the task of building a new reference group and self-conception in the recruit. Similarly, anticipation of rewards for learning is extended in systems of graded statuses linked with tangible rewards, instruction in deferred gratification as a value, role rehearsal in advance of various status transition and by controlling access to membership groups to which the socializee aspires.

Despite the fact that all humans undergo some considerable socialization experience, expectations are frequently seriously in error; that is, the expected behavior is not forthcoming. (This is often described in another way: a person is said not to live up to expectations, or not to fulfill role expectations.) When at least one of the parties to interaction defines the situation of action as subject to commonly applicable rules, expectations that err in anticipating behavior (or behavior that fails to meet expectations) are potentially disruptive. There are several alternatives open to persons in such a situation.

3.4 Conflict and External Control

The person whose expectations were not confirmed may reassess the discrepant behavior of the other to see if it could be assigned a meaning that does not threaten the definition of the situation he holds. Failure to meet expectations may be attributed to something that excuses the individual. He may, for example, be viewed as responding to higher priority considerations that override the interaction that has been disturbed. Or his status may be invoked to excuse him from compliance (the forgetfulness of the aged, the candor of the child, the fickleness of women (or men), the blindness of love, the ignorance of the newcomer, etc.). A stranger who is known to be a traveller or tourist may be allowed to flaunt local custom of dress, food habits, deportment; a foreigner who is viewed as a settler may be obliged to conform to local custom.

The erring behavior may also be labeled as "sick." The characteristics of the sick are that their impaired performance is not due to their volition but to inability; that they are exempt from any normal obligations (they may qualify for not working, being in bed, collecting benefits, etc.), they are subject to more permissive handling from others (demands and tastes are catered to, behavior of others accommodates the ill person) and they are expected to cooperate in a process of management or cure, and when restored to health are expected to return to role incumbency. Labeling someone as sick is in a sense defining him as deviant, but the deviance is contained and is itself subject to another set of expectations (defining the sick role) and hence the predictability and complementary of the situation is restored. Leslie Wilkins calls our attention to the added convenience of this explanation for the established system. The sick-role explanation for problematic or erring behavior may absolve social institutions from criticism. Wilkins refers to this as using "individuals as scape goats for systems" (Wilkins, 1965, p. 78).

When none of these considerations can be sustained, however, the person or group whose expectations are frustrated must more radically restructure or redefine the relationship between himself and the person whose behavior is not conforming.

We must pause to review an important assumption underlying what will follow. Sociologists who assume that social systems tend to be integrated by norms define deviance as a violation of patterned expectations commonly held throughout the system. Parsons writes:

> From the point of view of the social system deviance is a motivated tendency for an actor to behave in contravention of one or more institutionalized normative patterns. From the point of view of the actor, deviance is the tendency on the part of one or more of the component actors to behave in such a way as to disturb the equilibrium of the interactive process. (Parsons, 1951, p. 250)

This view assumes an established, existing institutionalized pattern; it assumes an internalized value pattern in the participants. Whether this is a reasonable or plausible assumption in many situations of action, particularly those involving crime and delinquency, will be examined later in this book.

Assuming a normatively regulated situation, the person whose expectations were not fulfilled may renounce the expectation. On the other hand he may attempt to correct the "erring" behavior of the other; or instead of either of these, he may become ambivalent and combine both. He may even support the other's nonconformity and join him in the abandonment of the rule. Or he may attempt to redefine the situation to allow the other to correct his nonconformity. Or he may promise to reward the other if he again conforms to patterned expectation. He may seek to coerce or threaten the other into conformity, or, finally, he may seek to remove the other altogether from the scene of action by expelling, confining or killing him.

The success of any but the last of these efforts depends in part on the existence of some sort of ties between the nonconforming person and the person whose expectation embodies the norm. Even something short of an institutionalized, common value system may still provide a point of leverage for the exercise of informal control.

Howard Becker approaches this problem by asking why more people do not deviate more of the time from rules. The answer for Becker lies in the degree of commitment many persons develop to a social position, reputation, or relationship. To the extent that individuals have investments in a given status quo, they will seek to avoid or conceal deviant conduct.

It follows that where common values or commitments are nonexistent or attenuated, "deviance" is a term that is less and less useful, since the argument for regarding one value pattern as "normative" for the system becomes weaker. A social system characterized by a plurality of contending values can be said to recognize and label deviant behavior only in a sense that is relative to each of the subgroups and solidarities in the system. What prevails in a fully pluralistic society is not deviance and control, but diversity and conflict. Jack Douglas has carried the implications of a pluralistic society even further. Douglas criticizes sociologists and anthropologists for proceeding on the assumption that common values are perceived and rules do exist. He notes two assumptions in much of sociology.

> (1) the social meanings . . . were assumed to be the same for all members of society, including the officials who constructed and imputed the categories, so that one could expect a direct relation between the official meanings and the general social meanings, and (2) the social meanings were assumed to be nonproblematic for all members, including official . . . but a social category, such as "crime" or "suicide," can be said to be socially problematic when its meanings or uses by members of the society involve disagreements, uncertainties or conflicts. (Douglas, 1971, pp. 80, 101)

3.5 Rule-Breaking Among Youths: Estimates from Self-reports

Criminology is the study of crime and delinquency. It would be plausible to assume that crime and delinquency research would draw heavily upon empirical observations of criminal and delinquent behavior. Students of the field would observe how persons carry out acts of this type, how they conduct these activities in the wider contest of social life, how novices enter the activities and learn to perform, how delinquents succeed or fail, mature into criminals, or drop in and out of the ordinary class patterns of adulthood, and so on. Such research is fundamental in biological disciplines and in some social sciences such as developmental psychology and anthropology.

But criminologists seldom observe even a single instance of law violation, and few are ever present when law violations are planned.[2] The behavior of delinquents is indirectly inferred from interveiws or questionnaires administered to captives, or surveys asking if certain stipulated rule violations have occurred. Other sources are even further removed: police versions (usually themselves second-hand accounts of citizen complaints) or pleas of guilt entered usually in the context of plea bargaining. The sociology of crime and delinquency might be significantly altered by direct observation of delinquents in natural settings.

These difficulties in juvenile delinquency records have caused some researchers to turn to "self-report" data. Self-reported delinquency is measured by responses to questionnaires that pose descriptions of various acts that are more or less in violation of prevailing statutory definitions of delinquent behavior. Given the great latitude of discretion possessed and exercised by agencies or officials who define instances of juvenile delinquency, it is not surprising that very large majorities of virtually every sample of young persons thus surveyed admitted to at least occasional conduct that violates the laws, and could be regarded as *potentially* delinquent acts (Gold, 1970; Hirshi, 1969; Nye, 1958; Short and Nye, 1958). The value of such surveys is considerable, but it is important that this value and these data be distinguished from socially defined delinquency and the consequences that follow from such official determinations.

The data we do have are scattered. A number of studies provide some self-reports and observations. We will concentrate on these. Their implications are clear. "Numerous investigators have shown delinquent conduct to be far more widespread than official records indicate. Large proportions of all populations studied admit at least some acts for which they could have appeared before court" (Hood and Sparks, 1970, p. 27).

A study of men and women in New York State in the 1940's revealed 64 percent of a male sample admitted doing something that under

[2]A few exceptions include D. M. Downes' *The Delinquent Solution* (New York: The Free Press, 1966), Laud Humphreys' *Tearoom Trade* (Chicago: Aldine Publishing Co., 1969), Malcolm Klein's *Street Gangs and Street Workers* (Englewood Cliffs, N.J.: Prentice-Hall, Inc., 1971), James Short and Fred Strodtbeck, *Group Process and Gang Delinquency* (Chicago: University of Chicago Press, 1965) and Lewis Yablonsky's *The Violent Gang* (New York: Macmillan and Company, Inc., 1962). For some discussion of methodological problems in observing illegal behavior even among captured or paroled persons, see Gene Kassebaum, "Strategies for the Sociological Study of Criminal Correctional Systems" in *Pathways to Data*, edited by Robert Habenstein (Chicago: Aldine Publishing Co., 1970). Although not an observation study, Martin Gold's *Delinquent Behavior in An American City* (Belmont,California: Brooks-Cole Publishing Co., 1970) provides interview data on offense behavior in a general population.

certain conditions could have been prosecuted as a felony. Another study estimated between 38 percent and 46 percent of a sample of Midwest school children violated the criminal law. Hood and Sparks report two British studies showing substantial percentages of London school children admitting theft. Short and Nye, (1958), in still another Midwest study, found large percentages of a general sample of youth reporting undetected delinquent behavior.

Several facts have emerged from self-report data on rule-breaking. First, although the percentages of rule violators is very high, often the items measuring rule violation are trivial, ranging from inanities like "defied parents to their face," "kept something I have found," "have stolen fruit," to vaguely defined offenses that could connote serious or trivial acts, such as "I have stolen from a cafe" (What? An ashtray? The contents of the cash drawer?). Secondly, while large percentages of the samples report doing something illegal at some time, fewer children report persistent rule violations. These data show more rule violations among males than females, and more persistent and serious law violation among children who have been officially picked up or adjudicated than among children who have not.

Quite possibly the best—certainly one of the three best—of the self-report studies to be published is by Travis Hirshi in a monograph entitled *Causes of Delinquency* (Hirshi, 1969). Hirshi's study draws on questionnaire responses of a sample of 4,077 children entering eleven junior and senior high schools of a predominantly working class urban region in the greater San Francisco Bay Area in 1964, and from school records and police rap sheets on members of this sample (the survey was not anonymous). The measure of the self-report rule violation was a score derived from the following items in the questionnaire:

1. Have you ever taken little things (worth less than $2) that did not belong to you?
2. Have you ever taken things of some value (between $2 and $50 that did not belong to you?
3. Have you ever taken things of large value (worth over $50) that did not belong to you?
4. Have you ever taken a car for a ride without the owner's permission?
5. Have you ever banged up something that did not belong to you on purpose?
6. Not counting fights you may have had with a brother or sister, have you ever beaten up on anyone or hurt anyone on purpose?[3]

[3]For the above questionnaire, note that four of the items are from Dentler and Monroe, and two of them are from Nye and Short. Several other items from these previous studies were not used because they were not sufficiently serious to denote delinquency. It is of interest to note the triviality of some items used in previous studies by listing the items discarded by Hirishi: Have you ever driven a car without

TABLE 3.1

Number of Official Offenses, Number of Times Picked Up by Police, and Number of Self-Reported Delinquent Acts, by Race (in percent)

Number of Acts (or Reported Contacts with Police)	*(A) Official Offenses*		*(B) Self-Reported Police Pick-up*		*(C) Self-Reported Delinquent Acts*	
	White	*Negro*	*White*	*Negro*	*White*	*Negro*
None	81	57	65	57	56	51
One	10	19	18	20	25	25
Two or more	8	23	17	22	19	24
TOTALS	99	99	100	99	100	100
	(1335)	(888)	(1302)	(833)	(1303)	(828)

Source: Travis Hirshi, *The Causes of Delinquency*. Originally published by the University of California Press, 1969; reprinted by permission of The Regents of the University of California.

Responses to each item were to be in terms of one of four stipulated alternatives: 1. never; 2. more than a year ago; 3. during the last year; 4. during the last year *and* more than a year ago.

The Hirshi survey shows that self-reports of rule-breaking, self-reports of being picked up by the police, and official records of police are correlated, but that the official data considerably underestimates the frequency of rule (law) violation. This exaggeration is greater for black children than for white.

White boys were less often officially delinquent (as defined by police record) than blacks; were slightly less likely than blacks to report being picked up by police; and were very nearly equal to blacks in self-reported delinquent acts (Table 3.1 above).

Martin Gold's study of delinquent behavior in Flint, Michigan administered a 51-item list of actions ranging from praiseworthy (honor roll for good school grades) to robbery and arson (Gold, 1970). Positive response to an item brought a series of probes that elicited information about details of the offense behavior. Gold, drawing on the extensive resources of the Institute for Social Research at the University of Michigan, made a series of crosschecks for validity of self-reports and was satisfied that errors in reporting are low and are in the direction of under-reporting.

a driver's license or permit? Have you ever skipped school without a legitimate excuse? Have you ever defied your parents' authority to their face? Have you ever bought or drunk beer, wine, or liquor? (Include drinking at home) Have you ever had sex relations with a person of the opposite sex?

He constructed two indices: one is a count of "delinquent acts that youngsters most seldom conceal—trespassing, assault, stealing a part of a car or some gasoline, hitting one's father, hitting one's mother, drinking alcoholic beverages without parental knowledge or permission, running away from home, gang fighting, shoplifting, larceny and fornication." The other index is derived from Sellin and Wolfgang (1964), which is weighted by severity of offenses. The components of this index are trespass, threatened assault, property destruction, assault resulting in medical treatment, theft of part of a car or gasoline, theft (other), arson, shoplifting, and driving away a car without permission. Gold rejects the dichotomy of delinquent versus nondelinquent children, and reports only 17 percent of the sample did not admit to a chargeable offense within the previous three years. His data suggest no consistent preference or specializing of kids on selected offense.

"According to (the) data, Flint youngsters simply did not specialize. Among the hundred most delinquent of them the fewest different varieties of offenses committed by anyone was four, and there were only five youngsters of the hundred who committed as few as four kinds" (Gold, p. 33)

It may be a peculiarity of Flint, the times (data were collected in 1961), or the investigator that apparently no questions on drugs were included, nor do the words "drugs" or "narcotics" appear on the book's index. More puzzling is that apparently no respondent mentioned glue or paint sniffing, marijuana, amphetamines, barbiturates, or heroin in any of the interviews.

Gold's data show that overall, more girls than boys report few or no delinquent actions, although he is of the opinion that girls may have been more reticent than boys in self-reporting. He finds several offenses traditionally assumed to be "girls' offenses" (running away, incorrigibility, and fornication) to be nearly as often admitted by boys (Gold, p. 65).

The Flint survey found older children slightly more frequently delinquent than younger ones; property theft peaked earlier than assault and drinking. These data on age, and the earlier rate increase in girls, lead Gold to surmise that physical maturation may be a factor in increasing delinquency (Gold, p. 7).

Social Class

The data relating self-reported delinquent behavior to social class are somewhat equivocal, but the evidence would seem to indicate smaller differences among classes in behavior than the official rates show. Hood and Sparks state:

> Many studies have shown an absence of, or a negligible correlation between social class and the proportion of respondents admitting delinquency, but others have found significant positive correlations. For example, Short and Nye's and Dentler and Monroe's high school studies found no differences between boys from low, medium or high status family backgrounds. The Utah enquiry concluded: "most respondents on one status level were no more or no less delinquent than most respondents on another." The same conclusions were found by Edmund Vaz in a Canadian small town, by Akers in a large Ohio city and by Voss in Honolulu. The Scandinavian studies produce similar evidence. In Norway, Christie concluded: "Instead of any concentration of high degrees of self-reporting at the lower ends of the class scale we found a slight but persistent tendency in the opposite direction." These results were mirrored in Finland. Voss in Honolulu and Arnold in Texas reported that crimes of property destruction were higher in the upper socio-economic groups and in Utah the middle status delinquents who were incarcerated were especially frequent offenders. (Hood and Sparks, p. 55)

Gold used a scale of prestige of occupations of the fathers of his respondents to assign each child to a social status category. He concludes that the frequency and severity of delinquent behavior are greater among lower status boys than for high status, but that girls of higher and lower status families do not so differ (Gold, p. 73).

> Of lowest status (white) boys, eight percent are in the least delinquent category on Index F, (less serious acts), where 35% of the highest status boys are found. The proportion of highest status boys falls from 35% in the least to 11% in the most delinquent category. Middle status white boys occupy intermediate position on delinquency Index F.
>
> White boys show same pattern on Index S (weighted re: more serious). Among non-white males, the F index did not correlate well with status, but the S index did. (Gold, p. 75)

Gold observes however:

> . . . real as the relationship (between status and delinquent behavior) appears to be, it is slight and official records have exaggerated it. . . . (These data suggest that) treatment and prevention programs aimed exclusively at lower class targets miss a lot of heavily delinquent youngsters. (Gold, pp. 76–77)

Hirshi, in the study of Richmond, California, interprets his data as indicating that "there is in the present sample no important relation between social class as traditionally measured and delinquency," and again "I suggest the maximum relation the skeptic can reasonably claim is defined by the relation between social class and official delinquency which is not very strong" (Hirshi, pp. 75, 81).

However, an inspection on his data provides some evidence to the contrary. The tables exclude blacks, and are based on white boys only (thus truncating social class). Looking at the white data, we see a steady decrease in delinquency as father's occupation varies from lower to upper middle, whether this is measured by self-report or by officially charged offenses. The rate for official delinquency in upper middle-class white boys is 2/3 the rate for lower-class boys. When father's education is substituted for father's occupation, the delinquency for the boys with fathers of less than high school education is twice the rate for boys whose fathers are college graduates (.35 as compared to .17), with again no reversals in rates over the five categories from low to high education. Hirshi, after minimizing the importance of these data, goes on to state:

> . . . yet the relative importance of social class as traditionally defined and measured as a determinant of the commission of delinquent acts should not be construed as showing that social class is unimportant in other aspects of delinquency. It is of the essence of social class that it can create differences in reward where none exists in obedience to rules. The evidence that the lower class boy is more likely than the middle class to end up in juvenile court and in the reformatory is no more open to doubt than is the evidence that he is less likely to end up in college. (Hirshi, pp. 81–82)

Race

As with social class, Hirshi's data show that police records differ between races more than reported delinquent behavior differs.

Hirshi sees differential school success as influencing some of this difference in rates but adds: "The present data also support the conclusion that Negro-white differences are exaggerated by differential police activity" (Hirshi, p. 81).

Gold's conclusions are consistent with Hirshi's: ". . . Negroes in Flint confessed to no more delinquent behavior than white youngsters, and the validation data testify that they were equally honest" (Gold, p. 29). Gold's analysis shows that racial differences in seriousness and frequency of delinquent acts that do exist vanish when social status differences are held constant.

The self-report studies all show the selective process of law enforcement, and show that official statistics are a considerable underestimate of the actual frequency of rule violation. They also show a tendency for frequency and seriousness of offenses to be correlated (those who admitted to more frequent violations also admitted to more serious). Finally they show that adjudicated offenders admit to more offenses and more serious offenses than youth who have never been arrested (Hood and Sparks, p. 61). If law enforcement tends to pick up children who commit offenses more often, they are likely to be dealing with those who commit the more serious offenses. However, other considerations may well influence the probability of arrest and charging, which will be examined in Chapter 6.

Chapter **4**

THEORIES OF DELINQUENT BEHAVIOR AND CRIMINAL ROLES

4.1 The Search for Causes

People have attempted to understand phenomena of crime in much the same way as other phenomena are understood. Specific facts are used to construct generalizations, which can then be related to systems of concepts that are regarded as established. The history of human society provides a wide range of theories of crime and delinquent behavior, many appearing more than once in the history of both academic and legal thinking about crime. In fact, there are so many contenders for acceptance as explanations of delinquency that it may be useful to state some criteria that should be met by an adequate theory.

The theory should first of all distinguish the objective of explaining law-violating or deviant conduct from the objective of accounting for *rates of officially labeled delinquency* or crime. Many causal theories falsely assume a continuity between these, regarding the latter as merely an imperfect sample of the former.

Law-violating behavior that is either unknown to the community authorities or ignored or not acted upon by authorities is by all indications in total more prevalent than officially recorded or adjudicated law violation. But there are possible situations in which on the basis of official rates of law violation, the community surmises higher rates of law violation or more serious offenses than in fact prevail. Officially designated delinquency implies action by law enforcers or persons upholding their conception of the rules of the group. One study has commented:

> If our concern is with official delinquents, then investigations must encompass a broader spectrum of phenomena. In addition to indicating whether official delinquents, and their acts, differ from law abiders and undetected law violators, and their acts, investigations must take into account the acts and judgments of the agents of juvenile justice. The factors that lead to official labeling, as well as those that lead to law violating acts, must be explained. (Empey and Lubeck, 1971, p. 148)

Secondly, causal theories must separate the criteria of delinquency from the attributes or variables used to account for the delinquency. Failure to do so is circular reasoning, where the signs of criminality are also the diagnostic signs of the presumed cause. The abuse of the term "psychopathic personality" is a case in point. Michael Hakeem, reviewing textbooks on psychiatry, comments that a well-known text on psychiatry teaches that to place a subject in a category of psychopathic personality "the antisocial behavior of the patient should be the principal manifestation of the disorder." Another textbook advises that "no diagnosis of psychopathic personality should be made in the absence of punishable or censurable acts episodically carried out."

Causal theories must be explicit about the range of *offense* behavior they purport to explain. Does the presumed explanation pertain to all law-violating behavior, or only to violent offenses, property offenses, use of prohibited intoxicants, or violation of child-conduct laws. Does the theory apply to youthful offenses only, or is continuation to adulthood implied? Does the theory account for rate-producing behavior, and if so, is it police arrest rates, court commitments for males, females, or both?

Finally, theories of deviance or delinquency must keep separate the characteristics of the rule violator *prior* to efforts at control (adjudication, confinement, punishment, correction, treatment, etc.) from the characteristics of the youth observed *after* he has become a probationer, inmate, or parolee. (See Lemert, 1967, on the distinction between primary and secondary deviance.)

"The literature on delinquency theory," comment Cohen and Short (1966), "consists largely of arguments between partisans of 'psychological' and of 'sociological' theories." The actual data and even some of the explanations of these two camps frequently overlap, however, and we must be wary of overstressing the contrast. An explanation asserting that a boy has a greater chance of becoming a delinquent if he is rejected by his parents and accepted by a street gang may be phrased in the terms of personality and social psychology or in terms of ecology, small groups, and sociology. We must look at the data and explanations, not at the academic partisanship. Increasingly, it is apparent that characteristics in the situation of action, in the actor and in the rules and their enforcement all add influences to the production of delinquent phenomena.

4.2 Backgrounds to Current Theories: Physical Affinities

Contemporary efforts at understanding delinquency represent a departure from a previous tradition of thinking that enjoyed prominence for more than a century. The rise of positivistic philosophy reverberated in the 19th century as a dominant fact of intellectual life. The widespread applications of physical science, the triumph of evolutionary theory in biology, and the extension of natural science into the practice of medicine and the new discipline of public health contributed to a climate of thinking that sought solutions to a great number of problems of scientific (i.e., physical) investigations. The study of crime in the positivist approach may have had diverse beginnings but is conventionally dated from the appearance of the first and very influential publication of the Italian criminologist Lombroso. (But for earlier scientific works on the causes of crime, see below, pp. 53–54.) Lombroso put forward a theory that attributed criminal behavior to the influence of primitive traits that were evolutionary throwbacks (he called them *atavistic*) to an earlier, subhuman past.

Perusal of Lombroso's books (often quoted but seldom read) reveals what today seems a naive mixture of physical measurements (head shapes and cranial ratios, distribution of bodily hair, nose and ear shape, finger characteristics) with the blatant racism of 19th-century Western Europe. Pictures of dark Sicilian men and women stare from the pages with captions of "murder," and "prostitute." Descriptions of criminals in terms of despised physical, racial and regional characteristics (the dark, the short, the hairy) reinforced popular prejudice and justified many of the class discriminatory procedures of the time. Assumed equation of certain common Mediterranean Negroid and Oriental traits with primitivity and brutishness reveals the ideological convenience of the Lombroso school. More importantly for our study, the positivist school turned attention away from the *crime* and focused on the *criminal.* For a century after Lombroso, criminology became not the study of the unlawful actions but the study of the characteristics of the offender. The aim of criminology became the search for the criteria, or defining attributes, of the offender and the potential offender.

It is astonishing that Lombroso, although sustained by the philosophy of scientific investigation, was not tested by scientific means. Although it was theory that contained testable elements, it was not subject to systematic empirical validation for decades. It remained for a British statistician named Goring to provide factual data that did *not* support the claims of physical stigma and atavistic traits as the cause of crime. Goring's research showed *no* significant differences in physical traits of British and Scottish prison inmates and samples of noncriminals in the British Isles.

Goring's embarrassment of Lombroso marked the decline but not the demise of psysicalistic theorizing about delinquent behavior. Ernest Hooten (1939) published in the 1930's and 1940's books presenting a melange of methodological and conceptual confusion that advanced the thesis that body type was associated with criminality. Although his work is almost totally without merit, a more serious and carefully done example of neo-Lombrosian thinking may be found in the works of Sheldon (1949). Sheldon cited a line of somatotype classification that goes back to Hippocrates, presented a modern method of measuring and typing human physique, and linked this with a theory of "temperament," and then correlated both with delinquency. Sheldon assesses each individual in terms of a profile of three bodily components: endomorphy (round, visceral, fat), ectomorphy (skeletal, thin), and mesomorphy (muscular) and proposed that delinquents tended more often to be high on mesomorphy. Sheldon and Eleanor Glueck's (1956) voluminous research publications carried Sheldon's idea along with a number of other theories. The sampling and the definition of delinquency in their works have been extensively criticized and physical theories continue only as a distinctly esoteric theory of delinquency causation (See Cohen, Lindesmith, and Schuessler, 1956; and Cohen and Short, 1966).

Goring's own work demolished the thesis of physical types only to replace it with a theory of a logically similar sort; Goring also searched for the differentia specifica by which the delinquent could be isolated as a type, but he stated that this fatal flaw in the makeup of the offender was *mental.* Such an offender was

> one who is found to possess low degrees of general intelligence; or to hold extreme disregard for truth, for opinion, and for authority; or to be unteachable, unemployable, profligate, lazy; or to display marked preferences for undesirable company; or to be very impulsive, excitable, restless, uncertain, passionate, violent and refractory in conduct; or to be careless in business, neglectful in responsibility, false and malevolent in speech, filthy in habits, and nearly always inebriate. (Goring, in Hartung, p. 43)

It will be noted that while the theory stipulates mental deficiency, the traits above range far more widely into mood, behavior, and moral and aesthetic attributes. However, a number of studies of Zeleny (1933),

Vold (1958), and others (Shulman 1961; Neumeyer 1961) disconfirmed Goring in much the way that Goring originally upset Lombroso.

The real significance for the student of delinquency is the extent to which the physical theories of Lombroso correspond to what might be called "popular logic." These theories articulate a spirit of an age, depicting the criminal or the delinquent in a few easily recognizable signs that symbolize the criminal status. The underlying appeal of the physical theories—and to some extent the "subnormal mental" claim—is that they are in accord with what the public took to be the essential features of criminals. These theories depicted criminals in the stereotyped and heavily colored way that everyone could recognize, similar in a sense to the iconographic conventions by which artists represent personages or characters in paintings. The physical theories picture the offender in terms familiar to a world view of a certain age or class of people. They embody the common-sense assumptions that evil behavior must surely come from a flaw in the offender, that these flaws have a direct meaning that can be discerned (the mark of the brute) in the characteristics themselves. There is nothing inconsistent with having an iconography about what are essentially social conventions in the depiction of villainy; we have examples of highly specific procedures for recognizing and testing for witches and techniques for dealing with werewolves; the difficulty of establishing the existence of these signs as conclusive proof of the trait they were supposed to identify was not immediately an obstacle to the acceptance of the idea.

Although the early searches for the distinctive physical or mental traits of the criminal type were not successful, a third line of endeavor has been extremely important. One of the problems with the physical theories was the difficulty of postulating the way in which the supposed physical cause exerted its malicious effect. Since the laws defining offenses vary from place to place and from one time to another, how does the gene or body type issue forth in biologically determined delinquencies? The successor to physical theory in the positivist search for the distinguishing marks of the offender provides a much more interesting answer to this question than its predecessors. This is the line of thinking that asserts that delinquent behavior is an expression of emotional disorder or a distinctive personality pattern.

A number of different positions have emerged. On the most general level, almost any view of the causes of criminal behavior admits that emotional characteristics of persons may be involved in certain law violations. But to assert the relevance of "personality" factors to delinquent behavior says little. Of course, personality is relevant to behavior. The question is how much and in what way? Psychological or psychopathological explanations essentially say that personality characteristics are *crucially* involved. The research interest in determining the extent to which a particular combination of personality characteristics is distinctive or predictive of delinquent rather than law-abiding behavior is much more to the point, and so far the data, despite decades of research, are still ambiguous.

The purest statement of the claim is that offenders have distinctive personality traits that mark the offender from the nonoffender. The important test of this claim is to be provided by studies that seek to demonstrate that offenders as a group score differently on measures of personality as compared with nonoffenders as a group.

Karl Schuessler and Donald Cressey (1950) assessed 113 studies of personality differences between criminals and noncriminals done prior to 1950. The results failed to establish the personality components of criminal behavior. Criminals and noncriminals often had largely overlapping distributions on test scores. Also, test results do not distinguish between personality traits causing criminal experience and traits that could be produced by criminal experience.

The Schuessler-Cressey review was done a long time ago. Moreover, it strove to be inclusive and has been criticized for not rejecting a number of poorly designed or interpreted studies. In an attempt to remedy this, as well as to bring the data up to recent years, the literature from the end of the Schussler-Cressey review through 1965 was assessed by Waldo and Dinitz (1967). They surveyed U.S. journals and classified articles on personality and delinquency according to the manner by which personality was measured (objective, projective, and performance) and the quality of the methodology (control of background variables, sample size, and comparisons between delinquents and nondelinquents). The authors found that studies using objective tests such as the Minnesota Multiphasic Personality Inventory and the California Psychological Inventory most often showed some differences between delinquents and nondelinquents. Performance and projective tests distinguished less often and less consistently. The results of the best of these, the MMPI-CPI group, are interpreted as support for the contention that the personalities of delinquents differ in some way from those of law-abiding persons. The authors register a number of important reservations however. First, after noting that statistical significance was reached in some studies by differences in responses of the delinquent and nondelinquent groups to only four items out of a total of fifty, they state:

> Although this represents statistical significance it is difficult to ascertain the degree of theoretical significance involved. Since one item of the scale is "I have never been in trouble with the law" a positive response to this

> item alone would tend to discriminate statistically between delinquents and non-delinquents if the sample were of sufficient size. (Waldo and Dinitz, 1967, p. 156)

They also quote Volkman's reminder that the MMPI is a self-descriptive inventory, which asks the respondent to answer a variety of items related to habit (19 items), family and marriage questions (12 items), sexual attitudes (16 items), religion (19), political attitudes, including law and order (46), and social attitudes (72) (Waldo and Dinitz, 1967, p. 156, quoting Volkman, 1959). Waldo and Dinitz also note that some studies fail to control for other variables in the responses differences, such as institutional setting *per se*, that many studies did not employ random samples of delinquents and nondelinquents, and that differences within delinquent and nondelinquent groups were sometimes greater than mean differences between the groups. They end by stating that the results are "far from conclusive." It is striking then that two reviews of published studies of personality differences between the law-violating and the law-abiding, which taken together reviewed 207 studies ranging over several decades of research, are unable to provide any firm basis for the claim that there are distinguishable and characteristic features in the personality of the offender.

Although the search for demonstrable differences in the psyches of offenders as compared with nonoffenders has proven fruitless, the continued appeal of the claim that disorderly or undesirable conduct must have something to do with disordered or problematic personalities has produced more complex formulations of this argument. One argument holds that although problematic personal traits are essentially shared by delinquents and nondelinquents alike, these traits, in combination with certain other social conditions in the environment of the individual (e.g. poverty), yield a higher probability of law violation; another more complex argument holds that widely distributed traits and conditions, in combination with certain policies of public notice (e.g. local law enforcement policies toward violence or violent types), may result in a high probability of delinquency. The appearance of these arguments marks the difference between the first half of the 20th century and the second as far as speculation in this area is concerned. These more complex arguments lead to considerations of differential treatments for different types of offender personality problems, or different combinations of personal traits and social or collective situations requiring (or excusing) differential dispositions made of delinquent cases.

The confusion is reduced considerably by a rough typology put forward by David Matza in two stimulating books, *Delinquency and Drift* (Matza, 1964) and *Becoming Deviant* (Matza, 1969).

One type of theory of the causes of deviance Matza calls *affinity* theory, a word that implies a close connection, an inclination, or attraction. Affinity arguments cite a set of personal attributes or conditions that in themselves increase the probability that persons will be propelled into delinquent conduct. The simple physical, mental, and personality theories just reviewed are examples of criminal affinities located in the individual. Sociological affinities are exemplified in social conditions such as low income, dilapidated housing, high unemployment census tracts, which have been shown to be correlated with crime and delinquency rates. A number of persons living in a situation regarded as problematic or inadequate will acquire a set of problematic personal traits or habits as a consequence. The mechanism is seldom clearly specified.[1] Such a view points out "bad" antecedents to deviant behavior and assumes simple contact with these conditions results in delinquent behavior. Unlike the notion of contagion in public health, there is no germ theory of disease to provide a mechanism and an explanation.

4.3 Ecological Studies

Many of the affinity arguments were derived from early ecological studies showing differing collective rates of crime or delinquency in various areas of a city. In some cities with histories of foreign immigration, successive waves of immigrants . . . Irish, Italian, European Jew, southern U.S. black and Puerto Rican . . . occupied the same or overlapping residental areas; it was held that although the cultural backgrounds of these populations changed as one group moved out and another moved in, the slums retained fairly consistent high delinquency rates. It was concluded that something inherent in the social or physical conditions of the areas transmitted the delinquent behavior.

The ecological approach actually predates the positivistic (physical) theory. Yale Levin and Alfred Lindesmith in a 1937 article (Voss and Peterson, 1971) take note of the ecological studies of crime carried out in England between 1830 and 1860. These early 19th-century studies documented that youthful and adult criminals were disproportionately located in densely populated urban or metropolitan neighborhoods characterized by deteriorated housing, overcrowding, and recent in-migration. These latter conditions in turn were seen to be related to the rapid growth and dominance in Great Britain of the manufacturing system. The phenomenon of the juvenile gang was cited as a special problem in 1850. Joseph Mayhew's *Criminal Prisons and Scenes of Prison Life* (1862) brought forward a mass of evidence relating rates of crime to social characteristics; Levin and Lindesmith pointed out that Mayhew explicitly discussed and

[1]Although in view of some rather extensive and closely reasoned material by Shaw and McKay (1969) toward this end, Matza's dismissal of the mechanisms in affinity theories must be regarded as an overstatement.

rejected the physical or constitutional theory of criminality many years before Lombroso's famous book was published.

The early British studies were emulated in the United States by two large surveys supported and published by the Russell Sage Foundation in New York: *The West Side* (New York) *Studies*, 1914 and the *Pittsburgh Survey*, 1914.

The Chicago sociologists Clifford Show and Henry McKay, beginning in 1929, produced an important ecological study of records of juvenile courts that had widespread influence in the U.S. for two decades. They concluded:

> *1.* There is marked variation in delinquency rates between different areas in Chicago.
> *2.* Rates of delinquency and adult crime vary inversely with distance from city center.
> *3.* Truancy, delinquency and crime rates are positively correlated.
> *4.* High crime rates are found in areas of physical deterioration.
> *5.* Crime rates remain stable over time especially in high rate areas, despite changes in population.
> *6.* Recidivism varies directly with delinquency rate. (Voss and Peterson, 1971, p. 13)

As important as their positive findings, however, have been the problems that have become clearer in the critiques and replication attempts stimulated by the Shaw and McKay studies.

It is striking that the most salient aspect of the research of Shaw and McKay, that is, that they studied urban *areas* by analysis of area characteristics, should have been so frequently overlooked in efforts to understand the behavior of individuals. Their data were based on census districts; the delinquency measure was the number of males less than 17 years of age[2] (per 100 of all males of same age) who were alleged to be delinquents in petitions to juvenile court. One set of their findings relates this measure of male delinquency rate to (a) distance of census district from the center of the Chicago central business district; (b) to the proportion of dilapidated buildings and level of pollution in district; (c) mean monthly rental or equivalent for buildings in district; (d) income of residents of area. The relationship is an inverse correlation in each instance.

Kobrin, in a perceptive critique of Shaw and McKay, related the several empirical foci of their interests to several types of data and concepts. He cites three primary sets of data: (a) basic data establishing differential rates of delinquency in relation to area characteristics; (b) correlation of crime rates with social characteristics of communities ("heterogeneity and instability of the population, characteristics intensified by the presence

[2]In one early study it was 16, a fact commented on below, p. 56.

of marginal, criminal, or unconventional persons, reduced the capacity of the population to act collectively in the solution of common problems by reducing its social solidarity. Inability to engage in common action was conceptualized as community disorganization"); and (c) community demoralization, reduced control of children, widespread approval of adult law violations, active and pervasive street gangs, and a tradition of juvenile delinquency (see Kobrin, in Voss and Peterson, pp. 107–8).

The ecological research of Shaw and McKay is impressive; moreover it is supplemented by a number of intensive biographical case studies (*Jack Roller*, 1930; *The Natural History of a Delinquent Career*, 1931). Yet together the area data and the case histories do not sustain the weight of the specific statements in their theory.

A paper by W. S. Robinson (1950) makes a crucial distinction between correlation measures based on measures made on individual persons and correlations based on a group of persons. Robinson shows by examples and by statistical reasoning that the two kinds of calculation do not necessarily lead to the same correlation on the same variable. For example, a correlation based on census tracts, correlating the percentage nonwhite with the percentage illiterate, yields a very high correlation coefficient (in Robinson's example, .95). On the same population if correlation of race (black and white) and literacy is calculated on measurements made on the same individuals, the coefficient is low (in his illustration, .20).

Robinson's article should be consulted for the underlying reason,[3] but the implication is clear for the Shaw and McKay ecological studies: so long as we are concerned with properties of area, the relationships reported between group proportions are informative and reasonable. If we are primarily concerned with the behavior of individuals, the ecological correlations are not informative and are not a substitute for individual measurements.

It would seem that part of the time Shaw and McKay are explicitly concerned with area characteristics; thus

> it is clear from the data included in this volume that there is a direct relationship between conditions existing in local communities of American cities and differential rates of delinquents and criminals. Communities with high rates have social and economic characteristics which differentiate them from communities with low rates. (Shaw and McKay, 1969, p. 315)

But at other times Shaw and McKay are reasoning about individual and small group (interpersonal) processes.

> [The delinquency] tradition . . . becomes meaningful to the child through

[3]Basically, it is because individual correlation is a function of internal table frequencies, but ecological correlations are derived from marginal frequencies.

> the conduct, speech, gestures and attitudes of persons with whom he has contact. (Shaw and McKay, p. 316)

Still another concern is salient in the work of Shaw and McKay: the inference that community disorganization is associated with high rates of delinquency and crime.

Even the area characteristics cited by Shaw and McKay are not always consistent with their conclusions. Jonassen, 1949, in Voss and Peterson, 1971 challenges their conclusion that ecology and location impose more or less constant rates of delinquency on successive waves of immigrants that move into and through the city over time.

Jonassen shows that a change in the age definition of delinquency in their time data (males ages 10–15 for one series, 10–16 for another) introduces some error, and that a number of factors that may very well have changed over the years (1900–1906 and 1917–1923) in Chicago were not assessed in their study. Finally their own tables (in *Social Factors in Juvenile Delinquency*, pp. 87–89) show,

> Comparing [the tables] it will be seen that in [one] area, Germans, Irish, English-Scotch and Scandinavians show a rate of delinquency lower than might be expected by their presence in the population, in both series; while the Italians show a rate very much higher than should be expected. And [in another area], the Slavic group and the Italian group in the early series show a disproportionate amount of delinquency, while the other groups contribute their quota of delinquents or less than might be expected on the basis of their presence in the population. (Kobrin, in Voss and Peterson, 1971, p. 141)

Other weaknesses in the classics of Shaw and McKay are clearer to the reader now than in the 1930s. The measurement of zones from city center in miles, irrespective of any consideration of naturally occurring boundaries or socially recognized communities, makes possible the inclusion of dissimilar neighborhoods in one area. Heavy reliance on case histories of lengthy delinquent careers is not a safe basis from which to generalize to the majority of youth in even the high delinquency-rate community. The total exclusion of females leaves half of the youth totally unaccounted for, and ecological argument is embarassed by the low rates of delinquency for females recorded by the agencies. Perhaps the most troublesome lapse of all is the lack of concern with the policies and day-to-day operations of law enforcement and criminal (and juvenile) courts. The role of these agencies in the definition of offenses and the disposition of cases is not discussed even speculatively.

The ecological studies took a different turn with the publication of a monograph by Bernard Landen (1954). He studied Baltimore and concluded that the Burgess zonal hypothesis did not fit Baltimore, that area characteristics (proximity to business and manufacturing, distance from city center, etc.) did not correlate with crime in Baltimore in the way suggested by the Chicago studies and that even measures that did correspond to the Shaw-McKay theory (housing quality, socioeconomic variables) should be reinterpreted. Using a multivariate statistical technique (factor analysis) he concluded that the stability or instability of a population (he used the term *anomie*) caused delinquency. Many have questioned Landen's interpretation of his own data. Bordua in 1959 attempted to replicate the Landen study on Detroit data. He found partial confirmation, but observed,

> Future studies in a similar vein might profit by a more critical look at the "anomie" concept as used by Landen. In the obliquely rotated factor analysis referred to previously, Landen located a cluster of indicators that he named the "anomie" factor. These were the delinquency rate percent of non-white and percent of homes owner occupied. Landen himself points out the tautological nature of such a finding if we seek a causal solution. He treats all three as indicators of an underlying situation "anomie" which he defines as a condition in which social norms do not regulate conduct. Clearly then, anomie cannot cause delinquency. Delinquency is a species of anomie.(Voss and Peterson, p. 184)

Chilton (1964) in yet another replication (Indianapolis) with Baltimore and Detroit for comparison, uncovered an important computational error in the original Landen study, which leads Chilton to conclude that the study is "equivocal."

Rosen and Turner (1967) criticize Landen's methodology, showing that his factor analysis does *not* yield independent dimensions, and hence his claim that delinquency is unrelated to economic situation is unwarranted.

The ecological theories carry the implication that socioeconomic class and minority group status underlie much of the geographical correlations with delinquency. We are in a better position than earlier students to see that simple physical features of the community probably have little to do with delinquency, and that merely exchanging tenements for housing projects has not produced lower delinquency rates, and in some cases—the Pruit-Igo project in Saint Louis being perhaps the classic, penultimate instance—has brought an increase rather than a decrease in delinquency.

Suttles (1968) has provided a recent contribution to the long Chicago tradition of urban ecological research in an unusually perceptive monograph reporting research on the near West Side area of Chicago. Spending three years living in a low-income area of Italian, Mexican, Puerto Rican, and black residents, Suttles combines intensive ethnographic observation with full coverage of a "natural" urban area. His account begins with an analysis of ethnic segmentation in social solidarity and use of territory, and from there moves to an account of the place of youthful gangs in the life of the slum community. Suttles characterizes the urban slum he studied as a provincial area where "social relations are restricted to permit only the safest ones" (Suttles, p. 8). The frequently observed working-class reluctance to use the home for gatherings of any but relatives is documented here. Further he sees the segmentation of the populace along sex, age, and ethnic lines as further steps to reduce what are regarded as risks of contact. The restriction of social relations provides some measure of relief from the anonymity of a partially transient population and also permits some information to be gathered on otherwise potentially hazardous companions.

> . . . slum residents can assuage at least some of their apprehensions by a close inquiry into each other's personal character and past history. Communication then should be of an intimate character and aimed toward producing personal rather than formal relations. In turn, social relations will represent a sort of private "compact" where particularistic loyalties replace impersonal standards of worth. (Suttles, p. 8)

The extent to which this slum population is divided into ethnic solidarities is documented in many ways: ethnic differentiation in clothing styles, recreational establishment clientele, gang hangout areas, churches, language, public behavior, and area of residence.

The pluralism of the urban slum is recognized by Suttles to provide less of a normative basis (common values in terms of which deviance is defined) than a set of expectations, interpersonal and intergroup strategies, and sanctions based on reputation and situation.

Suttles observes that the area contained about 32 named male street gangs and six female groups between 1962 and 1965. He draws attention to the fact that sex differentiation and segregation is the most important and pervasive cleavage in social relations throughout the area, followed in importance by age, ethnicity, and residence.

The adolescent street gang is seen as a primary group that affords some small universe of responsiveness and esteem in a transient world of front stoop gatherings, huge housing projects, and urban renewal bulldozers.

Such a detailed accounting of territory and social structure allows Suttles to relate offense behavior and victimization to community characteristics. He documents differential policies of police handling juvenile complaints depending on the ethnicity of the offender. He concludes that interpersonal conflict tends to be mainly in the Adams area, and property offenses outside this area.

Ecological studies do not explain the appearance of any particular child in the juvenile court or jail, but these studies have made important contributions:

a. They provide descriptions of area differences in various official and unofficial rates of delinquency and police activity. The social characteristics related to these differences are problematic—to be accounted for by any causal theory and to be addressed by any effective program related to crime and delinquency.

b. The ecological studies based on correlations between proportions or percentages of area residents should not be confused with nor taken for descriptions or explanations of individual behavior.

c. The descriptive, ethnographic study of ecological areas provides the data on social context for law-violating behavior and law-enforcement behavior. This is an inescapable socio-cultural-political context necessary if the delinquent gang is to be distinguished from minority youth protest or police harassment of blacks or chicanos or "hillbillies."

d. Ecological-community studies focused on the community rather than on the "delinquent" or the gang provide information on the interaction between adjudicated or accused deviant and the nonlabeled members of the community, and provide data on the noncriminal opportunity structure in the area.

e. Community studies have the potential for more detailed and realistic understanding of police and legal operations within that sector of the populace.

4.4 Affiliation Theories

Affiliation theories stipulate that persons associating with those whose values favor law violation will themselves become disposed to violate the law. People are viewed as likely to take on the characteristics of the groups they join or are most strongly associated with. The affiliation argument is metaphorically linked with the idea of conversion, the adoption or receiving of an individual into a solidarity.

Affiliation is a fundamental concept in sociological and social psychological theories of delinquent behavior. The term affiliation originally referred to taking someone into a family, uniting or attaching in close connection those who were previously unattached. Matza defines the underlying process as one by which an individual is converted to conduct that is novel for him but established for the group. Indeed, the affiliation argument works best if we ignore the question: where does the *group* get its values, or its conduct?

Affiliation theories are of two types, which may be called positive and negative affiliation. Positive affiliation theory asserts that persons who associate with individuals or groups holding values favorable to law violation will themselves be likely to embrace these values and violate the law. This principle, best known in the form of a statement by the criminologist Sutherland as "differential association," is based on general ideas of social learning. It assumes that crime is learned behavior, and that this learning takes place in small groups with which the individual seeks membership. Persons take on the crimes common to the groups they join.

Consider the data provided by participant observation studies of how people learn the habits of work in factories. One such study (Bensman and Gerver, 1963) was conducted in an aircraft manufacturing plant. One phase of the study centered on the manner in which new employees were socialized into the use of a prohibited illegal tool, the *tap*. The tap is a device by which two connection holes may be rethreaded so as to properly align. The result of tapping, however, is to structurally weaken the part in question (in this operation because it destroys the effectiveness of "stop nuts" used to safeguard bolts in the airframe). The mere possession of a tap by an employee was recognized by the contract as grounds for dismissal. It is thus an offense clearly prohibited in the rules, with sanctions (dismissal) threatened in the event of noncompliance with the rule.

New employees, encountering a difficulty in work, seek assistance from an experienced workman. After seeking a legitimate resolution of the difficulty (say, aligning the holes in two sheets of metal) the experienced worker would resort to the use of the tap, meanwhile lecturing the novice on the need for discretion in its use. If the employee stays on, after a few weeks he may have had a number of occasions for seeking the assistance of a more experienced worker who has a tap. At some point the novice may be loaned the tap to use himself. He may even be told by the foreman to use a tap. When the new worker gains more experience he buys his own tap. Full acceptance is signaled when a foreman or other employee borrows the newcomer's tap for his use. Even government inspectors were involved in the use of taps. But the prohibition is not total and the fervor of the inspector is shortlived.

Inspectors sometimes reprimanded a new worker caught using a tap, and sometimes a new inspector reprimanded a worker for using a tap, but dismissals are rarely reported. The tool crib of the shop even had tap extractors for use when a tap broke off in a hole. These could be checked out by employees without consequences despite the illegality of the tap.

The point of this study is clear. Discreet use of the tap is a condition of belonging to the work group; a novice is initiated into the use of an illegal device as he is introduced into the group itself. Indeed, for a novice to steadily refuse to adopt the use of the illegal tap would be deviant and imperil his standing in the group.

It takes little extension to apply this observation to a school situation where a boy moves into a peer group with an established practice of glue sniffing or store theft, or a boy joining a gang in which a boy's reputation and self-respect are related to manifestations of dependability, courage and "heart" as demonstrated in gang fights.

Whether the situation described above is a reliable model for more generalized social situations is a matter for further investigation. Affiliation arguments, nonetheless, account for a person's behavior by locating his interpersonal ties and the consequent learning based on the values and expectations of the group within which he maintains his ties. This suggests that deviance and conformity, like most other things in the world, are relative matters. Conformity to group expectations may constitute deviation from societal rules; the rule conformist or law-abiding person may be considered a group norm deviant. There are four possibilities if we consider that conduct may be sanctioned positively or negatively by the group, and be in conformity or defiance of the law of the wider society, as shown below:

TABLE 4.1

Effect of Membership in Small Group (Gang) on Law-Violating Conduct

		The Relation Between Group Activities and the Law	
		Group in Conformity with the Law	*Group in Conflict with the Law*
The Relationship Between Individual Conduct and Group	*Individual Conforms*	group membership leads to law-abiding behavior	group membership leads to law violation and delinquency
	Individual Violates	alienation from group likely to lead to law violation	alienation from group likely to reduce likelihood of law violation

Affiliation arguments, as we have considered them so far, link membership in deviance-sanctioning groups with law violation. A second form of the affiliation argument, however, links rule violation and nonconformity with social isolation and nonmembership. We saw in the example of the airframe plant that an aloof or rejected individual in the work group would not learn the plant's law-violating behavior (the use of the tap). However, in other cases, nonmembership also facilitates flaunting of group norms. Failure from an early age to affiliate with a family group may result in particular insensitivities to certain rules or expectations prevalent in the community.

Positive affiliation explanations do not account for either the presence of the illegal activity in the group in the first place, or the specific motivation for joining the group, although the theory is compatible with other explanations of why individuals join groups. It links deviance with membership in a deviant group.

Negative affiliation theory is the reverse of the positive argument. Instead of explaining delinquent or criminal behavior by discovering to what groups a person belongs, negative explanations argue that the absence of ties to a norm-bearing or group permits an individual to act in violation of that norm. This perspective suggests that persons with weak ties to other people, to the conventional segments of the community, are free of the reach of the moral sentiments embraced by those persons or that segment, and hence are psychologically free to flaunt that rule.

Some research provides specific support for affiliation theory. Consider the Cambridge-Sommerville Youth Study, which began with the idea that one could make a reduction in the delinquency rates of working class youth in these semi-rundown areas of Boston if the kids were channeled early enough into relationships of companion and advisor (that is, a model) with a sympathetic adult. Accordingly, approximately one thousand boys in their early teens were referred to this project by schools, churches, police, and so on—all of whom had been designated "predelinquent," though no uniform criteria were employed in arriving at this judgment. It was felt, however, that all the children selected would benefit from some type of social counseling.

To this initial group was added a corresponding group of so-called "normal" children (not thought to be predelinquent, though again no uniform criteria were used) and eventually, 325 pairs of children, some of whom were "likely delinquents" and some of whom were not, were gathered for the study itself. Some received special counseling, some were exposed only to normal services and interactions—the studies continuing from 1939 to 1945. Thus the study began keeping records on these kids before they developed any delinquency.

In attempting to relate its findings to affinity and affiliation arguments, the Cambridge-Sommerville Study rated the neighborhoods in which the subjects lived according to community organizations, dilapidation, prevalence of gangs, and so on, arriving at four neighborhood "types." The subsequent delinquent records of the study groups were then tabulated solely in relation to the neighborhoods in which they had lived, rated from "good" to "worst." The probability that a boy will be convicted or sentenced is highest for worst neighborhoods. This result, however, may reflect the discretion of the judge in assessing the prospects of the juvenile offender on the basis of his background (does the kid live in a "good" or a "bad" neighborhood). We should also recognize that the neighborhood-type spread in this study is much narrower than would be found in an entire city: the "good" neighborhood in this study, for example, representing a clean, quiet, working-class neighborhood, not an affluent middle-class suburb.

The Cambridge-Sommerville Study also tabulated gang membership with subsequent delinquency, the data showing that 75 percent of regular gang members developed subsequent criminal behavior, while 30 percent of nonmembers developed similar patterns. Intermittent gang members were in the middle, 50 percent. While these figures tend to support affiliation theories of delinquent behavior, we must remember that these arguments do not account for the social phenomenon called the "gang," and thus offer incomplete explanations at best.

The main focus of attention in this study was the characteristics of the families in which the children were living at the time of the study; to this end, a number of tables characterizing home atmosphere in terms of selected adjectives were constructed and utilized. We must note that a very conventional idea of what constituted home atmosphere was employed: at this time, the war had siphoned off most male social workers and most younger people in general; thus the ratings were made primarily by the more elderly females who remained (those whose ideas were likely to be the most conservative). Nevertheless, four types of home environment were distinguished: (1) *cohesive,* if mutual family affection and sharing in activities was evident, not much arguing; (2) *quarrelsome but affectionate,* if there was a lot of conflict but cordiality prevailed; no real violence done in the heat of arguments; (3) *quarrelsome and neglecting,* conflict-ridden with parents neglecting even the physical needs of their children and disliking each other, and (4) *broken homes,* in which the parental bond had been broken by death, divorce, or other disruption. These results clearly suggest that there may be (on the basis of this study at least) (McCord, McCord, and Zola, 1959, p. 83) something worse than a broken home; the highest probability of subsequent criminal behavior ending in conviction was found to be associated with the quarrelsome/neglecting home atmosphere. The study therefore went on to analyze father-child relationships, distinguishing five father-types: (1) *passive,* not participating in family management; (2) *warm,* affectionate toward his children; (3) *neglecting,* rejecting; (4) *cruel,* imposing harsh punishment; and (5) *absent,* departed or dead. Least delinquency-prone offspring were expected to result from relationships with a warm, affectionate father; most delinquency-prone offspring were expected to come from relationships with cruel fathers. The results, however, indicated that *neglecting fathers* produced the highest percentage of delinquent offspring.

The Cambridge-Sommerville Study reanalysis by the McCords thus explains some delinquent behavior by charting nonviable bonds between the delinquent person and his early sources of affiliation.

Travis Hirshi, whose survey of Richmond, California junior and senior high school boys we considered briefly in Chapter Two, advances an affiliation theory of delinquency. Delinquent boys, he suggests, are but a special case of the general proposition that "the essence of internalization of norms, conscience or super ego . . . lies in the attachment of the individual to others" (Hirshi, 1969, p. 18). Hirshi's survey data link self-reported law violation with reports of closeness of relationship of the child to his parents: the closer the relationship, the less his delinquency. The basic data appear below:

TABLE 4.2

Reported Intimate Communication with Father

		Little Communication				*Much Communication*
Frequency of delinquent acts (self-report)	None	39	55	55	63	73
	One	18	25	28	23	22
	Two or More	43	20	17	15	15
		100	100	100	100	100
	Total Cases	(97)	(182)	(436)	(287)	(121)

Source: Table 19, p. 91, in Hirshi, 1969.

Subjects' report of closeness of mother's supervision yields a similar correlation with delinquency. The finding is irrespective of the social-class level of the parents. Other findings are consistent. Those boys indicating concern for approval of middle-class persons (such as teachers) report lower levels of rule-violating behavior.

The influence of affiliation with delinquent models is also demonstrated in the Hirshi data. Boys reporting having close friends who have been picked up by police are themselves more likely to report higher levels of delinquent behavior.

Commitment to conventional institutions (school achievement, liking high-school experience, etc.) contributes to low delinquency scored, and in conjunction with affiliation with parents and combined with no close friendship with boys who have been picked up by the police, produced high probability of nondelinquency. Hirshi summarizes his argument:

> The child with little stake in conformity is susceptible to predelinquent influences in his environment; the child with a large stake in conformity is relatively immune to these influences. The greater the exposure to "crimi-

nal influences" the greater the difference in delinquent activity between high and low stake boys. (Hirshi, 1969, p. 161)

4.5 Theories Combining Affinity and Affiliation

A substantial line of theorizing and investigation has postulated more complex explanations of delinquency in terms of lower-class culture, deprivation, blocked opportunity, low achievement and strain, peer dependency, gangs and deviant youth subcultures, and finally, resulting delinquency. In a monograph that contributes to the clarification of several arguments and the specification of certain difficulties in all of them, Empey and Lubeck identify a basic, if complex, theory uniting class, individual frustration, and delinquency.

> Born into conditions of poverty and deprived of the kinds of intellectual and interpersonal experiences that are necessary for achievement in a success-oriented society, lower class children are terribly handicapped, if not doomed to failure. The result is a growing sense of frustration that not only alienates some of them from conventional rules and expectations, but turns a significant number to membership in delinquent groups where the tendency is to repudiate basic values. Deviant norms, alternative sources of satisfaction and illegal activities are the result. Delinquency has been spawned. (Empey and Lubeck, p. 3)

This complex argument weaves through a tradition of studies on lower-class culture (Monahan, 1957; Hirshi, 1969; Miller, 1958; Cohen, 1955; Cloward and Ohlin, 1960). The argument is not always stated in the same way. Miller for example asserts that lower-class values are different from middle-class values; Hirschi and Matza (1964) affirm on the other hand no great alienation of lower-class youth from many middle-class values. Cohen and Cloward and Ohlin believe in an essential continuity in values, but postulate that blocked opportunity among the deprived and the despised leads to frustration, anomie, and rejection of lawful control by some lower-class youth.

Empey and Lubeck test a formulation of this theory by a large set of statistical correlations on four samples of boys: adjudged delinquents from Los Angeles, delinquents from Utah, nondelinquent (never arrested) boys from Los Angeles, and nondelinquents from Utah. The Los Angeles data were apparently collected ten years after Utah data. Delinquent samples were repeat offenders, incarcerated by juvenile authorities. They correlate measures of social class, achievement, strain, identification with delinquent peer groups, and delinquency. The results failed to support the hypothesis that social class was correlated with achievement, strain, identification with peers, or adjudged delinquency (See Empey and Lubeck, 1971, Chap. 4). The delinquents in both samples were drawn from various levels of the class structure, although it must be noted that these samples are numerically small and that scant attention seemed to be given to how representative each was, particularly of ethnic minorities. Nonetheless, their data are consistent with some other studies. They cite Polk (1967), who summarizes research showing inconsistent relationships between individual class status and delinquent behavior. They also cite the self-report studies of Nye and Short, Gold, and others, which show no correlation between class and law-violating behavior. Regarding class, Empey and Lubeck caution

> This conclusion is not meant to suggest that class differences do not exist, especially when ecological rather than individual measurement is used. But what it does imply . . . is that our understanding of delinquency and other adolescent difficulties might be enhanced if we concentrate our search upon other determinants for which social class, by itself, may be a poor clue. The fact that delinquency is not limited to the lower class suggests that we might discover as many differences within classes as we discover between them. (Empey and Lubeck, p. 48)

Empey and Lubeck did find that low performance was associated with measures of strain, that poor school performance was weakly correlated with peer group identification, that "identification with delinquent peers was associated with adjudged delinquency," (p. 67) as were strain and lack of achievement. Poor grades in school were particularly predictive of subsequent delinquent behavior. The authors go on to comment

> Contrary to theoretical expectation the achievement and strain measures tended to be more highly related to delinquency than were the indicators of peer identification. (Empey and Lubeck, p. 121)

Empey and Lubeck, in the later chapters of their book, go on to consider features in the community and in the juvenile justice system that affect the probability of being adjudged delinquent (Empey and Lubeck, Chap. 2). The perspective that gives such factors greatest priority has recently been referred to as labeling.

4.6 Labeling

Matza mentions a third argument, which he calls signification. A more common sociological term for this is *labeling*. Labeling theories shift the focus of attention still further away from the offending individual than did the affiliation arguments. Where affinity explanations scrutinize the offender for characteristics in him or in his situation that cause delinquency, affiliation arguments look out to the interpersonal bonds the individual has formed, or the failure of such bonds to be formed at all, and labeling looks to the enforcer of rules rather than the violator. According to this view, rule-violating behavior becomes socially significant and meaningful only when individuals are designated as "offenders" by some group or agency. An individual so labeled may accept the role; more importantly, the significance of his conduct is assessed by others according to that label. The labeling argument may be characterized by the root metaphor *stigmatizing*. Both affiliation and labeling presume interaction; linking the individual with other people.

Labeling theory takes as its problem how rule-violating behavior is converted into socially recognized deviance. It seeks to explain the actions of someone or some group who publicly defines acts and persons as in violation of rules, and some office that brings sanctions against offenders under certain conditions. The first assumption of labeling theory is that residual rule violation is going on in the population more or less continuously. The second assumption is that people tend to act in accordance with the conception others have of them, and over time other people act toward a person in accordance with his reputation, public identity, or dominant status characteristics. Labeling theory has relatively little to say about episodic acts of violating rules. It has more to say about the process by which an individual develops a consistent pattern of behavior in violation of rules. It suggests that stigma, exclusion, and special roles for delinquent or criminal tend to confirm or validate a status as deviant and over time move the incumbent of such a special status further from the mainstream of community life. Getting a youth to think of himself or herself as delinquent, or an adult to think of himself or herself as criminal, and getting others to deal with such persons in terms of this persistent status, perpetuates a criminal career. This is particularly the case when sanctions include displacement from the community for long periods of time. Employment difficulties of the ex-convict, for example, create difficulties for him, in turn increasing the probability of violation of parole, in turn increasing precautionary restraints on him, in turn pushing him further out, and so on.

The business of the special agencies for regulation of conduct of children is to control behavior that has been picked out by some agency or office as problematic. By picking it out, an agency may establish limits on the problematic behavior, but it may also confirm the deviant status. The long-term delinquent or repeat offender cannot be understood without considering the possibility that the effect of social control is to produce deviance; that delinquency may be a response to control.

This is not to say that the rule violation would disappear if the definitions of the delinquent character of that behavior were to disappear. But it would no longer be criminal.

The affiliation argument, as we saw, takes two forms: the first says that an individual (or "'actor'') establishes interpersonal bonds, he acquires novel behavior; the second says that as an individual is excluded from a group or from strong interpersonal relations, he will not acquire the ways of behaving established for those other persons. Combining these two, we see according to affiliation theory that if an individual is cut off from groups that observe the law, and if additionally the individual is drawn into groups whose values sanction law-violating conduct, such a person is doubly likely to violate the law. In such a situation nothing special need be posited about the individual himself.

The labeling argument points out that the actor who is labeled deviant, delinquent, or criminal by others in fact becomes confirmed in the deviance when this label defines the reactions of others toward him. The labeling argument implies two things: that the meaning of behavior is determined by an outside label, and such labeling leads to a definition of delinquency (that is, without labeling there is no official delinquency), and that an individual so labeled may react to the label itself. This reaction, called secondary deviance, may be different from the original rule-violating behavior.

4.7 The Concept of "Deviance" and the Problems of Understanding Social Control

The sociology of "deviance" has denoted a perspective in the social sciences for the past twenty years. "Deviant" has come to be an important, or at any rate frequently used, term. Early usage was careful enough: deviance was one of a set of concepts comprising an analytic model. Deviance denoted behavior of one acting person, regarded by another person as an undesirable departure from a commonly held norm or institutionalized expectation (Lemert, 1947; Parsons, 1951; Merton, 1957).

The elaboration of this simple model represented a reaction to an earlier trend of interpreting various conventionally or officially designated misbehavior as indicators of social pathology or disorganization of family, small group, or community (Mills, 1943; Gordon, 1958; Matza, 1970). This approach took cultural assumptions from various sources: small-town nostalgia, Christian-liberal values, white middle-class economics, and official mandates of various welfare, medical, law enforcement, and correctional agencies. It maintained a strong identification with the operating aims and problems of control of police, military, government, church, and welfare agencies and frequently adopted, as a definition of "deviance" or "social problem," the prevailing official perspectives on actual or "potential" prisoners, patients, and clients. It took the existence of conventionally designated deviants as given and asked: how did these people get this way?[4]

Merton and Parsons were explicit that "deviant" could mean nothing without a careful statement of *what* norm was taken as the expected, and *from what* (or whose) perspective the action in question was defined as deviant.

> . . . there is a certain relativity in the conceptions of conformity and deviance. . . . It is therefore not possible to make a judgement of deviance without specific reference to the system or subsystem to which it applies. The structure of normative patterns in any but the simplest subsystem is always intricate and usually far from fully integrated; hence singling out one such pattern without reference to its interconnections in a system of patterns can be very misleading. (Parsons, 1951; pp. 250–51)

Nonetheless over the years deviance has been converted into a term for a general type of behavior, and "the deviant" has become not an analytic term among several in a model, but rather a kind of character or social type. We have become accustomed to speak of deviance as "behavior that does not conform to the norms" and leave it at that, resting ultimately on the faith that somewhere a consensual base of "norms" exists.

There has been a growing awareness that this truncated and imprecise use of the term has diluted its original promise, and that the ease with which the term is bruited about may obscure a number of important situations in which the concept of deviance is irrelevant or inaccurate. Such situations include those where

a. shared norms do not prevail (no consensus, many values),
b. the norm evoked is not applicable or relevant,
c. groups are in open conflict over what value is to prevail,
d. control is imposed for purposes other than enforcement of norm cited.

Moreover the use of "deviant" as a character designation often disregards the relativity of deviance to time, place, and circumstance. These are not trivial qualifications. It is precisely in order to take into account variation of time and place, and to recognize value conflicts, that the deviance-control model was formulated. By emphasis on the *deviant* term in the model, sociologists eluded the main issue, which involves the confrontation of *perspectives*.

That issue was revived by efforts of Becker, Lemert, and others to draw attention to the concepts of *labeling* (the act of designating a given

[4]The "sociology of deviance" was also a departure from what sociologists regarded as classical psychodynamic theory (Freudian and neoFreudian) of deviant behavior, and its presumed emotional determination by intrapsychic characteristics derived from early childhood experience. But for an argument that the sociology of deviance is still preoccupied with those questions, see the critique by Liazos (1972).

action as deviance) and *enforcer* (the perspective from which control is exerted).

The nontrivial import of this manner of using the term *deviance* is to distinguish between process and status. Deviance in this sense is *not* synonymous with "being different," or "being distressed."

The terms *norm, labeling, enforcer,* and *deviance* define deviance as conduct labeled as undesirably departing from a norm that the labeler believes should apply to the deviant, for which enforcement is potentially available. Labeling is a *political* act in a political context.

Labeling requires an effective means of public symbolization of the changed status of the deviant, particularly focused in *charges* and *sanctions* (Garfinkle, 1961).

The *labeler* categorizes behavior as departing from a norm. The characteristic actions of a labeler are (a) making a charge and (b) developing an argument that interprets another's behavior in a way that justifies displacing him into a new and more problematic social status (temporarily or permanently). The effect of the changed social status is to (c) typically render the incumbent more susceptible to surveillance, control, or manipulation. The *deviant* is the person who acquires a role on the basis of this position. The *enforcer* is the agency or individual who carries out surveillance, control, regulation or treatment of the deviant; who in general applies sanctions, usually creating a public record (or written case record with limited readership). The objective of the general enforcer is to stigmatize deviance; the special role of treatment is to transform the deviant.

4.8 Implications for the Study of Deviance and Control

The utility of the deviance concept depends on the deliberate use of all the terms of the model—labeler, norm, deviant, enforcer —as sources of direction and sensitivity in data collection. The employment of these terms in a study of juvenile delinquency or crime leads to observation of the role of police and court officials in developing a decision about the character and probable future career of the youth brought to the court (Emerson, 1969; Blumberg, 1967). It turns attention to the source of the court's mandate (Platt, 1969) and the implications of a particular mode of juvenile court organization (Allen, 1965).

One of the elements of the model helps distinguish the emergence of institutionalized deviance from other, more casual forms of social evaluation. That is the concept of *enforcement*. The application of sanctions by an impersonal authority and the creation of a written record depicting the individual's problematic history and character are crucial elements in the social production of deviants. Obviously the relative *power* of enforcer agents and agencies is an important variable in the study of any given area of deviance and control. The power (considered both absolutely and in comparison with actual or potential countervailing power elsewhere) may be transitory or enduring; it may be restricted or diffuse. The degree of elaboration of an organizational framework is another variable of power. An organization has varying capabilities to assemble data, conduct activities and distribute information and classification, with varying levels of effectiveness in affixing a label to the individual in question.

Aside from the magnitude of power is the question of the *kind* of power possessed by an agency. It can be a pure or mixed form of power to detect, apprehend, classify, punish, confine, or change offenders. Where more than one form of power is exercised, there is the possibility of interference; for example, power to punish may interfere with power to detect or to change the behavior of the offender.[5]

A second important axis of variation is the level of *consensus* on the relevant norm that prevails in the social system in which the process is going on.

The joint distribution of these two attributes provides a starting hypology of possible consequences of criminal labeling.

TABLE 4.3

Implications of Various Combinations of Power and Consensus on the Control of Deviance

Power of enforcer	Consensus on "norm"	Consequence
High	High	The effective creation of outcasts and criminals
Low	High	Ostracism or vigilantism
High	Low	The creation of suppressed deviant
Low	Low	Segmental solidarity; politicization of issues

[5]There are theoretical and empirical grounds for believing that the influence of a group over its members is correlated with the cohesiveness of the group. One would thus expect greater behavior change induced in self-selected groups whose members wish to remain in the group. This is contrary to the prototypical correctional institution that receives unwilling inmates, confines them, and extends the period of confinement in instances of noncooperative actions or misbehavior.

4.9 Criminalization and Decriminalization

Effective *criminalization* occurs when an organization is available to formulate laws, to rationally manage and apply power, to record information, classifications, and decisions, and to bring the coercive power of the State against law violators. The enforcer organization has greater power to affix a label if it has a *range* of powers—to detect, apprehend, punish, confine, or exert efforts to change behavior and behavior propensities.

But the proliferation of formal organizations also contains the latent possibility of rapid *de*criminalization through corresponding, though conflicting and opposing, political processes. Such a process holds up to question the norm, challenges the legitimacy of the criminal label, agitates for a redefinition of the action, and if successful, applies a collective, political interpretation in place of a moral or clinical explanation of differences in behavior. Because of this political basis of criminalization and decriminalization, it is to be expected that mass societies (urbanized, industrialized, democratized, bureaucratized) should have higher crime rates and more rapid change of what is defined as crime than do nonindustrialized, communal societies.

The result of successful decriminalization is the displacement of an interpretation of "crime" with an interpretation of "opposition" or party, movement, and so on. Decriminalization is a process of removing a label, just as criminalization is the process of applying a label. Pluralistic society displays a dialectic of criminalization and decriminalization processes.

Chapter 5

JUSTICE AND CORRECTIONS

5.1 The Correctional Impulse

Communities have always had to provide not only the words defining good and bad conduct, but also the guidelines and the offices that would be used in dealing with certain forms of bad conduct. Social control has always existed to be exerted when the rules became too hotly disputed or when treated too casually. History provides no examples of persisting and viable societies that have long been indifferent about fundamental questions of expected and unexpected behavior.

Naturally enough the young have borne a great deal of the burden of various surgings and ebbing in the fashions in social control styles. Children, being born into families, are immediately susceptible and accessible to authority. Their initial plasticity invites direction, their energy and curiosity presses against the ruts of established tradition, and their lack of investment in the system makes many rules not as much to their convenience and protection as they are to the security of the vested interests of their elders.

Societies and communities have differed in the extent to which the uplift, guidance, and chastisement of the young has been the diffuse concern of many individuals and groups, spread along the lines of lineage and affinal ties, or centralized in official agencies. No doubt there are cycles in this as in other matters, and by going far back in time we find the adolescent barracks of Sparta, the Catholic orders, the boy monks of Burma, and the men's house in Africa or the Pacific. But on a simpler scale, we find rather close at hand a comparison that sheds some light on contemporary American society. We cannot go back much beyond the 19th century before recognizing that the society then did not regard youthful conduct and misconduct in the same terms as we do and did not develop the institutions and program which we have made central to the control of delinquency.

David Rothman (1971) calls attention to the invention of the prison, reformatory, orphanage, and insane asylum in Jacksonian America: The purpose of the asylum, the prison, and the youth reformatory was the imposition of discipline for the purpose of the correction of the unlawful, and, if possible, the rehabilitation of the erring or the deranged. The courts and the police, as well as private religous and charitable organization, became concerned about the looming social problems of an increasingly urban and commercial America.

5.2 Delinquency as a "Social Problem"

Children have always indulged in conduct that to varying degrees was distressing or threatening to other segments of the community. In modern times, industrial societies have come to regard childhood misconduct as constituting a social problem, and a great deal of time, money, and force is expended in attacking it by local and national governments.

There is nothing inherently self-apparent about a social problem. A situation, a group characteristic, or individual behavior comes to be regarded as a social problem through a process of collective behavior. Social problems are pinpointed by collective definitions supplied by mobilized public opinion. Public opinion designates something as a threat to legitimate values, norms, or law. Public perception of a physical or moral threat from a situation or group may be the occasion for defining a social problem and for organizing action to counter the threat. The process is not straightforward; it is characterized by selectivity, controversy, and compromise. In a general theoretical discussion of this process, the sociologist Herbert Blumer commented:

> A social problem is always a focal point for the operation of divergent and conflicting interest, intentions and objectives. It is the interplay of these interests and objectives that constitute the way in which a society deals with any one of its social problems. (Blumer, 1971, p. 301)

The times in which we live have provided us with a body of assumptions and expectations about social problems. There is a remarkable level of agreement, at any one time, about the kinds of social problems that confront the nation or the community; popular journalism, professional social science, and the language of bills and acts in legislatures speak, if not with one voice, at least in a chorus. Although there are different solutions proposed for social problems, and although there is some dissent about priorities, it is striking how well the terms are accepted.

"Delinquency" is one such word. When appended to the word "juvenile," it connotes youthful law breaking, violence, and gang threats to the safety of the neighborhood. It is often thought to be the first stretch of a road to crime. The public feels it is the business of the courts and police to cope with this delinquency, and their failure to do so is believed to be related to the rising crime rate in the country today. The causes of delinquency are debated and variously ascribed to physical constitution, personality or character disorder, improper or inadequate socialization, broken homes, weak fathers, rejecting mothers, slums, poverty, status problems of youth, urbanism, comic books, child-centered families, bad companions, and so on.

The measures proposed to counter this menace are also varied: they include early identification and segregation of the pre-delinquent, the use of amphetamine drugs and tranquilizers on school children, adults playing the role of Big Brothers, psychotherapy, group counseling, Little League baseball, special discipline programs in school, special schools for the unruly, behavior modification via Skinnerian conditioning, correctional institutions, jail, probation, mental hospitalization, "getting tough," "cracking down," corporal punishment, etc.

We will examine in detail some of these theories and schemes for control.

5.3 Adult Crime and Criminal Justice

There are two essential ingredients in any crime. There must be a definition of a specific offense or violation of a criminal law, for which a penalty is provided, and there must be a report or allegation, stating that a particular instance of such an offense took place. The report may or may not identify an offender; the report may or may not identify a victim; the crime may not have a victim; the act may or may not be rare; and it may not be unpopular or widely regarded as deviant, repellant, or inexcusable.

A crime is thus different from several other kinds of prohibited or disapproved actions. Without being in violation of a law, an action, however strongly disapproved, is not defined as a crime and does not have legitimate criminal consequences for the perpetrator. The concept of crime assumes the existence of a State, functional government, or authority with an effective claim to a monopoly (or near monopoly) on prosecution and punishment of actions held to be offenses against the community. The claim of this monopoly accompanied the early assertion of government itself. The significance of early criminal law, such as the Babylonian Code, lies not in its severity—it was not more or less severe than practices before and after Babylonians—but because the Code defined crimes not as private matters but as the king's business. It is this quality of being defined as a crime in *law* that is criterial to criminal offenses, not some intrinsic quality in the act itself. An act may be a crime in one place and not in another; it may be a crime if done by one class but not by another; it may be a crime at one time and not at a later time. An act can become a crime or cease being a crime by passage or repeal of a law, or by Supreme Court ruling. Abortion in the United States is a case in point. For decades prior to 1970 it was a serious felony; after repeal of the law in question it became merely elective surgery. An act may be widely practiced in the community and still be a crime; gambling almost anywhere in the United States is such a case.

A criminal law is a statement legitimately established by a person or group empowered to do so (usually a government body as, for example, a legislature) that defines an offense against the State or the community.[1] It differs from ordinances or regulations that do not impute criminality to violators. Crimes by the same reasoning differ from injuries (torts) and disputes, where one person claims he has been wronged by another person. The latter may and often do involve courts of law and may result in penalties, but these are regarded as civil disputes, individual matters and not criminal. Thus if a person sustains injury in a fall on another individual's property, he may recover damages (money payments in compensation for an injury), but the affair confers no criminal status on the person who pays the damages, however great the amount may be. The parties to such a dispute may agree to settle the matter privately; the victim and the criminal have no option to do that except in certain

[1]"The rationale of the criminal law," writes Packer in his *Limits of the Criminal Sanction,* "rests on three concepts: offense, guilt, and punishment. These concepts symbolize three basic problems of substance as opposed to procedure in criminal law, i.e., (1) what conduct should be designated as criminal; (2) what determination should be made before a person can be found to have committed a criminal offense; (3) what should be done to persons who are found to have committed criminal offenses" (Packer, 1968, p. 17). This compares closely with a definition of Donnelly, "Criminal law is a process for deciding what should be labelled criminal, what official responses should accompany this designation, and what persons or agencies, under what conditions and circumstances, would be authorized to make and give effect to such determination" (Donnelly, Goldstein, and Schwartz, *The Criminal Law*, p. 1). Thus crime is "forbidden conduct for which punishment is prescribed and which is formally described as a crime by an agency of government having the power to do so" (Packer, 1968, p. 18).

minor matters in which, with the knowledge and approval of the court or the police, restitution to a victim may result in charges being dropped or a case dismissed. But it is clear that the State may continue criminal proceedings against an accused even if the victim is uninterested in obtaining conviction and punishment, and conversely, the loss sustained by the victim, and the question of restitution or damage awards, is irrelevant to the prosecutor of crimes.

The role of criminal law is to distinguish between private disputes and public wrongdoing. It monopolizes the prosecution and punishment in the latter; a man, if robbed and beaten by another, may not simply get assistance and chase down the robber and administer punishment; this the State reserves for itself and indeed may proceed against the victim who takes "the law into his own hands." Even the police are theoretically enjoined from administering punishment (widespread evidence and reports of police illegalities in this matter will be reviewed elsewhere in this book).

The cause of crime is thus to be found in the existence of law. This may seem to violate common sense; one may insist that even in a Stateless community, "robbery is robbery," hence a crime. But that is too simple; if that society is invaded or colonized, for example, and the law imported does not extend its protection to natives, seizure of land or valuables may simply be the actions of a good settler, and the capture of people into slavery merely the spoils of war. Cultures abound that define as moral obligations actions that other cultures define as serious crimes. Societies comprised of various differentiated communities may exhibit little consensus on the meaning of many actions; only where one or another position has impressed itself into criminal law and law enforcement will noncompliance result in crimes or criminal identification. The views of Jews and Moslems regarding the eating of pig, the views of Brahmans regarding the eating of cows, and the views of North Americans regarding the eating of puppies are clear expressions of disapproval and condemnation, but carry no criminal implications in the United States. Eating or smoking opium is prohibited by State and Federal law however, and does carry criminal penalities. If the United States went theocratic overnight by a new religious movement, and the laws changed, opiate use in rituals might become an obligation, and eating beef might become at least a heathen misdemeanor.

The implications of this legal foundation of crime for jurisprudence are numerous and important; for the sociology of crime however, the relevance is chiefly to the theoretical explanation of criminal conduct (the causes of delinquent or criminal behavior) and the implementation of programs of crime reduction and the treatment and punishment of the offender.

Definitions of crimes change over time. Two centuries ago, one of the more severely punished offenses in Puritan New England was blasphemy. Today however, official, even academic, interest in research on personality or ecological correlates of blasphemy, or whether behavior conditioning, psychotherapy, or group counseling reduces repeat offenses of blasphemy, would be low indeed. The politics of religious belief and its social meaning have changed so considerably that such questions appear pointless. We would instead invert the question by considering the conditions under which penalties might attach to the expression of unorthodox or irreligious sentiments.

In a similar sense, we must approach childhood's delinquencies and ask: what are the rules, and what are the agencies and policies that confer upon youthful misconduct its delinquent character, and open the way for corrective prevention?

Of course, it would be naive to forget that in the criminal law as applied to adults, there is a gap between theory and actual practice. Yet the theory does to some degree shape the actuality, and it does exist as a potential source of redress and reform from time to time. The fundamental doctrine of the law in theory is that it deals with conduct, and only conduct. Criminal conduct cannot be defined capriciously nor after the fact. Packer writes:

> (1) No one may be subject to criminal punishment except for conduct; (2) conduct may not be treated as criminal unless it has been so defined by appropriate lawmakers before it has taken place; (3) this definitional role is assigned primarily and broadly to the legislature, secondarily and interstitially to the courts, and to no one else; (4) definition of criminal conduct must be precisely enough stated to leave comparatively little room for arbitrary application. (Packer, 1968, p. 73)

Packer distinguishes a *retributive* position, which claims that the purpose of the criminal law is to exact a payment of a moral debt incurred by the erring criminal ("the retributive position holds that man is a responsible moral agent to whom rewards are due when he makes right moral choices and to whom punishment is due when he makes wrong ones" (Packer, 1968, p. 12). He contrasts this with a *utilitarian* position, which holds that punishment is justified and necessary *if* it reduces the probability of subsequent illegal behavior. The purest expression of a retributive law is to be found in religious dogma. In the Old Testament, for example, we have a ferocious expression:

> Whatever hurt is done, you shall give life for life, eye for eye, tooth for tooth, hand for hand, foot for foot, burn for burn, bruise for bruise, wound for wound. (Exodus 21:23–25)
>
> Whoever strikes his father or mother shall be put to death. (Exodus 21:12–15)

This dogma expresses not only retribution but asserts a kind of parity.

For property offenses an element of restitution enters; see for example, Exodus 22:2–4. In Leviticus, the distinction becomes explicit: "Whoever strikes a beast and kills it shall make restitution, but whoever strikes a man and kills him shall be put to death" (Lev. 24:21). Restitution and retribution share a quality of repayment; in articles of value in the former, in the person of the actor in the latter. In the Old Testament, retribution lies ultimately on the community as a whole, as the citizens of Sodom and Gomorrah discovered.

From time to time there are reactions to the ideology of retribution. One of the most articulate is by the British philosopher Jeremy Bentham. Bentham scorned retributive punishment, which he regarded as an outburst of temper rather than a reasoned response to a problem. (He called it sympathy–antipathy.) For the ideology of utilitarianism, the end of government was not the implementation and preservation of a moral code, partially perhaps because certain moral assumptions of European capitalists were never seriously questioned by the utilitarians. The purpose of government was the promotion of the algebraic sum of "happiness" in the society, by rewards and punishments judiciously applied.

The utilitarian position took no direct satisfaction from the punishment of sinners. Indeed Bentham seems to have had moments when he defined *all* punishment as evil. But punishment was excusable if it could be shown to influence behavior in the direction of the common good. He wrote:

> i. The general object which all laws have, or ought to have, in common, is to augment the total happiness of the community; and therefore, in the first place, to exclude, as far as may be, everything that tends to subtract from that happiness: in other words, to exclude mischief.
>
> ii. But all punishment is mischief: all punishment in itself is evil. Upon the principle of utility, if it ought at all to be admitted, it ought only to be admitted in as far as it promises to exclude some greater evil.
>
> iii. It is plain, therefore, that in the following cases punishment ought not to be inflicted.
>
> 1. Where it is *groundless*: where there is no mischief for it to prevent; the act not being mischievous upon the whole.
> 2. Where it must be *inefficacious:* where it cannot act so as to prevent mischief.
> 3. Where it is *unprofitable*, or too expensive: where the mischief it would produce would be greater than what it prevented.
> 4. Where it is *needless*: where the mischief may be prevented, or cease of itself, without it: that is, at a cheaper rate. . . . (Bentham, p. 843)

The modern variant of utilitarian thought in criminal justice is a clinical-behavioral perspective, which holds that "the commission of a crime is simply one signal among many that a person needs to be dealt with" (Packer, 1968, p. 12). The language of the latter view is more rehabilitative and clinical than legal and punitive, but as we will have occasion to note, ideologically a program can be rehabilitative in ideology and language but incapacitative and punishing in its effects. At any rate, what should be established here is that the juvenile justice system is a derivative of the clinical-rehabilitative line of thought.

The influences of psychiatry, psychology, and psychiatric-social casework has been the dominant ideology animating the juvenile justice movement in the United States. It has also been exceedingly important in attempts to reform or radically change justice procedures for adults as well. This impact in part derives from a general spirit of the times, in which professional and popular psychologizing of behavioral problems is characteristic of modern thinking. Part of the influence in justice procedures, however, is also the result of a concerted effort to apply the label of sickness to criminal and delinquent behavior. Michael Hakeem (1958) has provided a review of the extent of this influence and of the deliberate movement in forensic psychiatry behind it.

> The opinion of a psychiatrist can have a substantial or decisive influence in the determination of whether an offender is fit to stand trial, whether he is responsible for a crime, and whether he is to be executed or given a life sentence. It can play an important part in the decision whether to place him on probation or to send him to a correctional institution, the type of institution to which he is sent, his subsequent transfer to other institutions, and his activities within the institution. It can sway the estimate of his stability for parole or pardon. . . . (Hakeem, 1958, p. 650)

Some of the assumptions of the psychiatric view of delinquency in our justice procedures, causal theories, and specific programs express, in its purest form, the distinction between the contemporary correctional ideology and former philosophies of crime control.

The older retributive philosophy seeks its justification in an overarching moral code coupled with procedures for fairly and accurately establishing the guilt or innocence of the accused. Once guilt is established, retributive punishment is its own justification for those who believe in it. Beyond the offender's justified suffering, no further effect is required. It is sufficient that the guilty pay.

Utilitarian deterrence and corrective rehabilitation, however, are advocated on the basis of effects claimed. Measures of whether in fact these claims are realized, and these effects produced, are not merely incidental to these programs; on the contrary, they are essential to their meaning and are required for their continuance. Punishments that do not deter can scarcely be urged upon us because of their utility, and treatments that do not produce effects must be regarded as empty. It is therefore entirely fitting that the 18th- and 19th-century critics of penal codes and prisons should have been concerned with justice and injustice and have inveighed against inhumane punishments. The highest priority concerns of 20th-century evaluation of correctional programs revolve around whether the offender shows signs of change and whether the recidivism rate goes down or up. Modern correctional philosophy implicit in the origins of the juvenile court and explicit in the new ideology of adult criminal corrections is necessarily dependent on proof that its programs produce effects. It has nothing else to argue; without this evidence, or in the face of evidence to the contrary, modern juvenile and adult corrections is a pretense that falls short of justice and cure alike.

5.4 The Creation of Adolescence as a Social Category

Mass society has many features familiar to its members, so familiar as to be taken for granted as the "natural" order of things. But in a deliberate analysis of a given feature, this quality of being assumed natural, being taken for granted, should be set aside, so that the familiar may be scrutinized in an effort to account for its existence.

In mass society there are a number of institutional patterns that combine to confer upon young persons a peculiar status not found in most other societies. Mass society, through public education, urbanization, the reduction of the vitality of extended kinship systems, and the proliferation of regulatory welfare and law enforcement agencies, has created a period of great social significance between early childhood and what we are inclined to define as adulthood: this is the phase when a person is a juvenile, an adolescent, a teenager, a minor. Compared with the civil rights extended to citizens after the age of majority—the legal rights of children and youth are quite constricted, ranging somewhere between bondage and parole. The treatment of children varies from exploitation to benign and felicitous paternalism. Collectively our policy toward children is similar to colonialism in its mixture of good intentions, selfish interests, and inequality of powers. As in colonialism, there are hardliners and reformers, independent ideologies, rebels, controls, and much internal dissension on both sides. For some groups the arrangements have great convenience, for other groups they cause rancor.

Mass society sometime in the 19th century began to extend a mantle of control over the young, while at the same time it withdrew many rights formerly held by young persons. Minimum ages were established for many significant activities; compulsory free public education was instituted; a movement for the salvation and reform of children of the working-class poor developed from early welfare organizations.

One commentator draws attention to the utility of the child-saving movement to the long-run needs of the Industrial Revolution.

> Few of the reformers had any idea about the needs of children as persons and if they did none of it was reflected in the legislation they pushed

> through a reluctant parliament. Some of the more farsighted saw the need to give children education which would enable them to man more efficiently the machines of the developing industries of the future. Some also saw the need for protecting property against destitute children who were forced into crime in order to exist at all. The employing classes—the owners of the new mills who were aso the property owning classes—saw only one aspect of children's lives; their ability to work in the mills and make profits for the masters. (Berger, 1971, p. 155)

In the 19th century, biological explanations of hereditary criminality were popular in some circles; where they were not, the prevailing view was that urban, and especially immigrant, slums imposed an atmosphere of moral corruption, disorganized family and neighborhood life, and produced brutish and dangerous youth. And many reformers covered all bets by endorsing an eclectic theory of childhood criminality. Enoch Wines, a U.S. penologist of the late 19th century, said of lower-class urban children and their propensity for crime: "They are born to it, brought up for it. They must be saved" (Wines, 1880, p. 132, noted in Platt, p. 45).

What is perhaps most remarkable about correctional treatment plans for juveniles is the persistence and continuity of concepts and programs over a century. It is not too much to say that most of the principal ideas of 1970 juvenile institution programming were proposed by the 1870's. Compare, for example, Mary Carpenter's recommendation that juvenile institutions be run on a "cottage" plan (the euphemism was employed even then), with about 40 children in each institution (Platt, 1968, p. 50. For original see Carpenter, 1875). A call for diversion of children from court adjudication was public by 1878, as was the effort at segregation of youth from contact with hardened adult convicts, indeterminate sentence (until maximum of age 18), and an intention to intervene into the lives of not only the law-violating but the probable "predelinquent." From one of an annual series of Illinois reports, Platt quotes:

> If the prevention of crime is more important than its punishment, and if such prevention can only be secured by rescuing children from criminal surroundings before the criminal character and habits become firmly established, then it is evident that the state reform school cannot accomplish all that we desire, since it does not receive children at a sufficiently early age, nor does it receive children who still occupy the debatable ground between criminality and innocence who have not yet committed any criminal act but who are in imminent danger at every moment of becoming criminals. (State of Illinois, 1880)

We can go back much earlier, however. Alexis de Tocqueville and Gustav de Beaumont toured American prisons and related institutions and published, in 1833, a report entitled *On the Penitentiary System in the United States*. In this book they provide an account of the New York House of Refuge, established in 1825 (followed by Boston in 1826 and

Philadelphia in 1828), which embodied much of the language of the last half of the 20th century in its approach in the first part of the 19th century.

> The house of refuge, the discipline of which is neither too severe for youth, nor too mild for the guilty, has therefore for its object both the withdrawal of the young delinquent from a too rigorous punishment and from the dangers of impunity.
>
> The individuals, who are sent to the houses of refuge without having been convicted of some offense, are boys and girls who are in a position dangerous to society and to themselves: orphans, who have been led by misery to vagrancy; children abandoned by their parents and who lead a disordered life; all those, in one word, who, by their own fault or that of their parents, have fallen into a state so bordering on crime, that they would become infallibly guilty were they to retain their liberty.
>
> It has, therefore, been thought that the houses of refuge should contain at once juvenile criminals and those on the point of becoming such. . . . The magistrates who send the children to the refuge, never determine what length of time the delinquent must remain there. They merely send them to the house, which from that moment acquires all the rights of a guardian. This right of guardianship expires when the lad arrives at his twentieth year, but even before he has attained this age, the managers of this establishment have the right to restore him to liberty if his interest require it. (Tocqueville and Beaumont, pp. 138–39)

The program was thus anticipatory, nonaccusatory, interventionist, and employed an indeterminate sentence. Since it is so avowedly restorative and rehabilitative in intent and ideology, it is not surprising that an evaluation of treatment effectiveness was done in 1830 and reported in the same book.[2]

[2]It is useful to tabulate these data and note the number of cases on which no data exist. Using all cases, we can say that de Tocqueville and Beaumont establish that 35 percent of released boys and 50 percent of released girls could be shown to have definite signs of leading a law-abiding life. If the large number of boys on whom there are no post-release data are discarded from the analysis, and the ratings repercentaged, it would be possible to say 58 percent of boys show scores "more good than bad," "conducted themselves well," or were "excellent." This would probably be an underestimate of post-release delinquency, however, since youth who were regularly and conventionally employed would be more likely to be contacted in a followup. The following table displays these figures as given by de Tocqueville and Beaumont without, however, clarifying the meaning of their labels.

de Tocqueville and Beaumont Classification

	Males		*Females*	
	f	%	*f*	%
"Excellent"	41	.096	11	.107
"Conducted themselves well"	85	.199	37	.362
"Rather good than otherwise"	24	.056	3	.029
"Doubtful"	37	.087	10	.102
"Rather bad than good"	14	.032	3	.029
"Bad"	34	.079	22	.215
"Very bad"	24	.056	16	.156
Sub-total rated by T and B	259	.605	102	100%
No information	168	.395	—	—
Total released	427	1.000		

This sanguine opinion of the House of Refuge was not shared by everyone. Shortly after Toqueville's report, American criticism was voiced in terms that closely resemble the views we hold 100 years later. In 1857 in Massachusetts a conference heard the charge: "the great failure of these institutions is, not that we have not had admirable men to take charge of them but that we attempt to reform boys by prison discipline." The very name was seen as misleading. "We call it by sweet names (House of Refuge, Reformatory) yet it is nothing but prison discipline" (Rothman, 1971, p. 258). Rothman further reports that the inmates of juvenile institutions were disproportionately drawn from the lower class, foreign born, or second-generation foreign extraction, whose removal from the free community and confinement caused little distress to the respectable segment of the society. Thus by this date all the essential elements of juvenile correctional philosophy had been implemented. The years since have brought little new.

By the early 20th century a number of public and private agencies were empowered to adjudicate the fates of children who were regarded as problematic, undesirably deviant, failing to live up to the moral standards and legal expectations of the State and the ruling class of the community. Such children came to be regarded as "delinquent," a phrase still used to denote failure or neglect of a duty (such as unpaid accounts, unreturned library books, unpaid taxes). Childhood misconduct was henceforth not a private matter of family and community, nor were childhood offenses limited to the statutory crimes of adulthood; in a curious blend of welfare and control, childhood came to be subject to the powers of agencies and courts with broader and more diffusely defined mandates than those underlying adult criminal courts. Then, as now, the most salient characteristic of these children was that they were poor.

5.5 A Separate Justice System for Children

The development of separate processes for offenses of children is recent; the first juvenile court in the U.S. was established in Illinois in 1899.

The Supreme Court of the United States, in one of the most important decisions redefining the procedures of the juvenile court, commented on the development of the idea of a special children's court, and the shortcomings in the implementation of this idea:

> The early reformers were appalled by the adult procedures and penalties, and by the fact that children could be given long prison sentences and mixed in jails with hardened criminals. They were profoundly convinced that society's duty to the child could not be confined by the concept of

> justice alone. They believed that society's role was not to ascertain whether the child was "guilty" or "innocent," but "what is he, how has he become what he is and what had best be done in his interest and in the interest of the state to save him from a downward career." The child—essentially good as they saw it—was to be made "to feel that he is the object of [the State's] care and solicitude," not that he was under arrest or on trial. The rules of criminal procedure were therefore altogether inapplicable. The apparent rigidities, technicalities and harshness which they observed in both substantive and procedural criminal law were to be abandoned. The child was to be "treated" and "rehabilitated" and the procedures from apprehension through institutionalization were to be "clinical" rather than punitive.
>
> These results were to be achieved, without coming to conceptual and constitutional grief, by insisting that the proceedings were not adversary, but that the state was proceeding as *parens patriae*. The Latin phrase proved to be a great help to those who sought to rationalize the exclusion of juveniles from the constitutional scheme; but its meaning is murky and its historical credentials are of dubious relevance. The phrase was taken from chancery practice, where, however, it was used to act in *loco parentis* for the purpose of protecting the property interests and person of the child. But there was no trace of the doctrine in the history of criminal jurisprudence. At common law, children under seven were considered incapable of possessing criminal intent. Beyond that age, they were subjected to arrest, trial and in theory to punishment like adult offenders. In these old days, the state was not deemed to have authority to accord them fewer procedural rights than adults. The right of the state, as *parens patriae*, to deny to the child procedural rights available to his elders was elaborated by the assertion that a child, unlike an adult, has a right "not to liberty but to custody." He can be made to attorn to his parents, to go to school, etc. If his parents default in effectively performing their custodial functions—that is, if the child is "delinquent"—the state may intervene. In doing so it does not deprive the child of any rights because he has none. It merely provides the "custody" to which the child is entitled. On this basis, proceedings involving juveniles were described as "civil" not "criminal" and therefore not subject to the requirements which restrict the state when it seeks to deprive a person of his liberty.
>
> Accordingly the highest motives and most enlightened impulses led to a peculiar system for juveniles, unknown to our law in any comparable context. *In re: Gault*: President's Commission: Juvenile Delinquency and Youth Crime, 1967.

The "peculiar system for juveniles" was distinctive in two senses: its procedures did not involve the machinery of due process to the extent found in criminal courts, and the powers of the court included not only the punishment for violation of specific laws, but also extended to determining if a child is immoral, wayward, in need of supervision, incorrigible, or in an unfit home.

Precisely because of the high level of popular concern over perceived threats of juvenile crime and the persistent reports of the large percentage of serious crimes attributed to young offenders, it is important to stress the distinctive contrasts between juvenile and criminal justice agencies. Remington *et al.* divide juvenile justice administration into three phases of pre-court, adjudicatory, and postadjudication activities.

> (1) The pre-court stage of the juvenile system is marked by a commitment to solutions other than court processing and by a recognition of the great discretion accorded the police in taking juveniles into custody and disposing of the cases without referral to court.
> (2) The adjudicatory stage of the juvenile system has been characterized by a lack of procedural formality. In its concern for a treatment-oriented hearing procedure juvenile court theory minimized the traditional practice of a court hearing . . . to determine the facts of an occurrence and to set the framework for governmental authority to interfere with the juvenile's liberty.
> (3) The post adjudication stage of the juvenile system is characterized by great latitude and flexibility given to allow the individuation of treatment for the purpose of rehabilitation. This has been true of the adult system though there is increasing concern over the applicability of procedural due process requirements in adult correctional programs. (Remington *et al.*, 1969, pp. 952–953)

Remington *et al.* go on to comment that the ideology of rehabilitation has had several effects on juvenile justice proceedings including the non-adversary nature of proceedings, the broad discretion accorded officials operating on all levels, the extensive reliance upon the skills of behavioral scientists, particularly social workers, and the broad and vague coverage of substantive delinquency to include much noncriminal conduct. The salient difference between juvenile and adult justice systems is the presumption in theory in the latter that police judicial and correctional discretion in sanctioning offenders is subject to the counterpoise of constitutional safeguards of the accused, including certain important rights of the accused to confront, and if possible, confound, his accusers. To be sure, in adult criminal proceedings the exercise of police and court discretion and administrative decision making is very great. The difference is one of degree rather than difference in kind, but the extent of the difference is impressive. Also, as Miller *et al.* (1971, p. 1153) comment

> . . . in one sense, "juvenile justice process" is much broader than "juvenile courts" and the latter is simply one segment (although an important one) of the former. Numerous important decisions are made about juvenile law violators by police, schools and social agencies, without referring the child to juvenile court."

The powers of police and the juvenile court are available as resources, not only for the government in a mass society but also for various interested parties, group or individual, in situations of conflict within that society.

The disposition of cases appearing in American juvenile courts is not the outcome of the workings of a single uniform justice system; on the contrary, all the evidence from casual and careful observation, as well as that supplied by the language of various mandating legislation, indicates that policies vary widely across judges, jurisdictions, and types of offenses and offenders. Three landmark decisions of the Supreme Court of the United States, however, introduced a major clarifying vector into all these various juvenile courts, making it somewhat clearer on what side of a line each might be located. This line essentially marks the policy of legalism and due process for juvenile offenses from the policy of social welfare and *parens patriae* for juveniles regarded as delinquent.

In *Kent* (1966) the court ruled that a waiver of juvenile court jurisdiction (to an adult criminal court) must satisfy "essentials of due process and fair treatment." In *Gault* (1967) the court asserted that the accused minor had a right to notice to appear at an official hearing for specific charges, advice of counsel, confrontation and cross examination of witnesses, and the right against self-incrimination. In *Winship* (1970) the court stated that juvenile courts must require proof beyond reasonable doubt when disposing of cases of minors charged with an act that is a crime if done by an adult.

What was the effect of these three decisions, which seem to reverse a half century of broadly paternalistic juvenile court powers?

1. Some State courts (notably Illinois) interpreted Gault as mandating not only due process but proof beyond reasonable doubt as requirements of juvenile delinquency hearings (thus anticipating Winship).
2. Some State courts (notably California) and the National Council of Juvenile Court Judges sought to interpret Gault as not really undermining the belief in the broad mandate of juvenile courts to act as *parens patriae*, and not really requiring basic procedural changes. The Council of Juvenile Court Judges declared "the fundamental right of a child is not to unrestrained liberty but to custody" (Stapleton and Teitelbaum, p. 35, quoting *Juvenile Court Judges Journal*, 18: 1968, p. 107).
3. Varying degrees of compliance and noncompliance by the courts themselves. Reckless and Reckless reported a survey of Ohio judges who stated their opinion that their courts were already in compliance with Gault; the study did not examine the manner in which these courts conducted hearings (Stapleton and Teitelbaum, p. 36). A Washington Post survey of actual conduct in juvenile court hearings in the District of Columbia indicated significant departures from Gault's requirements (ibid.).

Neither of these provides data on the way the Gault requirements influence court hearings. The need for research into the actual effects of laws and appellate court decisions has become clearer in recent years, but there are still few studies of this kind. It is not possible to see exactly what if any effect Gault and Winship have had on courts.

Two studies may be cited.

Cayton examines juvenile courts in San Bernardino, California, and Topeka, Kansas. Both are urban courts, getting about 75 percent of their cases from police referrals, who in turn have a number of dispositions they could make. The court in California received about 33–36 percent of the cases contacted by police; the Kansas court received nearly twice as large a percentage (61–73 percent) of the total cases. California made heavy use of "intake" screening and probation officers; Kansas involved the prosecutor as well as probation staff at intake. California made less use of informal supervision, twice as frequently as Kansas filed official petitions bringing the accused under supervision of court. The conduct of hearings differed in the two courts. In San Bernardino hearings were held by referees, with the accused handled by probation officers. There was no court reporter and no transcript beyond orders issued by the referee. Only in the infrequent contested hearings did the hearing bring in witnesses and defense attorney. Most cases were not contested, and hearings were concerned with a "social report" by a probation officer, who made recommendations nearly always accepted by the referee.

Kansas hearings were more formal and held in court before a robed judge. Prosecutor and defense confronted one another in an adversary proceeding. Like San Bernardino however, most of the hearings were uncontested, and in practice the probation officer was responsible for recommendations.

During the five years 1964–1968, the two courts differed in the way each dealt with youth accused of delinquent acts. San Bernardino referred more of the cases to court than did Topeka; Topeka made more use of other dispositions and informal supervision rather than petition filed with juvenile court. Once the case reached court however, the San Bernardino court was more likely than Topeka to dismiss the case, or to place the youth on probation, while Topeka continued to make use of other dispositions and other agencies.

From the raw data published by Cayton, it is possible to compute the probability that a child accused of delinquency would ultimately be incarcerated. Table 5.1 shows that for the first year the San Bernardino case was more likely to be confined than in Topeka; the following year it was about equal; and for the next three years the Topeka case was increasingly more likely to be confined.

It is not possible to infer much about the justice or effectiveness of the court's action without more data about the cases. However, it is important to note that the court that at least formally would appear to more closely comply with the requirements of Gault did not dismiss more cases brought before it than the more traditional casework-oriented court did.

Possibly the most extensive study to date of the consequences of

TABLE 5.1

	1964	1965	Year 1966	1967	1968	
Total Cases	3115	3400	3796	4279	5090	California
N Incarcerated	28	43	30	50	14	
Probability of Incarceration	.0089	.0126	.0079	.0117	.0028	
N Cases	653	803	1003	1009	1163	Kansas
N Incarcerated	11	11	18	32	60	
Probability of Incarceration	.0016	.0136	.0179	.032	.0516	

Adapted from data reported in Charles Cayton, "Emerging Patterns in the Administration of Juvenile Justice," *Journal of Urban Law* (1971) 49:377–98.

defense counsel for juveniles is reported by Stapleton and Teitelbaum (1972). Their work addressed two interrelated questions: what difference does an attorney make in the disposition of cases before the juvenile court, and how does the introduction of counsel affect the conduct of delinquency hearings? We shall restrict our review to the first question.

The aim of the study was to contrast, on *randomly assigned* samples, the effects of cases represented by defense counsel with cases not represented by defense counsel, in each of two courts. One court "more nearly typifies the traditional juvenile court philosophy, with its social work orientation and concomitant de-emphasis of legal procedures." The other court differed in that "adjudicative and dispositional processes are clearly distinct, and a finding of delinquency, if one is made, is carefully noted. Tests of admissibility of evidence are more consistently applied . . . and there is less reliance on a 'social report at the adjudication stage' (Stapleton and Teitelbaum, 1972, p. 57). The study was limited to delinquents, excluded females entirely, excluded homicide cases, and boys whose parents had initiated the charges. All cases were drawn from poverty areas as defined by the 1960 census.

The design was compromised by attrition of both experimental (attorney) and control (no attorney) samples. Some youth randomly assigned to a control group obtained counsel through their own efforts, and some youth assigned to the experimental group declined the offer of counsel. The vitiation of each sample in this way amounted to a loss between 11–39 percent of the cases in that sample. The authors decided not to purge the samples of the improper cases, but compared them including the errant cases. Aside from the costly failure to retain clean separation on the experimental condition, random assignment did successfully result in batches of cases that did not differ on offense, age, race, previous court record, number of petitions filed, judge hearing the case, and home situation. However with substantial numbers of cases in each category that do not coincide with the label of the category, the capacity of the design to produce clear conclusions is seriously compromised.

The authors title their two courts "Zenith" (the court with a more legalistic approach) and "Gotham" (the traditional juvenile court). Table 5.2 below shows that the presence of defense counsel increased the number of cases dismissed in the legalistic court (Zenith), but that in the traditional court (Gotham) there were not substantial differences between cases with counsel and those without. Note however that the Gotham and Zenith courts differ primarily in the great use of continuance in the Gotham court (traditional juvenile court philosophy); both courts put about the same proportions of their cases on probation or into confinement (a finding we noted in Cayton's data). Thus the meaning of the table is somewhat unclear without further understanding of the "continue" category. Moreover, as in the Cayton study, it is not possible to determine the effect of either court procedure (with or without counsel) on subsequent behavior.

There is still widespread popular support of the need for special juvenile courts to curb youth. Indeed, at the present time the juvenile court is under strong cross pressures to increase its early preventive intervention in the lives of young delinquents (and even "predelinquents"); however, on the other hand it is pressed to lessen the iatrogenic side effects of official labeling, and from still another quarter to dismantle much of its special apparatus of age-specific powers and return the accused youthful offender to the protection of the laws of statute and pro-

TABLE 5.2

Outcome of Cases

	Zenith Court		*Gotham Court*	
	Experimental	*Control*	*Experimental*	*Control*
Dismiss	49.8	40.0	18.5	19.2
Continued	9.9	3.9	30.5	34.5
Probation	31.6	43.9	40.3	40.4
Commitment	8.7	12.3	10.7	5.9
	100	100	100	100
	(323)	(310)	(243)	(255)

Source: Stapleton and Teitelbaum, 1972. Table 3, p. 66.

cedure that are supposed to prevail in the criminal court and in civil suits.

> The juvenile court was designed to save children—not punish them. Only "neglectful" parents were deemed appropriate targets of punishment. Unfortunately, the laudable intentions of the founders of the court movement have yet to be translated into reality. The United States Supreme Court, in 1967, reached this conclusion; so too, did the Task Force on Delinquency of the President's Commission on Law Enforcement and the Administration of Justice. Both governmental bodies ruled that juvenile court dispositions were, in effect, sentences that bore a remarkable resemblance to the outcomes of adult criminal proceedings. The Supreme Court was appalled at the idea that 15-year-old Gerald Gault could be deprived of his liberty for up to six years without the benefits of due process of law found in adult courts. The majority was persuaded that the consequences of judicial decisions should be considered, not just the ideals of the founders of the juvenile court. (Lerman, 1971, p. 36)

The present period is one of disenchantment with the higher ideals of the juvenile court. Whatever the promise of the early years of this century that by handling the erring child in the manner of the stern but sympathetic parent, the budding criminal could be returned to the path of a law-abiding citizen, the decades since have been disappointing on two counts. We have not seen great inroads made on rates of juvenile delinquency; on the contrary, the rates have climbed. Secondly, we have not seen the harshness of the adult criminal justice system modulated for the child; on the contrary, we beset the Supreme Court with appeals to restore or assert minimal civil rights for the children who come before the court for cloudy reasons to face largely administrative and summary sentencing from that court. Edwin Lemmert has noted:

> Roscoe Pound called the juvenile court one of the great social inventions of the 19th century. But the enthusiasms heralding its birth and early history have dampened considerably with the slow stain of passing time. Its later years have been those of unmet promise and darkened with growing controversy. Evidence that it has prevented crime or lessened the recidivism of youthful offenders is missing, and our sociological critics urged that it contributes to juvenile crime or inaugurates delinquent careers by imposition of the stigma of wardship, unwise detention, and incarceration of children in institutions which don't reform and often corrupt. The occasional early voice of the dissenting judge and of the frustrated lawyer has grown to a heavy swell of modern contention that the juvenile court under the noble guise of humanitarian concern and scientific treatment of the problems of children too often denies them the elements of justice and fair play. (President's Commission: Juvenile Delinquency & Youth Crime, 1967, p. 91)

For this reason, the sociologist must examine the specific correctional programs to which the child is sent by the juvenile justice agencies.

Chapter **6**

DELINQUENCY CONTROL PROGRAMS IN THE COMMUNITY

6.1 An Overview

Programs are special efforts to achieve an intended effect by the expenditure of resources and work in a particular way. When an organization commits resources to a program, it is implied that resources allocated in this manner are regarded as better spent than if allocated in another manner. Programs represent their task and justify their efforts by means of philosophies of delinquency causation and delinquency control. Such philosophies are important because of the sheer numbers of persons reached. In the United States, it has been estimated that one of every nine children (one out of six males) will be referred to the juvenile court at least once by the age of eighteen.[1] Thus any philosophy that is taken seriously enough to be implemented may conceivably affect hundreds of thousands of persons.

Programs for the prevention, punishment, and control of delinquency have been self-consciously formulated and demanded throughout the history of the United States. Programs for the control or reformation

[1]A study in 1952 estimated 65 percent of all boys in high delinquency ghettos in Chicago are brought before court sometime between ages 10 and 17 (Kobrin, 1952). Wolfgang *et al.* (1972) found approximately one-third of a male birth cohort had at least one recorded police contact between ages 10 and 18 (see Chapter One).

of erring children are of course much older; they reach back a thousand years in western civilization alone, as organized programs, not merely as sentiments (see Sanders, 1970).

In Chapter 5 we reviewed retributive theories of justice, in which punishment is applied to the offender because it is believed he deserves it and because such punishment asserts the moral order of the society and the position of the social groups that stand behind that order. We have seen that explicitly retributive punishment does not depend on the production of certain effects to justify punishment, but that on the contrary the punishment that is "deserved" may sometimes be applied despite the recognition that it may produce bad results. Moreover, the punishment is at times so severe that it cannot produce any subsequent behavior change in the offender because the offender is no longer alive, or at liberty to exercise any choice.[2]

Among other philosophies, which are *utilitarian* in their interest in producing deterrent or reformative effects, we may distinguish varieties of priorities and varieties of modes of intervention in the lives of citizens.

Among utilitarian philosophies, the legal scholar Herbert Packer distinguishes between programs of "*crime control,*" which place top priority on the suppression of the frequency of crimes to a minimum, and a "*due process model,*" which stresses the protection of constitutional safeguards of the individual's rights in the face of the power of the State. Ideological statements attempt to incorporate both as desiderata, but typically, priorities emerge in political competition or in allocation of finite resources.

Older philosophies of crime control seek to deter crimes—either originally, or subsequent to an initial offense—through the threat or imposition of punishment.

> The most immediately appealing justification for punishment is the claim that it may be used to prevent crime by so changing the personality of the offender that he will conform to the dictates of law; in a word by reforming him. (Packer, 1968, p. 53)

Another and somewhat more recent philosophy of crime control also holds that the aim is to reduce criminal and delinquent acts to a minimum, but instead of a program of threatened or actual punishments as deterrents to more or less rational persons, this philosophy seeks to reduce the probability of crime and delinquent behavior by bringing about a change in the offender. Such a philosophy does not phrase its objectives in the language of sanctions but in the terminology of the

[2]Anthony Burgess' *A Clockwork Orange* is a novel that poses the moral dilemma of "treatment" removing the possibility of choice and hence rendering ludicrous (or tragic) the law-abiding conduct it elicits.

clinic. Instead of seeking to fit the punishment to the crime, it seeks to match the appropriate treatment to the offender.

Advocates of crime control are alert to the possibilities of increasing control through reducing the power of the potential offender to elude detection or evade capture, and they are impatient with any but minimal regulations of investigative and correctional zeal. Crime control takes the offender or potential offender as an object over which correctional and rehabilitative programs have some considerable measure of authority in the interests of the common good.

Due process oriented philosophy seeks to minimize reliance on the criminal sanction as the means of reducing the volume of crime. Moreover, its adherents hold to the view that the interests of the majority are protected by those procedures that extend a measure of protection to the offender, before and even after conviction for wrongdoing.

There is no inherent reason why crime control and due process models could not be compatible, since they seem to be two independent dimensions. Ideally, one could have a program located at Point 1 in the diagram below (see Table 6.1). But more often specific programs and their spokesmen can be located at one or the other dimensions, such as Points 2 and 3. The due process model does not place maximum emphasis on the control and suppression of crimes, but on the accuracy of detection and accusation, on staying within the lawful confines of procedural laws, and on maintaining civil life with a bare minimum of

TABLE 6.1

Priorities in Delinquency and Criminal Justice Programs

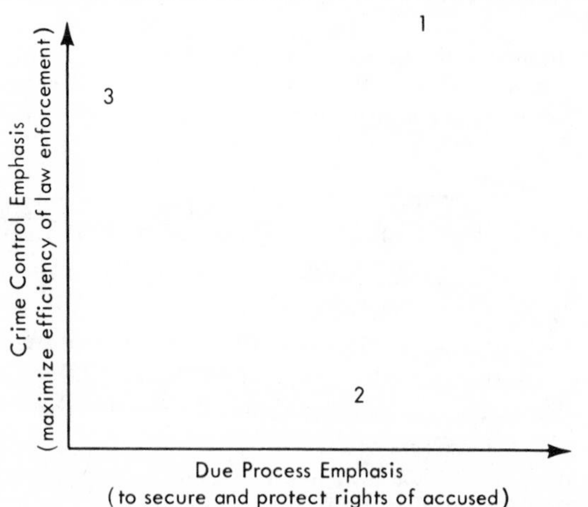

sanctioning by the coercive power of government. The crime control model is guided by the criterion of efficiency, and its proponents are willing to trade a measure of civil freedom for security. The due process model is guided by the criterion of justice under law, and its proponents are willing to trade a measure of collective security for individual freedom. That either or both may be mistaken in their expectations of what is actually produced by the programs should not enter into our consideration of their peculiarities at present.

Each of these beliefs in turn may embrace a conception of the offender or potential offender as either a more or less free moral agent and citizen, or as a person largely determined by personal and social conditions and hence further accessible to control by manipulation. If considerable simplification is allowed, a simple four-fold table expresses these philosophical emphases.

TABLE 6.2

A Classification of Criminal Justice Philosophies

Highest Priority:	*Assumption Concerning Offender Behavior:* *Voluntaristic*	*Deterministic*
"Crime Control"	(a) Vigorous law enforcement (b) Swift and sure punishment (c) Confinement of offender for community protection (d) Technological and legal support for law enforcement (e) Quasi-military weaponry and active surveillance of populace	(a) Early identification of "pre-offender" (potential offender) (b) Offender modification by conditioning, therapy, counseling, drugs or surgery (c) Civil commitment with strong and broadly mandated powers (d) Treatment programs in schools and community, both voluntary and compulsory (e) Environmental controls
"Due Process"	(a) Reduction in the use of criminal definitions and sanctions (b) Elimination of class, race, etc. bias in criminal justice administration (c) Minimal use of confinement, either pretrial or as sentence (d) Increase of political power of high crime rate individuals, communities and groups	(a) Improvement of life situation of high crime rate segments of population (b) Provision of more adequate services to which citizens eligible—education, training, political action (c) Offender, addict self-help organizations

6.2 The Voluntaristic Model

Legal bans, prohibitions, and other statements of customary and enacted rules define the permissible and nonpermissible. The threat of sanctions, and the administration of punishment, may have the effect of maintaining the nonviolator (or conformist), discouraging the person who seriously contemplates delinquency or skirts the edges of a delinquent act, or restraining someone who is already delinquent from committing a more serious delinquency. In these senses the deterrent effect is *preventive*. The other use of the word "deterrent" refers to the possible effect of sanctions on a person who has been found guilty of a delinquent or criminal act; in this sense the intention is that the sanction will discourage him or her from repeating the offense in the future, and we may say that the deterrence is *corrective*.

In considering that a law may act as a deterrent, one assumes that the population knows the penalties for law violation. But this may be only partially true.

> It seems reasonably safe to assume that for most serious offences the offender does not know the true probability of being caught, nor does he know the likelihood attaching to particular penalties if he were caught. The doctrine of deterrence would state that, if he knows these facts, his behaviour would be inhibited by heavy punishment. But may he not be deterred only because he has beliefs about what might happen to him which are incorrect? May not some people over-estimate the risk and the likely penalty, or under-estimate the gains? It is certain that people's actions are determined by what they believe to be true rather than by what is in fact true. There may be little association between fact and belief. Thus it may be possible to change behaviour in desired directions, not only by changing situations, but by changing beliefs about situations. In any event, it seems unprofitable to change actual situations if they are likely to be perceived as unchanged (Wilkins, 1965, p. 119) (See also Zimring, 1971, pp. 57, 58)

In all these instances the deterrence may be totally effective, partially effective (reduces frequency or seriousness), or totally ineffective.

The sociologist Durkheim (1915, 1947) clarified the general appeal of punishment to the conformist. The existence of explicit laws and the threat or imposition of punishment on the guilty reassures the conformist that his or her choice to observe and conform to the law is correct. If other persons flaunt without penalty the law he respects, it might raise doubts in his mind. The conformist may wonder if it is worth it to conform. Punishment asserts the authority of conventional values and debases the status of persons who transgress that authority. Where the conformist identifies with the offender, the intent of punishment is to reduce the offender, to neutralize him as a role model. For the conformist who identifies with the victim, punishment may satisfy his desire for revenge. For both, it affirms that the guilty differ from the nonguilty. Punishment sustains the solidarity of conventional persons and groups and bolsters the continued confidence of the law abiding in the propriety and advantages of conformity.

The distinction between the violator and the nonviolator is on the basis of conduct and hence is clear. The distinction between the violator and the potential violator is quite theoretical and not based on conduct, hence it is hypothetical and unclear. We use the term "potential violator" to mean a person actively contemplating a criminal or delinquent action, and concerning this hypothetical individual ask: In what way can threat of punishment deter the commission of an indictable offense?

Franklin Zimring approaches this question by considering several well-known differences in individuals and the circumstances in which they live that may have an influence on the effect of threatened sanctions. Persons are known to vary in the degree to which they are oriented to the future or the present. This distinction is between a preference for foregoing present rewards if this is a means to gaining a more substantial reward in the foreseeable future, versus a preference for rewards in the present even if this reduces or eliminates the likelihood of a more substantial reward later. In regard to punishment, future orientation means foregoing risk of future punishment by refraining from a prohibited reward in the present. Zimring notes that lower-class persons are reputed to be less future-oriented than middle-class persons and hence less deterrable. If this is so, it is highly possible that the realistic prospects of future reward following present restraint are sufficiently close to zero for lower-class persons that a preference for immediate consumption is learned. At any rate, it remains a conjecture whether lower-class persons are in fact less future-oriented or whether oriented to a more meager and less certain future.

Zimring also regards individuals and groups as differing in the degree to which they regard apprehension and punishment as likely to take place.

> In one recent study addressed to the optimist vs. pessimist theory, Daniel Claster asked a sample of delinquent boys and a sample of nondelinquent boys to estimate (a) the general chances of being apprehended and punished, and (b) their personal chances of being apprehended and punished, in relation to a variety of offenses. The two samples gave similar answers about the general chances of being apprehended and convicted, and about their personal chances of being convicted of offenses if apprehended, but the delinquent boys perceived their personal chances of arrest if they committed crimes to be significantly lower than the personal chances estimated by nondelinquents. These results might be evidence of the delinquents

> possessing, as Dr. Claster describes it, a "magical immunity mechanism" that serves to neutralize fear of punishment, and makes this group less susceptible to deterrence. It is curious, however, that the same mechanism does not appear in answers about chances of conviction after arrest. Moreover, it is possible that the delinquents' estimates of personal apprehension chances were accurate, and based on personal experience not possessed by the nondelinquent boys. So, available data fall short of establishing that personality traits associated with differential estimates of risk play any significant role in selecting those members of society who fail to be deterred by the threat of punishment. (Zimring, 1971, p. 37)

The effects of punishment as a deterrent have not been subject to careful empirical investigation, despite that it is a cornerstone in criminal justice and law enforcement. One study (Tittle, 1969) investigated the correlation of the number of offenses known to the police in each of the States with the general level of severity of punishments provided by law, and with the certainty that the law would be enforced. The measure of the latter is admittedly crude: it is the ratio of offenses known to the police in a given category to the number of commitments to state prisons for that offense. In general, Tittle found that the correlations varied greatly by category of offense, that severity showed no relationship to crime rate in and of itself, but that for some offenses the certainty of imprisonment was associated with lower crime rates.

Chiricos and Waldo (1970) provide data that do not replicate Tittle's results. Chiricos and Waldo examined national data on certainty and severity of punishment for six major crimes in 1960 and 1964. They found "little reliability in the relationship between certainty of punishment and crime rates" and "relationship between severity and crime rates are—with one exception—either positive or extremely weak. Moreover there is little consistency over time within offense categories" (p. 207). They fault Tittle with a statistical error and conclude that no study —theirs or others—has yet provided support for the contention that penalties deter crime.

Data on juvenile confinement are not adequate to provide a clear answer about possible deterrence. Information from studies of adult prison inmates show that longer sentences in prison are associated with greater rather than lesser probability of subsequent crime. A carefully done study of parole performance of first prison releases (since 1957) of persons originally committed for robbery was conducted by Jaman in California. The offense is a major cause of prison sentencing in California, with 42 percent of all adult felon prisoners in California being committed for that offense. Followup revealed that at 6-, 12-, and 24-month periods past release, those who served shorter terms did better than those serving longer terms. It was recognized that length of sentence could be influenced by factors also directly related to the parole violation risk of the individual. Accordingly the study controlled for age, ethnicity (race), and a multiple index of parole prognosis called the Base Expectancy. The study also recognized that differences in the parole situation would affect the results with, for example, higher chances of parole recidivism in a large urban area than in a rural area, or with varying degrees of closeness of supervision. The study controlled region to which paroled and type of parole supervision. A study of men paroled in 1965 was then done. In this latter survey all offenses were included. The results showed "percent of favorable outcome on parole among men who served less than the median time was *greater* than among those who served more than the median number of months" (Jaman, 1968). The argument that severity of sanctions does *not* produce a payoff of lowered offense level is also supported by the data on effects of the death penalty in the U.S. Homicide rates in states that have the death penalty versus those that did not have the death penalty were examined for the years 1920–1955. Findings showed murder rates varied widely over time, and that within each group of states having similar social and economic conditions and populations, it is impossible to distinguish the states with the death penalty from the states that have abolished it. Studies have also shown that trends in the murder death rate over time are similar with and without the death penalty, that abolition of the death penalty does not raise the homicide rate over the pre-abolition rate, and that the rate of fatal attacks on the police are the same in cities with and without the death penalty.

There are both logical and empirical reasons for concluding that the possible deterrent effects of prohibitions and punishments will vary by type of offense (see Chambliss, 1967). The more "rational" or value-producing (profit-oriented) an offense, the more likely it is that threat of punishment coupled with a reasonable probability that the punishment will be imposed will be associated with conformity with the law. Such crimes have been called by some authors (Zimring, 1971) *instrumental* as opposed to *expressive* crimes (the latter being assaultive offenses, or conduct offenses such as narcotic use).

Cross-cutting offense differences in the differential impact of punishment is the degree of investment or social commitment of the individual to a conventional style of life. To the extent that individuals are invested in a segment of the community, they are vulnerable to the stigmatizing effects of conviction and punishment. Those with jobs or who are on educational social escalators and whose families are law abiding face loss of present privilege and future opportunity and status by sanctioning. The threat of such loss makes the prospect of punishment more of a deterrent. This is the main thrust of Hershi's argument concerning achievement in school and frequency of delinquent behavior. Conversely, as Packer has remarked, "deterrence does not threaten those whose lot in life is already miserable beyond the point of hope" (Packer, 1968, p. 45).

6.3 Police and Juvenile Court: A Mixed Strategy of Punishment and Treatment

In Chapter 2 and Chapter 3 we discussed the juvenile court and its role in the definition of delinquency and the designation of specific individuals as delinquent. The court intends to bring about the correction and prevention of delinquent behavior. In this it is important to consider the crucial work of the juvenile divisions of police departments, formal and informal diversion of cases from the judicial processes, and the actions of the court itself.

The police play a decisive part in the intake of children and youth into the juvenile justice system, since their screening is early and accounts for the bulk of the cases sent to court or informally sanctioned. Miller *et al.* report that approximately half of the total contacts with suspect juveniles are settled informally by police. More important, of the remainder of cases, police referrals make up the majority of cases seen by the juvenile court staff.

> In most cases, a juvenile who is taken into custody will never see a judge. He will be released after a nonappealable screening process administered by individuals without legal training; he will not be represented by counsel, nor are the screening officials likely to acknowledge a right of silence. The result of the screening may be the creation of an official record of contact with the police or court or both, and, possibly, a substantial interference with the juvenile's liberty. This basic process is in use, in one variant or another, in virtually all cities. It is broken down into two stages, the first administered by the police and the second by "intake" departments attached to the courts. (Miller, 1971, p. 1247)

Detention is intended to be short-term confinement of a youth while the court prepares to review or hear his case. A youth may be ordered placed in detention for a variety of reasons: to prevent the youth from absconding; the family will not accept the youth; the youth is runaway; the youth is intoxicated, high, or addicted; the youth is deemed a threat to public safety, suicidal, or sick. Although there are standards asserting that minors shall not be confined or detained in adult jails, there is widespread violation of this in various parts of the country. Similarly, facilities designed for short-term detention often house minors for many days or weeks at a time.

The 1970 Uniform Crime Reports show police disposition of juveniles recorded as taken into custody (excluding traffic and neglect, both of which are very frequent). Of some 1,266,151 children taken into custody, 45 percent were handled and released without a formal referral to court; 1.6 percent were referred to welfare; 2.27 percent sent to other police; less than 1 percent referred to adult criminal court; and 50 percent referred to juvenile court. Thus informal screening and some form of treatment and release (interrogation, counseling, intimidation, etc.) is nearly as frequent as sending the youth to court.

In the city of Chicago in 1964, 98 percent of juvenile court cases were referred by police; in that year police reported contacts with 40,352 juvenile offenses, of which 26,978 were informally handled on the precinct house level, and 13,374 were passed on to juvenile court (Miller, 1971, p. 1248).

Understandably there is considerable interest in how the police informally handle so large a number of juvenile contacts, and what criteria are used to decide which cases shall be informally adjudicated by police, which shall receive no further sanctioning, and which shall go on to have their day in court. Since part of this process is so informal that it is outside the authorization of law, there is some delicacy about the questions that must be raised. The President's Commission findings, now nearly a decade old, revealed that on any given day in 1965 about 13,000 youngsters were held in "short-term" detention; they stayed an average of 12 days (which may or may not correspond to the reader's definition of "short-term detention") and over 400,000 youngsters passed through some period of detention during that year (not including sentences served in correctional confinement). Behind national figures lies great variation. Some jurisdictions are serious in minimizing the time a youth languishes in facilities not designed for lengthy stays; other jurisdictions resemble the account published in a recent study:

> The statistics tell a grim tale. In March, 1967, there were 186 boys and 64 girls in the Philadelphia Juvenile Detention Center. In March, 1968, there were 176 boys and 63 girls. These were not unusual months. As of March 27, 1967, 33 boys had been in the center more than 100 days, some as long as 650 days, awaiting suitable placement. Only 29 had been there for less than a week. Nevertheless, the fiction is maintained that this is a temporary detention facility. The official view is that children are not held more than three days pending trial. The files of the center show that some children are held a month and longer before trial and that few are released within three days. This situation prevails in almost every state and city in America. But the numerous research projects on juvenile court problems fail to reveal these obvious facts. Harvard Law School students made a study of juvenile court procedures under the sponsorship of the Walter E. Meyer Foundation. The report states: "In Philadelphia, if a child is held [in custody pending trial] he goes to the judge within 72 hours" (79 *Harvard Law Review* 792 [1966]). The authority cited is an interview with the director of the juvenile court probation office. In fact, many children are held for

> weeks pending trial. In a survey of one hundred consecutive cases, our office found that the average time of detention pending trial was sixteen days. The Harvard study makes no mention of this lengthy incarceration pending suitable placement. A similar study under the same auspices was reported in the *Columbia Law Review*. The authors of this report note that if the case is not dismissed on the merits, the first duty of the judge "is to determine that the youth 'requires supervision, treatment, or confinement'" (67 *Columbia Law Review* 340 [1967]). The plight of the child who needs treatment that is not available is totally ignored. (President's Commission: Juvenile Delinquency and Youth Crime, 1967, p. 120)

Although model juvenile sentencing law states that no child shall be confined in an adult jail, a survey found that 93 percent of all juvenile court jurisdictions (in places comprising 44 percent of the nation's population) had no facilities except the county jail to confine children. Only Connecticut and Vermont and the government of Puerto Rico report never using jails. Nine states prohibit jailing of children but do not always observe the law, and in 19 other states the law does allow adult jails to be used if there is some separation of children from adults. In a 1970 census of the 3,919 jails in the USA, 95 percent were reported to have no educational facilities and 86 percent to have no exercise facilities (*Freeworld Times*, February, 1972, p. 3). Thus this practice is on the face of it a serious problem, particularly since a juvenile has fewer means of redress such as bail. When juveniles are segregated from adults in a jail, they may also be segregated from attention as well. Physical and sexual aggression from other minors and suicide have been reported. The decision to place a child in temporary, prehearing detention is obviously an important judgment within the discretion of policemen.

Are the police less biased than the general population? The results of studies vary, some giving reason to believe law enforcement makes rather fewer distinctions of outright social, class, racial, religious, or political prejudice than others do in the same city; other studies show the police exercising not only the personal biases of the patrolmen but the political sentiments of the groups who employ them.

Piliaven and Briar studied police encounters with juveniles, in which the police officer had the discretion to dispose of the incident by (1) outright release, (2) release and a written field report, (3) official reprimand and release to parents or guardian, (4) referral to juvenile court, (5) arrest and detention. Observers rated the behavior and appearance of the youth in 66 incidents, found uncooperative demeanor resulted in most of the most severe (arrest, detention) and in most of the admonish and release cases. The authors comment

> Compared to other youths, Negroes and boys whose appearance matched the delinquent stereotype were more frequently stopped and interrogated by patrolmen—often even in the absence of evidence that an offense had

been committed—and were usually given more severe dispositions for the same violations. (Piliaven and Briar 1964, pp. 162–163)

They concluded that within broad categories of offense severity, police exercised discretion to charge or to adjust informally according to the demeanor of the apprehended youth (docile, respectful, or obsequious manners being more often rewarded with reprimand and release, displays of defiance or verbal aggression being met with arrest), appearance (signs of gang membership being associated with arrest and detention), and race (nonwhite being formally handled more often than white).

McEachern and Bauzer (1967) report data from a study in Santa Monica, California, indicating that

> police disposition of recorded offenses was almost exclusively a function of the offenses, and did not depend on such characteristics as sex, age, residential status, number of offenses in the subject's delinquent history, or whether or not he was on probation at the time he committed the offense.

A second inquiry into records in the Los Angeles Sheriff's department and data from Santa Monica showed approximately the same proportions of arrested white, Chicano, and black youth were dealt with by requesting petitions to go to court. This finding emphatically does not imply that the police made no distinction in contacts or arrests of youth of different races, but that once arrested there were no consistent differences by ethnicity in the probability of being referred to court. In another study Goldstein (1960) remarks that the *noninvocation* of criminal sanctions often was evident in police responses to multiple assaults in ghetto areas.

Wilson compared two cities having contrasting styles of law enforcement and compared the manner in which they enforced the law regarding juvenile misconduct. Comparing the frequency with which white and black juveniles were taken to court after a police contact, Wilson reports that in Eastern City (more traditional police) a black youth was three times more likely to be referred to court than a white youth after a police contact. However the overall rate of juvenile arrests in Western City (the more modern police force) was more than twice the arrest rate in Eastern City. Wilson comments somewhat wryly:

> In Western City [the more professional] the discretionary powers of the police are much more likely than in Eastern City [the more traditional] to be used to restrict the freedom of the juvenile: Western City's officers process a larger proportion of the city's juvenile population as suspected offenders, and, of those they process, arrest a larger proportion. (Wilson, 1973, p. 165)

Weiner and Willie, studying the rather special position of juvenile officer, computed correlations between socioeconomic status and race and the proportions of police contacts referred to court. They used census tract data and found that although lower-income youth and black youth had higher arrest rates, there was no correlation between race or social class and the percentage of cases sent to court by juvenile officers at the station. They attribute the lack of racial or class bias to the special work situation of the officer and the special organization supports sustaining him compared with the beat patrolman. Also, their data do not include information on the sentencing or the informal adjustment of cases not sent to court or to the juvenile officer in the first place.

When children are referred to court, they may or may not be found delinquent or persons in need of supervision. If they are not, they may be freed with or without a lecture, scolding, intimidation, or extra legal penitence, chores, or restrictions. If they are found delinquent, they may very well be sentenced to probation.

> Juvenile probation, which permits a child to remain in the community under the supervision and guidance of a probation officer, is a legal status created by a court of juvenile jurisdiction. It usually involves (a) a judicial finding that the behavior of the child has been such as to bring him within the purview of the court, (b) the imposition of conditions upon his continued freedom, and (c) the provision of means for helping him to meet these conditions and for determining the degree to which he meets them. Probation thus implies much more than indiscriminately giving the child "another chance." Its central thrust is to give him positive assistance in adjusting in the free community. (President's Commission on Law Enforcement and Administration of Justice 1967, p. 108)

Malcolm Klein (1972) reports data from a study of police contacts with alleged juvenile offenders in Los Angeles County, which resulted in the youths being diverted from deeper involvement with the justice system. He found great variability across police jurisdictions in the degree of diversion practiced. On the basis of the analysis to that date (with more planned to come) Klein wrote:

> A simple one to one relationship between departmental diversion practices and recidivism can not be established. A more complex relationship may indeed exist, wherein those departments inserting youngsters into the juvenile justice system early in their delinquent careers may be contributing to the development of more prolonged delinquent careers. If so, this is manifested not in whether offenders simply recidivate or not, but in how often. There is more support in these data for those who see diversion as a useful goal and insertion into the system as a detrimental stigma than for those who see diversion as rewarding misconduct and insertion as an effective deterrent. (Klein, 1972, p. 10)

By far the most frequently employed official means by which the court exerts its control in adjudicating a case in which a child has been declared a delinquent is probation. The statistical projections of the number of juvenile probationers by 1975 approach a half million at any given day. Although more adults are in prison or other confinement, the use of probation is quite comparable for both juveniles and adults. While of seemingly less severity than other sentences, probation is benign only by comparison with the ordeal of confinement, for studies of probation typically describe the high case load, absence of program, and largely negative character of the sanctioning. The probationer is described in the following terms by Emerson:

> The formal goal of probation is to improve the delinquent's behavior, in short, to "rehabilitate" him. This goal is short-circuited, however, by a pervading preoccupation with *control.* Reflecting insistent demands that the court "do something" about recurrent misconduct, probation is organized to keep the delinquent "in line," to prevent any further disturbing and inconveniencing "trouble." The ultimate goal of permanently "reforming" the delinquent's personality and conduct becomes subordinated to the exigencies of maintaining immediate control. Probationary supervision consequently takes on a decidedly short-term and negative character; probation becomes an essentially disciplinary regime directed toward deterring and inhibiting troublesome conduct. (Emerson, p. 219)

Terry (1967) tests the relationship of sex, race, and socioeconomic level to police disposition, probation department disposition, and court

TABLE 6.3

Youth Processed in Juvenile System

	Police	*Probation*	*Juvenile Court*	*Total*
Sex				
Male	7411	656	216	8283
Female	1611	119	30	1760
Ethnicity				
Anglo	7287	598	191	8071
Chicano	637	92	26	755
Black	1104	85	29	1218
*Social Class**				
Upper	737	49	15	801
Middle	1861	138	44	2043
Lower	6415	588	187	7190

Source: Terry, 1967.

*Lower status consists of Class V, VI, and VII of the Minnesota Scale, middle status consists of Class III and IV, and upper status consists of Class I and II. See "Minnesota Scale for Paternal Occupations" (Minn.: University of Minnesota Institute of Child Welfare, n.d.) (Terry, p. 86).

disposition on all offense records on file for the years 1958–62 in the Juvenile Bureau of an industrial city of 100,000 in the Midwest. On the first level of processing a complaint against a juvenile, the police could exercise judgement in the following manner: they could release the youth, refer to welfare or State welfare, or refer to Probation Division. Probation in turn could release the child, place him or her on informal supervision, send him to juvenile court, or waive jurisdiction to adult criminal court. Finally, the juvenile court could impose formal supervision or incarcerate. Terry cross-tabulated the exercise of this discretion by the three agencies with three characteristics of the juvenile: sex, ethnicity, and social class. These attributes divided as follows among the three agencies. Note the funnel effect exerted by the three levels, and its effect on sex, ethnicity, and class. The findings of Terry's investigation are fully reported in the tables accompanying his article, but for our purpose can be briefly highlighted in Table 6.4 below. He reports data that shows that females are somewhat less often referred to welfare agencies or the probation department than males; that females were more often put on informal supervision and less often referred for court trial than males, and were more often institutionalized by the court than boys. Terry regards this as due largely to the nature of the complaints against females, which was unreported by him but implied to be largely sex "offenses" and "incorrigibility."

Both Anglos and blacks are slightly more often released than Chi-

TABLE 6.4

Characteristic and Direction of Decision Making

Level of decision	*Sex*	*Ethnicity*	*Class*
police	fewer females released; more referred to welfare	more Chicanos referred to probation	more uppers released; more lower referred to probation
probation	more females informal supervision; more males to court	more blacks to adult court; more Anglos to informal supervise	more upper on informal supervise; more lower status to adult court
court	females more severely sanctioned (incarcerated)	more blacks incarcerated	more lower status incarcerated

Source: Terry, 1967.

canos, who were more often referred to probation than either of the other two racial categories; of those youth who were not released, blacks and Chicanos were more often sent to adult criminal court and once referred to court they were more often sentenced to confinement than were whites. Finally, lower-income youth were more often referred to probation and less often released by police than upper-income, more often sent to adult criminal court, and considerably more apt to be sentenced to confinement than upper-income. For the last, the percentages of lower-, middle-, and upper-income categories committed to confinement were 64.2 percent, 56.8 percent, and 46.7 percent. It is remarkable that Terry concludes from these figures that the severity of disposition is *not* a function of minority status or socioeconomic status. He comes to this conclusion by obtaining low values for a rank correlation coefficient (tau), but it would seem to ignore the consistency of the tabled results to conclude that female, nonwhite, or lower-income status does not increase a juvenile's chances of being dealt with more severely by the law. Yona Cohn, in a study of probation in the Bronx Children's Court (Cohn, 1963, in Garabedian and Gibbons, 1970) arrived at results consistent with the data of Terry. Examining 175 presentence investigation reports during the first six months of 1952, Cohn tabulated sex and race against recommendation of the probation officer.

> . . . A large number of girls [were] recommended for institutionalization and a small number of girls recommended for discharge and probation. While girls made up only one-sixth of the total, they constituted nearly half the group recommended to an institution; restated as a proportion, this means that three times as many girls as boys were recommended for institutionalization.
>
> For 30 out of 35 girls, the probation officer recommended psychiatric examination (diagnosis) or institutional treatment. Cross-tabulation of data for the 21 girls recommended to an institution reveals that most of them had committed delinquent acts against sexual taboos—acts which were generally considered decisive factors in arriving at the recommendation they received. The racial distribution of the total group . . . was three white children to one Negro child. Of these, fewer Negroes were recommended for psychiatric examination or discharge than for institutionalization. (Cohn, p. 193)

Disposition

What is the nature of diversion from the juvenile court or informal adjustment that is within the discretion exercised by the police? Indications are that it varies greatly from place to place. In this as in so many other aspects of criminal justice, one's chances much depend on where the offense happens to be committed or suspected. Miller *et al.* report that in the city of Tucson the police are limited to either referring to court or *immediate* reprimand and release; in Chicago the police make direct referrals to welfare agencies but make little systematic effort to enforce continued contact.

Another source of data should be included if the diagnostic and referral information were widely available: the psychiatric hospital. Unfortunately, estimates on the volume of cases of children and youth sent to mental institutions for alleged misbehavior are not easy to obtain. Although the most frequently listed official reason for referral is "observation for psychiatric evaluation" (that is, the child is sent to the hospital to determine if there is evidence of emotional disturbance), the unofficial motive is very often to remove the youth from the community instead of or in the face of impending legal difficulty.

6.4 Referral to Juvenile Court: Sentencing to "Treatment"

Once a child has been referred to court, he or she encounters a dual process of justice and "treatment." While the court is to some degree concerned with the determination of guilt, its major energies are devoted to making a classification of the youth. The juvenile court is the place where the State makes the opening moves in assuming correctional responsibility and even routine jurisdiction over youth. Much of the work of the court is carried out by administrative staff, in lieu of, prior to, and after a judicial procedure. The court has the initial problem of asserting public authority over the actions of a particular youth. The court must (1) decide if the youth in question is troublesome or troubled and to what degree; particularly the court must decide if it is confronted with a precriminal or merely an erring child; (2) it must frequently "back up" or legally support, by threat of greater sanctions, the efforts and attempts at control, of the school, parents, welfare agencies, or police; (3) it may decide to take direct action in removing the youth from his setting and place him in an institution or even in a foster family; (4) it may go beyond imposing its own restraints, label, and sanctions and waive its jurisdiction to an adult criminal court; (5) it creates a written record of the youth, his or her alleged offenses, and the disposition made.

The juvenile court is the agency of justice that most frequently assumes original, and often exclusive, jurisdiction of an alleged juvenile delinquency. In fact the court, as we have seen (Chapter Three), may assume jurisdiction over the child for a variety of reasons in addition to alleged law violation. Robert Emerson, in a study of a juvenile court in an eastern metropolis describes the internal workings of this agency. We draw heavily on his work because it represents a singular effort to provide observational behavioral data on the actual day-to-day conduct of court business. The court is concerned with asserting and maintaining public authority over the youth brought before it. The court is a backup authority for other individuals or groups in dealing with problematic conduct. The court is typically criticized or evaluated with respect to recidivism criteria, but in its operations it must take a number of other considerations into account. The court must act in such a way as to satisfy multiple demands for upholding the authority of the law, for being fair in the administration of justice, and in balancing firmness with sympathy for the child. The court must negotiate with other governmental agencies—according to Emerson's account, with the city—for programs (Emerson, p. 39), with the police not only for cooperation but access to cases (pp. 45–50), and with welfare both to be able to place wards of the court with welfare and to avoid excessive use as a dumping ground for troublesome welfare cases (pp. 70–71). The court is typically confronted with a high volume of work and proceeds on one level by categorization of cases. It categorizes two kinds of *trouble:* one signalled by a serious offense, requiring court action because of the feelings of the public elicited by the incident; and trouble signalled by a repeated pattern of behavior and the development of a reputation thought to forecast more serious criminal actions. The recognition of trouble is related to the courts classification of youthful character:

Emerson observes that the establishment of one of these classifications for a particular case takes place through intermediaries presenting denunciations or supporting testimony against or for the accused child. To an important extent, the Juvenile Court observed by Emerson serves as a sink for children who have been filtered through previous stages of welfare custody. The problem of what to do with a child who is regarded by other sources of custody as impossible to "place" is sometimes solved by sentence to the Youth Correctional Authority. Commenting on the Welfare Department's "group homes," Emerson presents the following case:

> The Boys Home serves essentially as a Child Welfare Department satellite, housing those older boys who have been rejected by the rest of the system of residential placements. The Child Welfare Department worker attached to the Home explained how its wards ended up there:
>
> That's simply this—some foster mother says "Out!" You get some boy 13 or 14, he's clipped $20 from her purse, or was masturbating in the bathroom and the little daughter saw him—any type of acting out which on second thought looks pretty normal. Anything like that will get them kicked out. (Interviewer:) And it's hard to find other foster homes for this

> type of kid? (Welfare Worker:) Most of the kids at the home have been pillar to post for several years. . . . They've been bouncing in and out of homes for years. (Emerson, pp. 64–65)

This transfer from the care of the Child Welfare Department to court and reform school—the dumping process—is initiated by filing a complaint against the youth, either for incorrigibility or runaway. For example, a child assigned to a group home may prove a disciplinary problem. The group home may press a petition of incorrigibility to permit the transfer of the child to a closed institution. The juvenile court faces the same dilemma that confronts all juvenile and adult law enforcement and justice agencies. On the one hand there is a presumption that the law defines proper and improper conduct and that justice should be administered—that law breakers cannot violate the rules with impunity, and that other community interests warrant protection and control of the law violator. On the other hand is the theory that failure to conform to laws is often the result of precipitating or disposing psychological interpersonal and community conditions, and that by role the agency, particularly the juvenile court, is to provide treatment, and other ameliorative services to the cases brought before it. The problem is made more acute by the relative lack of any treatment modality at the command of the court that has been shown to have real rehabilitative effect.

One way that the agency may solve the problem is to begin with a treatment approach and with repeated contact, escalate the severity of the dispositions into purely a punishment and control program. In order to justify this, the case must be discredited and shown to be unworthy of the "leniency" of treatment, to have "been given breaks before" or to have "wasted his previous chances." Even treatment specialists in justice and correctional settings redefine their professional role. One tactic is to conceal the fact that the interview is a clinical evaluation that will be reported to the court and affect sentencing. The psychotherapeutic exchange has traditionally been based on confidentiality. The patient can confess to any kind of deviant, disapproved, or pathological acts or fantasy, and should be able to depend on the psychiatrist to accept him *qua* patient. The court psychiatrist who reports information thus divulged to a State authority who may then use it to impose supervision or incarceration is playing a somewhat different game. The juvenile and adult convict comes to learn this and orients himself even more defensively, which in turn stimulates more dissimulation on the part of the clinical staff, in a cycle of indirection and deception (see Emerson, Chap. 9; Kassebaum, Ward, and Wilner, 1971, Chap. 5).

The dynamics of the presentence phase of juvenile court action is the establishment of either the "normal" character of the accused, or denunciation of the accused. In cases where a person outside the court presents the denunciation, sometimes an accused can refute the denunciation or even carry off a counter-denunciation (for example, where a parent accusing child can himself be accused of improper or provocative behavior). Since very often the denunciation is from a law enforcement officer, this strategy is only rarely successful.

> There is no faster way to discredit character than to direct a counter-denunciation against the police. These disastrous consequences result from the care shown by the court staff to protect the personal and moral character of the police from symbolic attack and damage within the ceremonial event constituted by the court hearing. This reflects not only the closeness of the court's working ties with the police, but also the fact that both police and court are part of the same legal structure. Both are concerned with the exercise of legal authority. An attack on the police, therefore, symbolically attacks the legal order which the court both represents and feels obligated to protect. An attack on the police represents a denial of the normative or moral order on which the court's activities are based. (Emerson, p. 275)

The final end of the court's actions is seen by Emerson to be the assertion of the legal authority of the social order the delinquent has been shown to have violated. The court, when convinced of the delinquency of a minor, seeks to get him or her to take the role of a wrongdoer. This is particularly an explicit aim if the courtroom behavior of the child indicates he does not accept his role. In such cases the posture of the defiant child must be humbled.

> . . . The courtroom ceremony is characteristically structured to thrust the delinquent into the status of wrongdoer: the delinquent is pressured to conduct himself in a repentant contrite manner and hence to acknowledge his own guilt and blameworthiness. But beyond this, the delinquent is not only thrust into this discredited and soiled role, but he is also subjected to systematic pressure to show full commitment to it. He is prevented from withdrawing or showing distance from the role of wrongdoer in any way that might stave off its discrediting implications for both character and self. (Emerson, p. 183)

The policy of juvenile courts in sentencing youth, and the long-term effects of different dispositions, is not adequately documented at present. There are formidable difficulties in making general statements based on fragmentary evidence available. Juvenile courts vary enormously in size, in the size and characteristics of their community of jurisdiction, in the political context in which they are located, particularly in the style of the relationships between the juvenile court and other agencies of government, and in the judges who run the courts. There may be a broad basis of support for the juvenile court among some segments of the adult community, although the matter is by no means certain. One study on several small communities shows that the public in these cities believed the juvenile court to be more "lenient" than it actually was, and the public preferred harsher penalties, as indicated by their preference for remand to adult court or incarceration in a reformatory as ways of dealing with sample juvenile cases. Their perception of the way the court was operating was incorrect however, and the public preference for penalties was in fact met or exceeded by the court. Although they attributed greater leniency to the juvenile court than it in fact exercised, what they did prefer was close to actual court severity. Juvenile court sentencing was studied by Scarpith and Stephenson (1971). They reviewed 1210 adjudicated 16- or 17-year-old males not previously incarcerated, not classified as severely retarded or mentally ill.[3] Each boy was brought before the County Juvenile Court and sentenced to one of four dispositions: probation (live at home), supervised work and group meetings but live at home, institution guided group interaction, live-in, state reformatory. Boys sent to reformatory were more often the less educated and came from families of lower income. A higher percentage of boys accused of offenses against persons were sent to reformatory than to other dispositions; differences on property and child conduct offenses (euphemistically called "offenses against public policy") were rather slight.

Black youths were more likely to be sent to reformatory than white. In view of the importance of race both as a social issue and to this finding of the study itself, it is somewhat surprising that the tables on race, offense, and sentence are not presented. The authors merely say that blacks committed to reformatory had more previous court appearances, were first seen at a younger age, and had different prior offenses. Reformatory sentences was more likely the lot of boys who had been brought before the court on several prior occasions, had previous petitions sustained by court, had been on probation previously, and were first known to the court at an early age. The study thus documents that reformatory is used as the sentence when the boy is black, lower-income, less educated, and with previous court and probation history. Vinter conducted a review of some 30,000 court actions in one state in 1960, and comments:

> . . . persons from minority groups or lower class families are differentially handled: persons from minority groups or lower class families are especially liable to be apprehended, to be charged, to be referred, to be adjudicated as delinquent, to be placed on probation, to be committed to institutions . . . these actuarial risks increase with age and seriousness of offense. . . . The same sources show that Negro youth and youth from lower socio-economic population levels are disproportionately liable to be

[3]The manner in which this sample of 1210 cases was chosen and the degree to which it is representative of the population served by the court or the court work load are not stated.

referred to juvenile courts, to be handled officially rather than "unofficially" and to be committed to State institutions. (Vinter, p. 87)

Wolfgang, Figlio, and Sellin (1972) provide valuable data in their monumental study, *Delinquency in a Birth Cohort* (see Chapter 2).

Wolfgang, *et al.* classified the disposition made of cases when contact with police was recorded. They categorized what was done into (1) remedial (where police handle the case informally, making a record but no arrest or referral to court); (2) arrest but no further judicial process; (3) adjustment or discharge in court; (4) court penalty such as probation or incarceration. The single most important finding was that nonwhite youth consistently got more severe disposition. This difference held up not only for the cohort as a whole (76.6 percent of white and 56.7 percent of nonwhite delinquents receiving remedial disposition) but also within social class, irrespective of differences in prior record, and whether the offense was "index" or "nonindex."

It is possible that remedial dispositions are used less frequently with nonwhites than with whites because nonwhites more often suffer disadvantages of poverty and limited resources; it is also possible that the more severe dispositions for nonwhites is a consequence of the higher rate of serious offenses among nonwhites. However, when both seriousness of offenses and socioeconomic status of accused are taken into account, whites still are more likely to receive the lighter disposition.

Race aside, the probability of a *first* court penalty is relatively independent of the number of prior offenses (at least up to five), but the probability of court penalties increases with each succeeding court penalty: a boy who has already received one court penalty is more likely to receive a subsequent court penalty.

What are the consequences of these dispositions? The data indicate that the more severe dispositions are more likely to be followed by a subsequent offense than are remedial dispositions. Does this mean that the court is accurate in deciding with whom to deal sternly (the persistent

TABLE 6.5

	White % *Remedial*	Nonwhite % *Remedial*
Low SES	71.8	56.5
High SES	80.3	58.7
One time offense	86.9	70.1
Recidivist	73.1	55.4
Nonindex	90.7	79.2
Index	51.8	31.6

Source: Adapted from data in Chapter 4, Wolfgang, Figlio, and Sellin, 1972.

TABLE 6.6

Disposition by Seriousness, SES, and Race

Seriousness Score and Disposition	*Lower SES*				*Higher SES*			
	Whites		*Nonwhites*		*Whites*		*Nonwhites*	
	N	*%*	*N*	*%*	*N*	*%*	*N*	*%*
Score less than 100:								
Remedial	1057	90.7	2195	83.9	1594	93.4	245	83.6
Other	109	9.3	421	16.1	113	6.6	48	16.4
Total	1166	100.0	2616	100.0	1707	100.0	293	100.0
Score 100 or more:								
Remedial	294	44.7	659	29.7	394	55.6	77	32.6
Other	364	55.3	1558	70.3	314	44.4	159	67.4
Total	658	100.0	2217	100.0	708	100.0	236	100.0

Source: Wolfgang, Figlio, and Sellin, 1972, Table 13.5. © by The University of Chicago Press.

recidivist, "hard core") or does it indicate severe dispositions produce the hardened repeat offender. Wolfgang *et al.* are aware that their data do not entirely resolve this question, but they do interpret their data as raising a question of the ultimate utility of more severe dispositions if the aim is to deter delinquency.

> Thus, we cannot conclude from an analysis of subsequent offensivity that the dispositions afforded juvenile offenders are serving the purposes for which they were designed. It would appear that on the one hand the judicial process has been able to screen the hard core offenders fairly well; on the other hand the judicial process and the correctional system do not seem to function effectively to restrain, discourage, or cure delinquency. Not only do a greater proportion of those who receive a severe disposition violate the law, but these violations are serious and rapid.
>
> . . . the type of the next offense—be it injury, theft, damage combination, or nonindex—cannot well be predicted by examination of the prior offense history, at least when that history is represented by our typology. There is practically no evidence to support a hypothesis of the existence of offense specialization among juvenile delinquents. (Wolfgang, Figlio, and Sellin, 1972, pp. 243 and 254)

The juvenile court is the point of contact for diverse officials and actors. The police, the citizen, or parent complainant, together with the accused youth and sometimes his or her counsel, come before a court referee, or a judge, assisted by probation officers and clinicians. The court mandate is broad, but its direct powers are limited. The court can do little directly to or for the child but place him or her in the custody of an agency (welfare, corrections, probation), remand him to his family, or shunt the case to adult criminal court.

The court in itself has not proven to be the effective device for the solution of the problems of the community versus youth. The President's Commission reported ruefully:

> . . . Studies conducted by the Commission, legislative inquiries in various States, and reports by informed observers compel the conclusion that the great hopes originally held for the juvenile court have not been fulfilled. It has not succeeded significantly in rehabilitating delinquent youth, in reducing or even stemming the tide of juvenile criminality, or in bringing justice and compassion to the child offender. To say that juvenile courts have failed to achieve their goals is to say no more than what is true of criminal courts in the United States. But failure is most striking when hopes are highest.

But to sense that the court has not worked as it should have or was hoped to work and to know to what extent the court fails, or why, are different matters. A few studies provide some reason for not rejecting the court.

Henry McKay, in a volume in the 1967 *President's Commission* series, reports a set of followup data from the Chicago of 1920. Examining a one-third random sample of males for whom first petitions alleging delinquent behavior were filed in Cook County in 1920, the study sought any record of subsequent arrest conviction or commitment for adult misdemeanor or felony. The length of the followup period is not stated in the report, which is an unfortunate omission, and although records of death were obtained, attention due to the boy moving from Illinois was apparently ignored. Any case that moved from the jurisdiction of the police and court records examined by McKay would be carried as a success regardless of his possible record elsewhere.

Of the sample purged of dead persons, 60 percent were arrested as adults; the proportion convicted of anything drops to 40 percent, and if commitment to jail or prison is taken as a criterion of recidivism, the figure is 23 percent (McKay, 1967, p. 109).

A majority of those who were arrested were arrested before they were 21 years old. A somewhat ambiguous finding concerns disposition by the court.

> Delinquents who appeared before the juvenile court only once and were dismissed by the court had an adult arrest rate of only 36.5, while those put under supervision, continued generally, or committed to an institution had an adult arrest rate of 55.8. For the group of boys with two or more delinquency petitions, variations by juvenile court disposition in the proportion arrested for all offenses were not in accord with expectation, but the proportion of those arrested for felonies was significantly higher for boys who had been committed. (President's Commission: Juvenile Delinquency and Youth Crime, 1967, p. 110)

Whether the court was correct in sending the precriminal to supervision or custody and discharging the youth who would probably go forth to sin no more, or whether the impact of probation and reformatory was deleterious and criminogenic, is difficult to decide from that finding. Three other early Chicago followups of juveniles are summarized by McKay many years later. They provide rough indications that between 50 and 60 percent of juveniles disposed as delinquents by the court are subsequently convicted of misdemeanors or felonies as adults, although a somewhat small number are committed to jail or prison. The absence of detailed tabulations by age or time from juvenile adjudication, or number of adult arrests for each person, makes it not possible to tell if many of the adult arrests are continuations of the youthful pattern and abandoned in the early twenties, or how many became persistent adult offenders. These figures, McKay notes, are not inconsistent with the results of Healy and Bronner's study of delinquents and criminals (Healy and Bronner, 1928), who reported 61 percent adult criminal records in a study of 421 boys from the juvenile court. McKay concludes his paper with the statement "the behavior of significant numbers of boys who become involved in illegal activity is not redirected toward conventional activity by the institutions created for that purpose" (McKay, 1967, p. 113).

Dunham and Knauer did a search of police arrest records in Detroit to determine if boys processed through juvenile court go on to adult criminal behavior. They selected a sample of males between the ages of 10 and 17 who were first offenders in the first year of each five-year period beginning 1920 and ending 1940. They found approximately one-fourth to one-third of each juvenile sample had been arrested by police as adults. Since there appears no consideration of possible attrition due to a youth moving away from the county, these data must be regarded as underestimates of the true percentage of former juvenile delinquents who are arrested as adults (Dunham and Kramer, 1952).

Chapter 7

DELINQUENCY CONTROL PROGRAMS: THE USE OF CONFINEMENT

7.1 Correctional Treatment Programs in Confinement

The reformatory and juvenile correctional institution is a legacy from the early history of the United States, dating back at least to the period of early urbanization up to the Civil War. The Age of Jackson stressed what was to be an American preoccupation for a century and a half: the positive formative influence of family upbringing, the mixed blessings of youthful companions, and the moral temptations of urban life. Childhood mischief was viewed as the seedbed of adult crime; the importance of youthful misconduct was to be gauged not by the gravity or triviality of the early offense, but rather by its significance as a predictor of subsequent criminal law breaking.

To develop a plausible argument for control and reform via organized agencies and places of confinement, the writers of the time amassed case histories that chronicled the progressive maturation of a nonconformist way of life from seemingly innocuous origins. Rothman states:

> The (case histories) demonstrated the dire consequences of even minor acts of disobedience. The delinquent moved inexorably from petty to major crimes. W. O. first stole one shilling from his father, then some items from a stranger, later robbed a watch and some broadcloth from a shop, and

> finally wrecked, burned and looted a house. E. M. began his career by pilfering small change from drunkards and graduated to highway robbery. J. K. went from pennies to dollars and C. B. from fruits and cakes in the kitchen cupboard to cash in store registers. What a careless parent dismissed as a comparatively harmless prank was a crucial event. A few pennis and sweets, as these biographies revealed, were the first symptoms of a criminal life. (Rothman, 1971, p. 77)

Of course it is to be noted that then as now the collection of such biographies proceeded backwards in time, from interviews with a confirmed adult felon that enabled one to reconstruct a career of prior activities. Thus, the manner of sampling precluded finding anyone who stole cakes as a child and did *not* go on to the gallows or the prison. There was little occasion for sampling at the input stage of the process, locating a number of children who pilfered the cookie jar and tracing their subsequent career, lawful or unlawful. Such studies were and are expensive and time consuming, to say nothing of being difficult. Nonetheless, for the Jacksonians as for us, the retrospective biographies served to justify already conceived theories of the causes of delinquencies.

From the Jacksonian period we get also the animating idea behind the prison and reformatory. The religious and political philosophy of the age stressed the plasticity and corruptibility of the young. Because of this belief in the plasticity and the potential perfectability of man, inhumanities such as torture and execution were no longer viewed as a reasonable way of dealing with law violation. The prison was seen as a better alternative, imposing restraint and penitence on the offender. However, the problem with previous prisons and lockups, such as the Newgates and Bridewells of England, was that they were congregate prisons housing in group cells the young and the old, male and female, novice and experienced outlaw, in circumstances where the inmate had to bribe and barter with his captors for the necessities of prison existence, where the discipline of the prison could be eased by the purchase of amenities of goods and services, and where continued interaction among prisoners led to exchange of information, planning of new offenses, and the reinforcement and confirmation of a deviant career. Reformers saw the solution to lie in the creation of a socially sanitary prison atmosphere where inmates would cease to enjoy even the scanty creature comforts of their own society. They would henceforth not have liberty within confinement to further "corrupt" one another, but would instead be obliged to labor in silence and discipline. The internal environment of the reformatory and penitentiary would be free of the moral contagion of the dissolute communities from which the delinquent sprang.[1]

[1]The confinement of children in the 19th century was for the most part under such severe regulations that much of the reformer's position might have seemed remote to the child prisoner. The records of an English jail show examples of disciplinary

In this hope there is a continuity from the 19th century to today. For decades both adult and juvenile corrections have repeatedly claimed that certain forms of supervision are "treatment" of the offender rather than punishment or control. It would be naive to presume that the use of the clinical phrases of the present era necessarily transforms punitive jails into rehabilitative clinics any more than they did in previous decades, just as it would be incorrect to gainsay many substantial changes in juvenile justice in the past 20 years. As an aid to separating ideology and claims from programs and effects, it may be useful to distinguish among three types of programs or services to persons regarded as needing special treatment.

---

measures taken against children, both those convicted of offenses and those confined for simple want of home:

CONVICTED CHILDREN

	Age	*Offense*	*Punishment*
A.A.	13.	Disobedience	1 hour in dark cell.
L.B.	14.	Neglecting to clean cell	1 hour in dark cell.
W.M.	12.	Turning round to look at another prisoner	1 hour and 20 minutes in dark cell.
W.M.	12.	Endeavouring to converse with another prisoner	Quarter hour in dark cell.
T.M.	10.	Ditto	Ditto.
W.L.	11.	Cutting table	9 hours in dark cell on bread and water.
W.S.	13.	Endeavouring to look at another prisoner in chapel	Deprived of dinner.
S.L.	14.	Talking in chapel	8 hours in dark cell on bread and water.

UNCONVICTED CHILDREN

	Age	*Offense*	*Punishment*
R.L.	9.	Improper conduct in chapel	1 hour in dark cell.
S.L.	14.	Turning up veil (girl)	1 hour in dark cell.
J.L.	12.	Disobedience of orders	Ditto.
J.L.	12.	Repeated disobedience of order	12 hours in dark cell on bread and water.
S.Y.	14.	Disobedience of orders and insolence	4 hours in dark cell and deprived of supper.
S.L.	14.	Ditto	Ditto.
S.L.	14.	Wilful damage	1 day and 4 hours in dark cell on bread and water.
I.N.	11.	Endeavouring to communicate	2 hours in dark cell
W.L.	11.	Cutting table	9 hours in dark cell on bread and water.
S.L.	14.	Talking in chapel	9 hours in dark cell on bread and water.
S.L.	14.	Ditto	21 hours ditto.
S.L.	14.	Ditto	2 days in dark cell and deprived of dinner.
I.L.	14.	Ditto	2 hours in dark cell and deprived of dinner.
G.N.	13.	Ditto	Ditto.
S.L.	14.	Endeavouring to communicate	Deprived of dinner.

Source: Joseph Fletcher, in the Journal of the Statistical Society of London 1851, quoted in Sanders, p. 178 .

Erving Goffman, in an ingenious essay on the "medical model" (Goffman, 1961, p. 321), draws attention to the similarities and differences between certain classes of professional service to clients and patients and the more prosaic work done for customers by repair trades. He then contrasts both of these services with the kind of treatment and control exerted over the inmate in public mental hospitalization. We may extend his thinking to include two other categories: welfare services and criminal corrections. Our task is complicated by the fact that adjudicated juvenile delinquents share some of the characteristics—and fate—of welfare clients, mental patients, and adult prisoners.

The idea of treatment, and terms such as "patient" and "client," presume a model that may be called "client-oriented" or *client-professional* interaction. A client engages an expert to perform professional service for him; the client initiates contact with the professional (e.g., physician, lawyer) and extends to him conditional control of the object for which his services were engaged (e.g., the patient's body or health, the client's legal affairs or portions of them). The nature of this interaction is limited by strict canons of professional practice and somewhat less strict obligations on the client. The professional is explicitly an agent acting on behalf of the client in the client's best interest. The notion of "malpractice" signals the distinction between acting in the interests of the patient and exploiting the patient through neglect or design. It is this client-professional relation that has similarities to the useful repair trades in which an owner engages a specialist to perform a service on some object belonging to the customer, acting in the interest of the customer. Here custom and law recognize obligations of proper conduct bearing on the person providing the service. The utility and prestige of such exchanges are both well established, and the terms "client," "patient," and "treatment," or "counsel," connote the rendering of service under conditions mutually understood and binding during the period of the relationship.

Another type of service organization developed in mass society. This exchange is *applicant-centered* rather than client-initiated. The applicant is either one who seeks benefits or relief to which he or she may be entitled, or begs charity because of extremity of needs. The agency determines the categorical entitlement or moral case for aid and renders services within the often negotiated terms of entitlement. The service may be terminated by either party; but major disputes may arise over discontinuance at the behest of the agent.

A third type of exchange may be called *correctional*, in which the State proceeds against a citizen whose conduct is found to be criminal, delinquent, or otherwise morally deplorable. Here an accused, convicted, or committed person seeks to defend himself or escape from the service to be rendered to him at the behest of the agency. The inmate, prisoner, or ward cannot terminate the relationship and has little power to defend any claims over the disposition of his person or liberty. The agent has custody of the inmate and acts on behalf of (and presumably in the interest of) the State.

The variation in correctional institutions in the United States is very great, ranging from converted residences with eight to 12 juveniles to huge reformatories for juveniles and prisons for youthful offenders, and even dual prisons for the incarceration of the hardest and most rebellious wards of the Youth Authority as well as the youngest adults committed to the adult department of corrections. The staffing and routine of the administration, and the internal, *sub rosa* organization among inmates, have been studied in a number of settings (Clemmer, 1947; Sykes, 1958; Cressey, 1961, 1965; Glaser, 1963; Ward and Kassebaum, 1965; Gialambardo, 1966; Irwin, 1970; American Friends Service Committee, 1971; Kassebaum, Ward, and Wilner, 1971). The common theme of most of the descriptions, including those done in modern institutions, is the disenchantment and cynicism voiced so frequently by both staff members and prisoners concerning the rehabilitative ideology and specific treatment programs.

Juvenile institutions have been found to exhibit most of the features of adult prisons: a hierarchy of power and intimidation, starting with staff such as cottage parent, and elite dominant older boys, and terminating with the errand runners, the raped, and the youngest "son" dependent on the protection or patronage of an older boy "father." Such studies have uncovered systems of barter and contraband, homosexuality both consensual and coercive, and alliances against staff as well as collusion between individual staff members and inmates. One juvenile institution may serve as a not atypical illustration. Fricot Ranch, an institution for boys operated by the State of California, has been studied by a succession of sociologists and psychologists (Fisher, 1961; Jesness 1965). Accounts over the years provide documentation that the institution routine is a dreary round of staff authoritarianism, inmate tribalism, and brutality and exploitation. Both Fisher and Jesness were staff members, and each had extensive acquaintance with the institution.

Jesness comments on the displacement of the lofty rehabilitative ends of the institution by the emphasis on custodial orderliness and discipline. In characterizing the day-to-day thinking of the staff, he emphasizes the preoccupation with obtaining and maintaining obedience and the assumption that this is best and perhaps necessarily accomplished by inspiring fear in the boys. The threat of punishment, including corporal punishment, is ever present, and its use is "constantly observable." These include both punishment of specific individuals, and collective reprisals on the entire residence hall. Likewise, Fisher characterizes the behavior among the boys as victimization and patronage and gives details of physical assaults carried out by staff on boys, and by some boys against other boys. Residence buildings are dominated by an elite inmate, sustained by a coterie of supporters, and ruling by intimidation and violence.

The displacement of treatment ideology by the realities of a preoccupation with custodial control is not of course peculiar to this institution.

Rolde and his associates provide a description of a maximum security institution that ostensibly serves as a "treatment facility" for young males in another state. The account details gross inadequacies of physical plant, heating, instruction, staffing, and programming. The main regulator of the round of daily activities is punishment. The main means by which punishment is administered include occasional corporal punishment by staff, *sub rosa*, unsystematic but frequent enough for mention; solitary confinement; and loss of privileges.

> Solitary confinement is one of the major means of punishment in the institution. It is frequently used for a wide variety of infractions, large and small. Boys are placed in small cells wearing their shorts and with no other possessions. The cells are bare except for a mattress and a single suspended light bulb. . . . Boys are placed in these cells for unspecified periods of time; 30 days is a frequent period of confinement, but longer terms are not unusual. (Rolde *et al.*, 1970, p. 441)

The striking thing about this report is that a series of private and public investigations by staff, local, journalistic, and federal investigating teams have repeatedly brought the same inadequacies and abuses to the attention of the Youth Authority without any significant changes in staffing, budget, plant, or program.

In studies of the juvenile correctional institution, one of the more firmly established findings is the development of patterns of informal social organization among inmates as a response to the deprivations of imprisonment. Studies of adult institutions have demonstrated the existence of differentiated roles nucleated around the struggle for goods and services in short supply, the articulation of an inmate code of values that asserts opposition to staff, and a variety of institution behaviors that are either deviant with respect to the rules and practices of the outside society, or so thoroughly grounded in the peculiarities of institution life that they highlight the isolated and artificial character of the inmate existence.

Begansky (1972) conducted a study of a small closed correctional facility in a western state. The primary program at this institution is behavior modification implemented by a "point" system. In this approach most amenities including extra food, cigarettes, candy, recreation, entertainment, and furlough are purchased by points amassed by school performance, work, good behavior, and special endeavors. Fines for infractions of regulations are also assessed in the point currency. In addition to fines, punishment includes loss of privileges or solitary confinement.

Begansky's study focused on a pseudo kinship network that existed during a considerable time period in the institution, and then, following a change in inmate population composition, passed into disuse. The network in question was a series of "father-son" linkages, the word "father" designating the dominant, patron, or exploiting role, and "son" denoting the subordinate, dependent role. An interview survey of the population of the institution was done at several points in time. Fifty percent of the boys occupied either father or son role during the survey and another 12 percent reported playing a role prior to the study.

Patronage and physical protection were given most often as the reason for these relations, followed by "goods" and "services." Fathers were found to be older and heavier than sons and had longer length of stay in the institution at the time of the study. The tendency of a boy to remain in a father or son role was relatively persistent for some time, but by the end of a series of surveys, a number of "sons" had left the arrangement to become independent or had been disowned by their "father."

After a period of approximately one year from the third wave of interviews, a fourth set of interviews was conducted. During the intervening year a change in court sentencing and parole policies reduced the variance and range of age and size of boys at the institution. Under these changed conditions the father-son system was found to have almost disappeared. Apparently as the risk of assault or abuse subsided in the inmate population, the need for a patronage network was reduced, and the arrangement ceased to be a part of inmate life.

One conspicuous characteristic of prisons themselves is that they harbor a high degree of illegal activity. Homicide and theft rates are very high in prisons, as are assault rates. Quite simply if the intention is to stop criminal behavior, the prison does not work. Public concern is seldom aroused much about this situation either way, testimony to the lowered moral claims of those who have themselves been labeled criminals. (There is an analogy to prostitutes: it is very difficult for a known prostitute to claim that she has been raped, though in reality she is at high risk and may have suffered forcible abuse.)

Recently, however, there has been an extension of the procedures of law into the prisons, in defense of victimized prisoners. In the Philadelphia municipal system, for example, suits against the city claiming forcible sexual assaults of young male prisoners have resulted in a large-scale investigation of this problem. The period 1966–68 was investigated by way of interviews of prisoners and staff, polygraph tests (which some staff refused to take), and so on, and results concluded that sexual assault in the Philadelphia jail system was virtually epidemic: nearly every slightly built young man entering the system had been approached sexually, and many are eventually forcibly and repeatedly assaulted, sometimes by groups. This investigation concluded:

> During the 26-month period, we found there had been 156 sexual assaults that could be documented and substantiated—through institutional records, polygraph examinations, or other corroboration. Seven of the assaults took place in the sheriff's vans, 149 in the prisons. Of the sexual assaults, 82 consisted of buggery; 19 of fellatio, and 55 of attempts and coerce solicitations to commit sexual acts. There were assaults on at least 97 different victims by at least 176 different aggressors. With unidentified victims and aggressors, there were 109 different victims and 276 different aggressors.
>
> For various reasons these figures represent only the top of the iceberg. (Wallace, 1971)

In the free community, on the other hand, the sexual assault rate on males is almost nonexistent.

Another departure from "normal" sexual patterns, again found in prisons, is the development of noncoercive homosexual behavior, especially among women. A study of one adult women's prison suggested that up to 50 percent of all inmates had actively engaged in homosexual behavior while in prison (Ward and Kassebaum, 1965). Naturally the question arises: Is it the prison environment or the people in prison that accounts for this rate?

By no means did 50 percent of these people have previous homosexual experience in civilian life. A small percentage had such histories; but some who engaged in homosexual activities on the outside were "straight" on the inside. The bulk of the inmates had no previous homosexual experience, calling attention to the characteristics of the institution itself, which could account for this departure from normal behavior; in addition, most of those studied reverted back to heterosexual patterns on release from prison. How can an institution that is set up to promote conformity produce such large amounts of deviant behavior?

An examination of the social structure of the reformatory and the routine programs conducted there does not carry us to the most relevant data for program evaluation. For this we must consider the correctional treatment model and post-release figures.

The correctional treatment model consists of the following: (a) upon conviction the task of deciding how long the prisoner is to remain confined is shifted from the judge to an administrative staff or a parole board; the inmate is tested and classified in prisons variously termed Reception-Guidance Centers, Diagnostic Centers, or simply Classification Sections, in order to assign the prisoner to a treatment program or place of confinement most appropriate to his problem and history; (b) the ambiguity surrounding both the length of time to be served and the criteria for release are strong pressure for inmate compliance with rules of institution and accommodation to correctional staff (thus a means of increasing docility in the confined population). The staff or parole board is to release the inmate when he is "ready"; (c) release to parole supervision extends the time during which the convicted adult or adjudicated juvenile is under direct control of the state; moreover, parole extends the boundaries of correctional control from inside an institution into the community at large.

Clashing with the treatment model are two important considerations. First, there is a prevailing concept of "just punishments," which requires that a person be confined a certain amount of time irrespective of the likelihood that he will commit another offense. Second, the custody and internal housekeeping needs of the prison, and the narrow range of treatment alternatives, influence classification. Whether an inmate is found suitable for "training in culinary work" and "group counseling" or works at a pay job in the spinning mill or becomes a plumber's assistant is often the result of what section of the institution must fill a job of a given type or has a vacancy in a pay job.

Almost every person who is sent to prison is subsequently released. As a consequence, there is great practical value in the prediction of post-release criminality and its correlates. But precommitment characteristics predict post-release returns to prison for any given commitment only to a limited extent, and information about the prisoner's experience or behavior in custody predicts parole outcomes even less accurately. Moreover, it is not really clear what is being predicted, since post-release criteria are typically either ambiguous or grossly oversimplified.

In a recent review of prediction efforts in corrections, Gottfredson comments:

> Criteria of delinquency, criminal behavior and of parole or probation violations are ordinarily quite crude. . . . Criteria may not depend solely on the behavior of the person about whom the prediction is made, but they also may depend upon . . . the behavior of the police and courts. . . . A designation as a "parole violator" is made on the basis not only of the parolee's behavior, but also on the response of the parole agent or the paroling authority. . . . In this situation, an increase in "parole violations" may reflect increased offending behavior by parolees, increased surveillance by parole agents or changes in policy of the paroling authority. (President's Commission: Juvenile Delinquency and Youth Crime, 1967, p. 173)

In the same review Gottfredson states "all currently available prediction methods still have only relatively low predictive power" (ibid, p. 181).

Treatment programs are special efforts within correctional organizations to reduce the probability of post-release returns to confinement. The major empirical evaluations to date seeking significant differences between treatment and control cases do not provide strong support for any important correctional treatment program (see Robeson and Smith, 1971; Kassebaum, Ward, and Wilner, 1971). Again, however, the criteria of parole success or failure are very unclear, and there is the disturbing possibility that the interpretation of the meaning of parole dispositions (e.g., return to prison) may be strained to fit the underlying psychological assumptions of current treatment programs.

Some of these difficulties result from a truncated view of the behavior of prisoners and parolees. Efforts at predicting are hampered by insufficient data on differentials in the life situations of parolees; a disregard of the characteristics of the formal organizations that have responsibility for the parolee; and a failure to deal in the analysis with the cyclical career pattern of the repeat offender. By gathering data on the parolee's environmental setting, studying the correctional and parole systems as organizations, and by dealing with the career of the offender over periods spanning more than one commitment, the behavior of the parolee may be better understood. An early statement of some of the questions are raised in Martinson, Kassebaum, and Ward, "A Critique of Research on Parole," *Federal Probation*, September, 1964. In that paper we argue (1) parole has been studied largely from the narrow focus of prediction of parole success or failure; (2) parole outcome has been regarded implicitly as simply a function of parolee behavior to the neglect of the parole officer as decision maker; and (3) the parole division has not been studied as a complex social organization. Paul Schreiber (1960) has commented on difficulties in using a criterion such as "recidivism" in comparing evaluations of correctional program effectiveness. Despite the ambiguities however, some measure of recidivism, properly interpreted is likely to be required in the assessment of any delinquency program.

7.2 Evaluation of Treatment Outcome

The whole point to correctional intervention in the lives of juveniles is the production of effects. The evaluation of the program's effects is incumbent on a society that permits such powerful intervention. The evaluation of correctional effectiveness is a special case of program or treatment evaluation. Whether the problem is to determine if a new analysis is a more potent pain reliever, or if in school small classes provide more learning than large classes, or if group therapy or conditioning techniques of behavior modification lead to a reduction in post-release criminal violation, the methodological questions are quite similar. The better program evaluation studies have been those able to utilize a longitudinal experimental design. Such studies are difficult to carry out in field situations, since they require:

1. An adequate control group with which to compare the persons exposed to the treatment program.
2. Controlled selection and assignment of subjects to the treatment and control conditions to insure initial comparability.
3. If possible the spatial separation of subjects in different treatment settings to minimize contamination of the independent variable.
4. A sufficiently representative sample to permit generalization of findings within acceptable confidence limits.
5. A uniform followup of all experimental and control subjects after completion of treatment, for a sufficiently long time to insure that returns to law violation, if they occur, will be detected.
6. Variables under study to include important attributes of subject and situations, and a realistic and relevant criterion for evaluation (see Kassebaum, Ward, and Wilner, 1971, Chap. 2).

The most common finding in correctional program evaluations is that the program's effects—compared with the absence of the program—are nil.

The trend in evaluation studies is clearest in adult corrections. Many of them have been done in the past decade, largely in the State of California and in the Federal Bureau of Prisons.

The accumulation of evaluations of treatment and training programs in close custody institutions has not demonstrated the usefulness of those institutions by the criteria of lowered incidence of lawlessness inside the reformatory, lowered recidivism after release from confinement, or greater success when used on parole. However, most of these studies varied the type of experience *in* confinement rather than the difference between prison and no prison.

One exception was a study done in Montreal. Here the experimental variable was not incarceration experience but parole versus unconditional release, and the subjects were not juveniles but adult.

> André Bourdon compared the experience of 247 men released on parole with 105 men released at the end of sentence without parole supervision. All were released from the Centre Fédéral Reformation in St. Vincent de Paul, Quebec, a medium-security institution for amenable prisoners, most of whom are serving their first term in a federal prison. The men studied were released between April 1957 and April 1959. Those released at end of sentence were considered recidivists if they were found guilty of any

> criminal charge, even if they were not reincarcerated. The parolees were considered recidivists if their parole was revoked either for an infraction of a parole rule or for a new offense. The prisoners released with and without supervision were compared, holding constant many of those variables cited below as being important in successful adjustment after incarceration.
>
> In general, Bourdon's findings were that the significantly higher rate of success among parolees compared with those released without supervision was largely a function of the selection process by which those most likely to succeed are chosen for parole. When supervised and unsupervised releases with similar traits known to be related to success and failure rates were compared, the failure rates were similar. (Arnold, 1970, p. 78)

A survey of 100 reports of correctional outcome reached a predominantly negative conclusion:

> It seems quite clear that on the basis of this sample of outcome reports with all its limitations, evidence supporting the efficacy of correctional treatment is slight, inconsistent and of questionable reliability. (Bailey, 1966, p. 156)

A series of studies done in California was elegantly summarized and interpreted in an article by Robeson and Smith, which reviewed evaluations of the effects of length of incarceration, the use of correctional confinement versus probation, treatment programs in prison, the closeness of parole supervision, and the differences between unconditioned discharge from prison and release on parole. Robeson and Smith conclude:

> In correctional practice, treatment and punishment generally coexist and cannot appropriately be viewed as mutually exclusive. . . . *The real choice is not between treatment on the one hand and punishment on the other, but between one treatment-punishment alternative and another.* Analysis of findings in a review of the major California correctional programs that permit relatively rigorous evaluation strongly suggests the following conclusion. There is no evidence to support any programs' claim of superior rehabilitative efficacy. The single answer to the question: "Will the clients act differently if we lock them up, or keep them locked up longer, or do something with them inside, or watch them more closely afterward or cut them loose officially?" is *"Probably not."* (Robeson and Smith, 1971, pp. 79–80)

The California Youth Authority's Community Treatment Program compared regular parole following incarceration (the "control" condition) with assignment of wards directly to small case load community probationary supervision (see Warren, 1966 and 1967). The finding of the study was that fewer experimentals than controls were unfavorably discharged or had paroles revoked. These results were criticized by both Robeson and Takagi (in Carter and Wilkins, 1970, pp. 233–259) and Lerman (Lerman, 1970, pp. 317–329) because this difference is demonstrably the result of greater readiness of the parole agents to revoke the parole of a control subject for a moderate offense while allowing the experimental case to continue on parole. This was seen as not unrelated to the desire of CYA to produce results that could have been useful in the defense of requests for program support.

An evaluation of correctional group counseling was done in the 1960's by Kassebaum, Ward, and Wilner. The study was able to utilize a longitudinal experimental design on a newly opened medium security prison in California. A total of 1800 adult men were randomly assigned to three treatment varieties and two control conditions. Measurements of program participation, inmate attitude change, and disciplinary rates were made in the prison over a two-year period. Approximately 975 men were released on parole from the program and were followed for a period of 36 months from release from prison. The study was not able to discern any differences between men in treatment programs and men in the same prison but not in the programs on attitude change, disciplinary reports, or on parole violation after release. Approximately equal percentages (from 50 to 60 percent) were returned to prison by the end of the three years from each of the treatment and control samples (Kassebaum, Ward, and Wilner, 1971, especially Chaps. 8 and 9).

Studies reporting no significant differences between "treatment" (exposed to a program) and "controls" (not exposed to the program) include Meyer, Borgatta, and Jones (1965); Empey, Newland, and Lubech (1965); and Adams (1971).

Followup of juvenile dispositions to probation or confinement have been done even less often and less rigorously than for adults. They nearly without exception ignore females. The few that have carried the followup from juvenile to adult have shown that a considerable percentage of persons who are adjudicated as delinquent when young do not develop criminal records as adults.

The meager data on juvenile parole suggests that the violation rate is as high or higher than for adults. Because of the extensive use of probation for juvenile offenders, this is perhaps not surprising, for the juveniles who are incarcerated and released on parole must represent a rather high risk group. Also, the younger a person is when first committed, the greater the probability of adult parole violation. Glaser published a two-year followup of Wisconsin juvenile parolees (1952–1954), shown in Table 7.1 below.

The younger at release, the more likely the parole was revoked; the overall rate is higher than some studies of adult parolees (Glaser gives 33 percent for an overall figure) but not much higher than the 50 percent Kassebaum, Ward, and Wilner report for men, or the 40 percent figures given for adult women by Carol Spencer (Spencer, 1972).

TABLE 7.1

Postrelease Violation Rates of Juveniles in Relation to Age at Release
Wisconsin 1952-1954 Juvenile Paroles Revoked Within Two Years of Release

Age at Release	*Males*	*Females*
12–13	78%	67%
14	54	58
15	58	40
16	50	33
17	44	40
18 and over	41	34
Rates for all cases	50%	39%
Number of cases	1,037	453

Source: Arnold, 1970, p. 7.

Post-institutional adjustment in the community was to be facilitated by a program of Mobilization for Youth in New York called the Reintegration Project (RP). Designed to ease transition, to reintroduce the youth into getting together with his family, get into school, or (if over 16 years of age) get and hold a job, and dissuade youth from reuniting with delinquent or criminal associates, the RP used small case load family counseling and active client advocacy. The 34 youths serviced by RP were compared with a control group of 24 cases who were serviced by the Home Service Bureau (implied to be a "standard" program). The youngsters had been sent up to reformatory for theft and burglary (32.8 percent), truancy and other trouble at school (29.3 percent), trouble at home (13.8 percent), fighting or assault (13.8 percent), and miscellaneous other charges (10.3 percent).

The RP became involved in the boys' families, a large number of which were simultaneously involved in a number of New York City's melange of medical, housing, public assistance, and community center agencies. The RP assisted family members to visit children when the latter were still in prison; and they dealt with problems of youth relating to both intact families and arranged foster placement for some cases where extreme conflict or the dissolution of the family removed it from further consideration. Employment was difficult to secure, and many young clients were poorly motivated to continue in wretchedly paying jobs.

Hettle Jones, from whose chapter much of this account is taken, comments on the bitter choice facing the young ghetto school dropout in the labor force:

It is interesting to compare what is expected in the way of dedication from a sixteen-year-old boy of limited background from a deprived family and what is expected from a middle-class, fairly well-educated youth. The middle-class teen-ager in America is required to be diligent in his schoolwork in the interest of future rewards, but his lapses are passed off as youthful spirits, and he is generally given much freedom to postpone arranging his own life. Responsibility, when it is assigned, is more in the nature of keeping the lawn trimmed than earning money to pay part of the rent.

On the other hand, the sixteen-year-old high-school dropout is not only required to decide, right here and now, exactly what he will be, but to do it with a minimum of "trouble." He is urged to be sober and serious, to work during the day at a job which usually involved some physical labor and then, if possible, to continue his schooling at night. We require of him the kind of motivation traditionally required of immigrants and their children, yet we make no promises that he will attain the stature of those who spend these years going to school and football games, even if he behaves as we wish him to. This is a hard role for a sixteen-year-old. The young black and Puerto Rican man of limited advantage knows full well that he stands hardly a chance of ever getting anywhere, especially since so few of the significant adults in his life ever have. The youth of the Lower East Side sometimes choose hustling for very real reasons. (Jones, in Weissman, 1969, pp. 83–84)

In the end the RP was modified into a preventive program working with the younger siblings of the youthful ex-convicts who were its original clients. It did not succeed in providing incremental opportunities to the delinquent youth, and a comparison of RP with the control cases fails to demonstrate any reduction in recidivism (See Table 7.2).

7.3 The Provo Experiments

Lamar Empey and associates more than ten years ago began a program of delinquency treatment aimed at boys (girl delinquents were excluded from this program) who had been previously re-

TABLE 7.2

	Total *n* = 58	*Experimental*	*Control*	*Home Service Bureau Annual Report*
Nonrecidivists	(34) 58.6	(20) 58.8	(14) 58.3	(666) 57.9
Recidivists	(24) 41.4	(14) 41.2	(10) 41.7	(485) 42.1
	100%	100%	100%	100%

Source: Hettle Jones "From Reform School to Society" in Harold Weissman (editor), *Individual and Group Services in the Mobilization for Youth Experience* (New York: Association Press, 1969), p. 90.

voked on probation. The theory behind the program was that delinquent youth derive their conduct from a peer group, that they are ambivalent toward the values and expectations of "conventional" society, and that "a delinquent subsystem simply represents an alternative means for acquiring, or attempting to acquire, social and economic goals idealized by the social system which are acquired by other people through conventional means" (Empey, 1972, p. 5). To be successful, the program must make conventional and delinquent alternatives clear, rewarding the former and punishing the latter, through peer group pressures rather than direct coercion by staff. Strict control was exerted over boys assigned a small, nonresidential program: failure to report daily on time and other serious lapses in rule conformity meant an immediate transfer to the state reformatory for boys. Boys were expected to participate in guided group interaction sessions (GGI), candidly and critically assessing one another, in the presence of staff adults. The intent of the program was to produce a minimal level of law violation during the program period and after discharge from the program.

The project attempted to use an experimental design, randomly assigning boys to treatment or control samples within each of two classes of sentencing previously decided upon by the juvenile court judge: probation cases and incarceration cases. Once the judge decided on whether the boy went to probation or reformatory, the design called for him to assign the boy either to the Pinehall Project, or to probation (or reformatory, as the case may be). However, so few cases were referred to the reformatory that the design for randomization of treatment and control cases within the incarceration sample had to be abandoned. The state reformatory had to serve as a control group, and Pinehall got all the boys slated by the judge for incarceration. Thus the experimental design was only partially randomized. A four-year follow-up was maintained on the boys assigned to either the experimental (Pinehall) or control (probation or reformatory) samples. The measure of effectiveness used was a simple ratio of the number of boys arrested divided by the number of boys assigned to the program (minus 1.0 to make an index that varied from 0 to 1. Complete absence of recidivism would yield an index of 1.0; everyone arrested would yield an index of 0. The results for each sample, year by year, are displayed in table 7.3.

Whereas the differences between the boys originally slated for probation (both Pinehall and actual probation) and the boys slated for incarceration (reformatory and Pinehall) are apparent after the first year, there are no differences between experimentals and controls within the probation group. For the incarceration group, the boys in the reformatory do somewhat worse than their counterparts who went to Pinehall, but we have seen that this is not a clean comparison as it is in the probation

TABLE 7.3

Programs Effects Based on One or More Arrests as Criterion of Recidivism

Treatment Variety	*Percent with One or More Arrest* *First Year*	*Second Year*	*Third Year*	*Fourth Year*
Probation Pinehall	.59	.52	.48	.42
Probation Control	.61	.54	.49	.46
Incarceration Pinehall	.55	.39	.36	.36
Incarceration Control	.40	.27	.21	.21

Source: Empey and Erickson, 1972, p. 187.

sample. Moreover, it is not clear whether the difference if it does exist is due to the positive impact of Pinehall or merely the avoidance of the deleterious effects of the "correctional" institution. If the criterion for recidivism is taken to be four or more arrests of more serious nature, the differences between programs are smaller, although again, incarcerated boys do worse. Thus the utility of the peer group pressures and regulations of Pinehall cannot be demonstrated by comparison with a comparable sample of boys assigned to ordinary probation, but the superiority of the community-based program over the reformatory is at least possibly demonstrated.

7.4 Civil Commitment

Disenchantment with criminal proceedings for both juvenile and adult offenders of certain kinds has found outlet in the possibility that a public health model of compulsory quarantine and treatment might be useful. Unfortunately, experience to date has not borne out the expectations held, and civil commitment is seen as a facade for correctional control.

Civil commitment programs were set up in response to two pressures: one from clinical specialists, who believed that treatment facilities could reduce the numbers of drug users; the other appellate courts, which were ruling that imprisonment for narcotic addiction was a violation of constitutional rights. The clearest case can be seen in California. In *Robinson* (370 US 660 [1962]) the Supreme Court ruled that a California law that made drug addiction a crime was unconstitutional. The reason cited by the Court was that addiction is a disease, and hence imprisonment violated the Eighth Amendment's protection against cruel and unusual punishment. The State responded by creating a civil commitment program providing compulsory confinement and "after care" for narcotics users initially under the Department of Corrections, with post-release supervision under the Parole Division. The law was quickly challenged; the program was operated inside ordinary state prisons for the first year or more, with persons committed virtually undistinguishable from other prison inmates by dress, program, cell, regulations, or privileges. The only difference during this period was the letter "A" preceding the prison inmate number. A former Chief of Research for the program, and a psychiatrist, writes:

> The provision [of the law] under which [an alleged narcotics user] was committed was located in the penal code; his commitment was to an institution under the jurisdiction of the Department and Director of Corrections; his commitment was for a minimum and maximum period (and further the maximum varied according to whether the addict was convicted in a municipal or superior court); for the purposes of punishing an escape from commitment an escapee is treated as "a prisoner committed to a state prison"; and primary discretion for the granting of paroles and the recommendation of discharges was placed in the Adult Authority, the same agency which grants paroles and fixes sentences for persons in a state prison. (Kramer, 1970, p. 10)

In lobbying for the enabling legislation, a Judge Burke asserted "the number one objective of this measure is to get the narcotic addict off the street" and a Captain Madden of the Los Angeles Police Department testified ". . . a narcotic addict must be isolated from the balance of society . . . so that he cannot contaminate others with his own vicious habit" (Kramer, pp. 9–10).

Research on the effect of the civil commitment program shows that not only was the program essentially penal in structure, but that it had no better results than prison. In a follow-up of 1,209 inmates released to parole, 50 percent had been returned to confinement within the first year of post-release, one-third were on parole, and the rest were listed as having violated various contract conditions of parole but had not been returned. When the follow-up period was extended to 36 months, one out of six former prisoners had been continuously on parole. Indications further were that the violation rate for the first year had increased after the program had been in operation for several years. Moreover the successes were not the typical heroin addict but were rather the tablet and cough-syrup users and other nonheroin users.

Despite unimpressive effects, the program has continued as a means of putting pressure on suspected drug users.

> . . . police [in Los Angeles] have literally snatched "known" addicts off the street; the policeman makes the declaration that the alleged addict was behaving suspiciously and states that to the best of the reporting officer's belief he is an addict. A five or ten minute examination is performed in jail usually by one or two physicians who earn a large part of their income from these proceedings. . . . When physicians at the Los Angeles County Hospital failed to render such opinions frequently enough, a cell block in the County Jail was declared a "hospital ward" and alleged addicts were admitted there for examination by physicians employed primarily for that purpose. (Kramer, p. 15)

Conversely, the very severity of the civil commitment program apparently caused some judges to impose short county jail sentences rather than invoke the heavy weight of the narcotics program.

Note: The New York program of civil commitment has been commented on thusly in the New York University Law Review:

> It is clear that the New York commitment statute fails to supply the alleged addict with the basic protections to which one in danger of losing his liberty is entitled. . . . Moreover the findings of the court . . . reveal that the narcotic addict on Rikers Island is being treated as if he were a criminal, in direct opposition to the demands of *Robinson.* (NYU Law Review, 1968, p. 1193)

Granted the severity of the civil commitment program, is there at least evidence that the program reduces the illicit use of narcotics? The available evidence is to the contrary. Robeson and Smith report a study of California's civil commitment program for narcotics users. A three-year follow-up of 1,209 persons paroled to outpatient status revealed:

> Seventeen percent received a discharge from the program after completing three continuous years on outpatient status.
> Sixty-seven percent were returned [to the Institution].
> Thirty-three percent received a new criminal conviction during their first release (22 percent misdemeanors and 11 percent felonies).
> Seventy-one percent were detected as having used drugs illegally (63 percent opiates and 8 percent other dangerous drugs or marijuana). (Robeson and Smith, p. 75)

The civil commitment programs for narcotics users rely on sweeping powers similar to those used to involuntarily incarcerated drunks, "defective delinquents," so called sexual psychopaths, and "sexually dangerous persons." These programs have been widely assailed for failing to provide safeguards against wholesale abuse of civil rights (Derschowitz, 1968, Kaplan, 1969), for failing to actually provide medical or psychiatric treatment (Nasatir *et al.*, 1966), and for being imposed on persons with a low probability of recidivism. In regard to the latter, and in summarizing its position on civil commitment programs, a publication of the National Institute of Mental Health states flatly:

> Special statutes under which so-called psychopaths, defective delinquents, sexual psychopaths and sexually dangerous persons are civilly committed should be repealed, as they fail to perform the basic function for which they were enacted—they do not select persons on the basis of dangerousness. They should be repealed for what they do accomplish—they allow for the indeterminante commitment of persons, many of whom are not dangerous, in some cases without a conviction of crime, without adequate safeguard for procedural due process. . . .
>
> Voluntary treatment programs for both narcotic addicts and chronic alcoholics are preferable to civil commitment procedures which function to deprive a person of his liberty without either adequate procedural safeguards or satisfactory treatment methods. (NIMH, 1971, p. 15)

7.5 Programming Controls via Operant Conditioning

The *deterministic-control* model is an important development in juvenile corrections. Most popularly called behavior modification (or "behavior-mod"), the most prevalent form derives from the operant conditioning theory of B.F. Skinner. (See Krasner, 1971; Jehu *et al.*, 1972 for review of current programs and problems as well as bibliography.) Essentially such programs assume that delinquent youth are in trouble because they violate rules or indulge in offensive behavior that is clearly seen by the community as wrong. To make the delinquent abide by the law it is necessary to train him to do certain things and not to do other things. It is in short a learning task, which can be reduced to the same elements of stimulus and reinforcement and conditioning as any rat or pigeon experiment.

Eysenck, in a review of conditioning programs, categorizes persons broadly into introverts (who may be prone to overconditioning and fixations) and extroverts (who may be prone to underconditioning). Introverts may be subject to disorders that tend to produce pain and trouble for the actor, and require therapy that desensitizes. Extroverts may be subject to disorders of behavior that cause pain or trouble for others, and may require reconditioning. The use of both contingent rewards and aversive treatment may be seen today in delinquency programs.

Krasner (1971) provides an introduction to the contingent reward program. Such programs place the prisoner in a living situation in which the amenities of daily living are dependent on certain output from the prisoner. The output may be school work, learning a module in math or language; it may be rule conformity, work, or other behavior. Points, usually in the form of tokens, are awarded and are used as currency for the purchase of various goods and services, including rest, privacy, or a day away from the institution. Krasner comments:

> Token economy programs are most recent illustration of broad application of operant conditioning approach to modifying deviant behavior . . . at the simplest level . . . it involves setting up of a contingent reinforcement program with three aspects:
>
> First staff designates certain specific patient (sic) behaviors as good or desirable, hence reinforcible. Second there is a medium of exchange, the token, that stands for something else, the back-up reinforcer. . . . Third, there is a way of utilizing the tokens. . . . These are the good things in life . . . and may range from food to being allowed to sit peacefully in a chair. (Krasner, 1971, p. 636)

One of the best known (and heavily funded) was the CASE Program (Contingencies Applicable for Special Education) at the National Training School for Boys in Washington, D.C. A characteristic of such programs is the scheme of imagery used to refer to the children and to their actions. One CASE report refers to "the principles of behavioral architecture," of "reshaping the lounge to act as a reinforcer" (i.e., charge entrance fee paid in tokens), and students are "sequenced" to provide only materials within their grasp at any given stage (see Institute for Behavioral Research Inc., 1966).

Unfortunately, few of the behavior modification programs have been proven effective at reducing post-release arrests or recommitments. Moreover, the possibility exists that the compliance learned to earn pennies in the institution may or may not carry over into civilian life (see Jones, 1964). More than any other form of program, behavior modification via operant conditioning requires carefully conducted parole followup.

> The "new look at corrections" involves specialized therapy and community-based programs in place of incarceration. One procedure borrowed from learning theory is to reward inmates for good behavior by giving them points which can be exchanged for money, clothing, trips, and so forth. At Draper Youth Center in Alabama, a programmed instructional system was established for inmates as part of the educational process. The CASE project in Washington, D. C., used reinforcement in therapy in the educational program of the National Training School. Inmates could earn points for good academic behavior, which could then be exchanged for food, clothing, rent on rooms, trips, and other such things. The control of behavior under such conditions is easy, and results are remarkable. This design depends on the "hungry rat" model of experimental psychology; a rat is reduced to eighty percent of body weight, and then food is offered as a reinforcement. The model is retained in prisons where subjects are in cages very similar to those in the psychological laboratory. An inmate who is hungry and has but one response to gain food will exhibit a high rate of responding.
>
> The CASE project altered the educational behavior of delinquents, but not the criminal behavior. How does one know that by improving the reading scores of delinquents one is thereby reducing the delinquent behavior? The crucial point is how the delinquent responds in a free operant

> environment. If a delinquent pushes a lever on a teaching machine to get rewarded in prison, will he do something similar when out? The President's Commission on Law Enforcement stated about CASE: "No research has yet been conducted on the maturity of inmates in dealing with analogous discretion in a free community upon release." (Jeffery, 1965, p. 89)

Aversive conditioning is also assuming greater importance, particularly in adult prisons but undoubtedly suitable for juveniles. The dean of hard-line conditioning theorists, Hans Eysenck, makes the interesting observation that aversive treatment dates back to John B. Watson's famous book *Behaviorism.*

> Watson's procedure for producing emotional reactions in Albert, a stolid eleven-month-old infant, was simple but effective. A white rat was offered to the child, and a loud noise was made at the moment when Albert reached out to touch the animal. Repetition of this association between a frightening sound and the white rat soon led to an emotional reaction to the animal alone. Little Albert's ultimate fate is not known, although is was Watson's belief that the newly acquired emotional responses would continue and would "modify personality throughout life." (Eysenck and Beech, 1971, pp. 543–44)

Aversion therapy is often commenced at the demand of others rather than the prisoner or patient, who does not suffer from his condition so much as the societal consequences of it. Hence such an individual is less motivated than a patient who seeks relief.

> Aversion therapy . . . is aimed at behaviors . . . which are socially undesirable, or undesirable in the patient's own long term interests, but which he finds reinforcing at least in part. Alcoholism, drug addiction, homosexuality, fetishism, transvestism, obesity, psychopathic and criminal behavior patterns all clearly fall into this field.
>
> Three main types of aversive stimulation have been used: (1) chemical, usually some drug like apomorphine, which leads to nausea and vomiting; succinylcholine chloride dehydride, which leads to paralysis of the skeletal musculature, including those muscles associated with respiration is another example; (2) electrical, that is shock produced by current from battery and (3) imagery, the patient is asked to imagine some fear producing or nauseating experience, and this [stimulus] often leads to actual nausea and/or anxiety. (Eysenck and Beech, 1971, pp. 575 and 580)

Eysenck gives reasons for predicting widespread use of electrical shock in programs of training, being easier to calibrate and capable of more frequent use with less clinical supervision.

The use of drugs to control behavior is well established in American prisons, and the use of aversive conditioning is merely an extension of the employment of chemical techniques against resistant inmates.

> Gerald B. Walsh of the Legal Aid and Defender Society of Kansas City charged recently that Missouri officials inject prison inmates with Prolixin after making clinical judgments that they are psychotic.

> This drug, a phenothiazine derivative, is advertised as a long-acting "parenteral behavior modifier" lasting about two weeks. It is manufactured by E. R. Squibb and Sons of New York as Prolixin Enanthate under the trade name Fluphenazine Enanthate.
>
> "The drug has been used on some inmates (in Missouri) for as long as two years," Walsh said, "and is equivalent to a 'functional lobotomy'." (Murton, 1972, p. 1)

In another prison, considerable ingenuity is exercised by the staff in making a clinical judgment that an inmate may be psychotic *but repressing the symptoms of his psychosis* and may thus be controlled on dosages of Prolixin. A writer from the Western Center on Law and Poverty, Los Angeles, states that the drug is: "Used for control purposes to undermine resistance and to quiet chronic complainers" (Murton, 1972, p. 1).

If this seems a bizarre reflection of *Clockwork Orange*, it is sobering to note the language used in an official publication of the State of New York:

> "Sociopath" Research Experiment
>
> One of the most difficult problems in prevention of recidivism is treatment of persons who are called "sociopaths" or "psychopaths." Such persons seem to have little regard for their obligations to society or for the threat of conviction and incarceration. It is generally believed that when their behavior takes the form of law violation, they will continue to offend again and again and thus will be persistent offenders. Recent research has suggested that these *persistent offenders do not learn as readily as other people from punishing circumstances, but that with the administration of certain medications their ability to learn can be improved.* If this be so, and if conviction and incarceration or some other sanction can be equated with *the laboratory simulation of punishment* (e.g., mild electric shock), chemotherapy may supply an important aid in preventing the recidivism of this hitherto undeterrable group.
>
> The central hypothesis of this experiment is that the so-called "sociopath" has a deficiency in the production of a hormone (adrenalin), and that such deficiency retards the ability to learn inhibiting impulses from fear-producing experiences. Hence, conviction and imprisonment, even when previously experienced, would not be a fear-producing device to inhibit future anti-social conduct (i.e., individual deterrence).
>
> The Committee has initiated an experiment seeking to explore this hypothesis in terms of *both the extent and duration of increased ability to learn from unpleasant experience* when the hormone, adrenalin, is administered. This experiment is presently being conducted at Clinton Prison under the direction of Ernest G. Poser, Ph.D., Professor of Psychology at McGill University in conjunction with the medical staff of Clinton Prison.
>
> The Committee believes that this research has enormous potential significance in preventing the recidivism of a group heretofore considered hopeless. (State of New York Committee on Criminal Offenders, *Report*, Albany, N.Y., June 1968, p. 8)

Despite Eysenck's prediction, chemical agents are arousing interest and concern among many who view with alarm the increase in aversive conditioning in United States' prisons today. In one California prison inmates have bitterly complained of the torture of receiving an injection that induces severe muscle relaxation similar to *curare* effects to promote negative conditioning while being reminded of aggression.

> *Anectine*, commonly used as a muscle relaxant in abdominal operations, mimics death by suffocation [by partial paralysis of respiratory muscles—G.K.]. Corrections authorities administered the drug to a handful [sic] of inmates at several state prison hospitals . . . while subjects experienced the sensation of drowning authorities told them they must not act violently. (*Behavior Today*, 65:3:23, June 5, 1972)

Active planning for feasibility studies of surgical implantation of brain electrodes, for both conditioning stimuli and monitoring behavior data are underway; at several prisons "corrective brain surgery" has been proposed, and at least in one prison in California, an application for grant funds to support lobotomies and other surgical alteration of criminals is a matter of record.[2]

Whether this is the threshold of an effective means of crime and delinquency control, or merely a stage in the development of further State control of citizens to a degree unimaginable 20 years ago is a disturbing question. We turn to a consideration of the implications of various strategies of delinquency and crime control in the next and last chapter.

[2]Although not aversive treatment, castration has been used to punish or discourage recidivisim of "sex offenders."

Chapter **8**

ALTERNATIVES TO A WAR ON YOUTH

> Ours is a time of obsession with law and order. One manifestation of this obsession is the development of what amounts to a virtual war on youth. (Kenneth Polk and Walter E. Schafer, 1972, p. 7)

8.1 Social Problems

Delinquency in the United States is widely believed to be a social problem that threatens the safety of the public street, the possessions of the propertied, and the sensibilities of the morally conventional. Youth, particularly the youth of the great cities, are viewed by their elders as violent, thieving, and disruptive, addicted to drugs and dreams and the open flaunting of nearly continuous violations of the moral standards of their parents' generation. Officials from the White House to the city council make public statements decrying the trends and calling for increases in funding and personnel for a war on delinquency.

It is not remarkable in itself that this should be so. All societies have been episodically distraught at the deviance and corruption of the young. It takes but the merest dose of reading historical accounts to reassure oneself that what is now seen as a raging problem has also been seen as a problem in previous periods. Each generation suspects its children and deplores a future to be ushered in by their evil ways. Time erases the recollection of previous crusades and alarms. It is nearly beyond belief but nonetheless true that there is to be found a serious, if strident, literature from the 19th century on the ravages of sexual cavorting and public immodesty brought about by the popularity of a new social dance called the waltz.

What is remarkable about our time is that the excesses of youth should be discernible amidst the clashes and violence of the adult portion of the society that so deplores delinquency. Although for over a decade we rained death, disfigurement, irreversible ecological disaster, cultural destruction, population displacement and round-the-clock, round-the-year terror on the men, women, children, and unborn of Indochina, we as Americans yet stand appalled at shoplifting and drug use. A society that has winked at the massacre at My Lai is concerned about street-corner gangs in Los Angeles and Detroit. A society that has countenanced the rape of Appalachia is upset over school vandalism. A nation of alcohol drinkers and pill swallowers passes savage laws for the suppression and punishment of marijuana.

Convinced that the community or nation confronts a social problem in the delinquent misconduct of its children and youth, the governing agencies of communities, and the national government, have developed a rhetoric of force and warfare, combined with the benign symbolism of clinical treatment, to combat deviance. So forceful is this language that careful calculation of some of the costs and side effects is necessary. In this sense it is similar to the calculation of the ecological effects of other social programs.

8.2 The Escalation of Conflict and the Lessons of Ecology

Fundamental to an ecological perspective is the recognition that in nature—and that includes the social biosystem of urban civilization just as the biosystem of a river—there are no isolated events. An action has a series of effects, carried along a complex chain of relationships. The crudest derivations from this principle are helpful in providing a basis from which to approach the problem of the maintenance of order in a free civil society.

The first derivation from the lessons of ecology is that the simple localized elimination of some life form or environmental feature is seldom without disturbance to whatever level of integration is possessed by the system in which it takes place. The simple application of brute force has been known to frequently create more problems elsewhere, or to introduce great disturbance without even solving the immediate problem.

This recognition comes slowly and painfully. We as a people have our roots in an era where the application of heavy technology to production problems and firepower to land-expansion problems were statements of pride. But today serious scholars and the public alike are becoming concerned that the outpouring of technology and energy for the single-minded pursuit of certain social objectives may have brought the world to the edge of environmental collapse—or indeed perhaps over that brink. The market for cheap coal created the strip mine; we are now attempting to calculate the cost of the effects of the strip mine. An interest in killing insects brought DDT; we are now attempting to recover from the effects of DDT, which is everywhere from the Greenland icecap to mother's milk. The ideal of Detroit sales campaigns for a car in every garage brought the freeway, at seven million dollars a mile of construction; we are now attempting to plan around the eight lanes of traffic clogging the immense spans and cloverleafs that have ruthlessly split human communities, whose cost has pre-empted funding of other transit systems. The field of criminal law enforcement itself provides examples nearer at hand. There are clear instances where the effect of a repressive or corrective measure has been to increase the very behavior it is intended to curb. Zinberg and Robertson, in an analysis of marijuana use, comment:

> Officialdom's very attempts to tighten up on marijuana have turned people on to other drugs. Operation Intercept in the fall of 1969 illustrates this. The Nixon administration attempted to cut off the supply of marijuana by initiating the largest search and seizure operation in American history. Everyone crossing the border into the United States from Mexico was stopped and searched. The supply of marijuana was sharply cut off, with the result that people who had previously used marijuana turned to whatever drugs were available. (The *New York Times* of Feb. 27, 1970, reported that) there was an upsurge in heroin use among suburban white middle class high school students shortly after Operation Intercept. (Zinberg and Robertson, 1972, p. 210)

A second derivation of the ecologist's perspective is that a problem does not cease to exist merely by being moved. Sewers flush away the odious waste of our cities, but it comes back on every tide, it eddys in our dying rivers, and it stings our eyes and nostrils in the smog of the metropolis.

A third implication is that nothing comes free in a world of action and reaction. The cost of a motorized society of air conditioners and high-rise living is being reckoned in either brownout and slowdown, or the continued ecological threat of thermal nuclear or air pollution from mammoth power generating stations, and the huge space requirements of power transmission corridors over an entire continent.

There is an analogous ecological cost in laws and law enforcement.

Resources are not infinite, and their allocation to one task necessarily subtracts something from other possibilities. The thrust of a particular program may (and probably will) generate stress elsewhere and will have to be carefully scrutinized and experimented on to detect hidden costs and damages wrought in its wake. Brute force and mindless assaults on "problems" in the single-minded pursuit of certain sociopolitical goals are as dangerous to the fragile structure of civil life as they have proven to be on the surface of our physical world.

These ecological lessons apply to crime control and always have. Schemes, past and present, for dealing with delinquents and criminals are in fact schemes for dealing with particular patterns of stressful relationships, and with clashes and conflicts between generations, classes, races, and the sexes. Proposed solutions imply different costs financially, socially, politically. The solutions proposed have different implications for the maintenance of traditional class and sex hegemonies, for maintenance or change in race relations, local government, the assertion and prevalence of values and codes of group solidarity, for the security or redistribution of property. The widespread application of compulsory psychological counseling, preventive pretrial detention, police surveillance, and correctional confinement under indeterminate or civil commitment procedures, or a decentralized community-based system of regulation and assistance to convicted delinquents or prelabeled probable offenders would each have pervasive effects throughout the governmental and cultural systems of American society.

The question for any society is under what circumstances are criminal (delinquent) definitions and criminal (delinquent) sanctions applied to problems arising in the behavior of people and the relationships between groups? What are the costs and what are the consequences of applying criminal sanctions to a given class of youth behavior? If for example a high intensity lighting system on all streets, a low-light TV scanning system, electronic monitors on all vehicles, and electronic audio bugs in all houses would reduce crime, would the cost in political and social terms be remotely bearable?

The realization that such ecological considerations apply to criminal and delinquency law and law enforcement is not a counsel for restraint; on the contrary, since we are already pyramiding controls upon controls, and escalating both the technology and the scope of their application, extensive and even radical changes must be contemplated in efforts to cope simultaneously with delinquency and the side effects of policies which oppose it. One possibility is a significant cutback in the application of correctional and legal sanctions to the solution of generation conflict, which reinforce traditional values concerning child and youth behavior, maintain traditional sex role differentiation, and postpone real solutions of problems of class, race, and urban communities. Another possibility lies in the expansion of civil rights of youth and the upgrading of the material and political status of those segments of the community that have the highest rates of offender and victimization in delinquency statistics and that bear the heaviest application of police and correctional power. Before either of these longer range measures must come a leveling off and reversal of the present trend to escalation of the conflict.

There are two senses in which it can be said that an escalation of conflict between youth and law enforcement is taking place at present: on the one hand, the employment of more advanced technology and tactics against criminal law violation in general has upped the stakes of confrontation between juveniles and the police. On the other hand, it is prefigured in the appearance of programs proposing more official adjudication and earlier intervention in the private lives of families and youths in an effort to prevent predelinquents from developing into delinquents, the effort to introduce preventive or corrective action earlier in the lives of "delinquent prone" youth, and an effort to control more youth in the community rather than incarcerating them.

The employment of heavier weaponry and military or quasi-military tactics against crime is not primarily directed against all forms of youthful delinquency, with the important exception of combating youth participation in political protest, particularly radical student and nonstudent youth participation in antiwar, race, political, or other demonstrations of various kinds. But even where the quasi-military interpretation of police functions is not directed against juveniles, it forms a context in which increasingly violent confrontations are more likely.

8.3 Surveillance and Hardware

Civilian police and justice systems are different and distinct from military controls. The most salient difference is that military operations are properly directed against an enemy, and police operations are in the interest of the citizens being policed. There are important carryovers however, and among these are the use of weaponry, tactics, and equipment developed and tested in warfare, most recently war in Indochina.

There is little doubt that a vigorous crime control policy has received a great deal of practical support from the development of military weaponry and technology, as well as certain tactics originally used in the "pacification" of populations in military conflict. We have become accustomed to police helicopters, devices for night vision, closed-circuit TV surveillance in banks, supermarkets, and shopping malls, the installation of high intensity illumination in certain areas, and the employment of vehicles, weapons, gasses, armour, and computerization that directly derive from the military. More spectacular military spin-offs include the use of drone planes (Air Force Pave Eagle) flying over remote stretches of the U.S.-Mexican border, relaying signals from sensors buried in the ground to a central computer made by Sylvania and originally used in Laos against guerrillas, in an effort to detect marijuana smuggling (Barkan, 1971). The same article also mentions the use of hidden sensors in a "maximum security" suburb of Washington, D.C., portable surveillance radar capable of scanning through brick walls, and recently declassified night vision sniper scopes made available to police through the Law Enforcement Assistance Administration as further signs of an escalation in technology for the control of citizen populations.

Indeed the logical conclusion of an unrestricted crime contrtol program is a military operation against civilian crime and delinquency. The distinction between a police force enforcing the law among its own citizens, and a military force waging war on some of them, is frequently blurred in the rhetoric of crime control and law-and-order appeals. The call for a "war on crime" may contain more truth than metaphor.

Another manifestation of the employment of heavier tactics of crime and delinquency prevention may be seen in the efforts of some to apply environmental engineering to this end. Often this is concerned with target-hardening efforts such as more secure locks and buildings and cars that are harder to steal (see Decka, 1972). But it also includes means of denying right of access to public space or free movement to various categories of low status or pariah groups in the community who offend not only the law but also middle-class sensibilities. The following example is not about school children but has a familiar ring. Environmental design may be a way of sanitizing the middle class against the poor, the old, the youth, and the unconventional.

> Why should [bus] terminals, like parks, produce crime, and what can be done in terms of urban planning and design to reduce the crime rate in these national crime areas?
>
> One interesting little quasi-experiment in crime control was undertaken recently at the New York City Bus Terminal under the direction of Mr. Jack Rosen, Director, Terminal Department, Port of New York Authority, and Mr. Marvin Weiss, Manager, Bus Terminal.
>
> Bus terminals, in general, are collecting spots for derelicts and petty criminals, and the New York City terminal is no exception. Indigents use the waiting room of the terminal for its benches, rest-rooms, heating, and air conditioning. Elderly Greek men (there is a Greek settlement in the neighborhood) use the terminal as a place for meeting and conversation. Homosexuals and alcoholics also use the facilities of the terminal, as well as using

> the terminal as a place to meet prospective victims or colleagues. Some men live out of lockers, so to speak, at the terminal for weeks at a time, paying twenty-five cents a day rent on a locker.
>
> Because derelicts and alcoholics are nuisances and interfere with the overall operation of the terminal, some measures were taken to cut down on antisocial behavior in the terminal. The center well of the terminal was a favorite spot for homosexuals and hustlers, who could view the flow of traffic from there. This area was cordoned off so that the problem people could not lean on the railing. Bench seats were replaced with bucket seats so that people could not sleep on the seats. Seats were also removed from the phone booths. The women's section of the waiting room was redecorated in light blue and pink, with more feminine accessories, and this kept the men out of the section. The level of lighting was increased in certain crucial areas, certain loading areas and exits of the building were closed at night, and the flow of traffic was contained in one controlled area. Corridors were sealed off and mirrors were placed at blind corners so as to eliminate surprise attacks in isolated sections of the terminal.
>
> These changes, though minor in nature, indicate the direction in which we can move to control behavior via environmental engineering. It is obvious that the environment of a bus terminal creates certain behaviors, so the remedy is to redesign the environment so as to eliminate the behavior. Future terminal construction should be carried out with security as one of the major considerations. (Jeffery, p. 218)

An unusually frank display of enthusiasm for the application of electronic monitors for the continuous surveillance and control of citizens convicted of crime or delinquency is set forth by Ingraham and Smith (1972). Advocating the further development and use of a device called a Behavior Transmitter-Reinforcer attached to a person and allowing a modified missile tracking station in the police department to receive data on the location and activities of the person under the surveillance, these authors claim that several capabilities would be supplied the police. It would enable 24-hour-a-day tracking of individuals with respect to certain prohibited areas or certain prohibited actions. It would allow for immediate capture of the subject. It would provide a recording of his behavior at previous periods prior to an investigation. It would be possible for the police to communicate with him by a tone, by a mild or punishing shock, or by lights. The authors leave little doubt that the hardware for this is at hand, and that the expense is well within government budgets. Moreover such devices can be small enough to be swallowed or surgically implanted inside the subject. They can be rendered beyond the control of the subject to deactivate them or be rid of them or the necessary supporting equipment. Such equipment or implantation could be a requirement for release or parole from confinement, or for probation in lieu of confinement, and hence could enjoy the facade of being "voluntary" (i.e., the subject could decide to languish in jail if he did not consent to have one installed.) In order that the State might be spared the temptations to use the equipment to gather information that might be ruled inadmissable in court (assuming the continued existence of constitutional guarantees of any privacy whatever), Ingraham and Smith recommend

> The parole authorities, if they be the users of this equipment, should have the discretionary power to revoke parole whenever they see fit without the burden of furnishing an explanation. (Ingraham and Smith, 1972, p. 44)

The ramifications of law-enforcement policy and the escalation of conflict can be documented in the 50-year preoccupation with the coercive control of certain forms of drug use in America. Much of the brunt of recent drug control programs has been borne by youth, and certain drug use in particular is strongly associated with age. In the fiasco over marijuana, but also in other forms of drug control and treatment attempts, the problems of generation conflict can be seen writ large.

8.4 The Marijuana Fiasco

"Victimless crimes" pose especially difficult problems to the task of arriving at accurate estimates of either conviction for or commission of the prohibited act. To the extent that no clean citizen-victim steps forward to complain, law-enforcement agents themselves must intrude on the conduct of suspected citizens and themselves serve as the (theoretically) offended party. Nowhere is the peculiar clash between youthful behavior and regulatory zeal more clearly seen than in the several decades of effort to enforce a prohibition on marijuana use.

The most recent available compilation of surveys of marijuana use provides estimates of the total frequency of persons in the United States who smoked marijuana at least once; the review concludes that between 15 and 24 million persons have used marijuana at some time (Subcommittee on Alcoholism and Narcotics, May, 1972, p. 8). The survey data yield different estimates due to variations in methodology. Variation in use by age groups and by region is marked. The western states report higher percentages of persons using marijuana than do other regions of the U.S. A study by Perry, Cisin, and Blater (1971) shows that of all persons aged 18–21, users amounted to 12 percent in the Northwest, 11 percent in the North Central, and 12 percent in the South, compared with the West, where 37 percent of youth are listed as having used marijuana. Two separate studies of persons 18–21 years old in San Francisco and in Contra Costa County reported figures of 32 percent and 35 percent respectively, which compare very closely with the overall percentage estimated for the region. Similarly, a separate study of persons in New York State 14 years and older reports 11 percent of the population had been or were using marijuana, which is consistent with the figure of 12 percent reported for the North Central States by Perry, Cisin, and Blater.

A 1971 study of Josephson *et al.* sampled persons 12–17 years of age and developed somewhat higher estimates of marijuana usage for three regions as follows: Northeast, 20 percent, North Central, 13 percent, South, 11 percent, and West, 23 percent. Both are as yet unpublished and are summarized only in the report of the Subcommittee on Alcoholism and Narcotics: thus the contradiction in estimates remains at present unresolved.

There is no doubt that age is the most dramatic correlate of marijuana use, and that the age of 30 or 35 years represents the great divide in this country between pot and martinis. Education, or at least school and college campus social life, is also associated with marijuana smoking. Only 2 percent of persons aged 35 and older use marijuana, compared with 22 percent 18-to-24-year-old nonstudents, 22 percent of high school students, and 42 percent of college students.

Kaplan's survey of high school youth in San Mateo County, California, showed increases in marijuana use with advancing grades and over a period from 1968 to 1969. Another study of college students runs the estimate higher. As of 1971 [at a West Coast University] 69 percent of undergraduates had used an illicit drug; 19 percent had tried LSD, and 21 percent were using marijuana regularly (weekly or more often) (Blum, 1972, p. 2–3).

Blum's voluminous studies document how widely distributed is drug use in all age groups. (Note that certain drugs, like alcohol or prescription barbiturates, are not criminalized as are marijuana and LSD.)

> The San Mateo County study for 1971, based on questionnaires given to over twenty-two thousand students in public and parochial schools, indicated that 59 per cent of high school boys reported marijuana experimentation and 44 per cent reported regular use (ten times or more during the past year); in contrast, 48 per cent of the girls reported experimentation, and 31 per cent reported regular use. Amphetamine use was at a peak for girls during their sophomore year (27 per cent) and for boys during the senior year (27 per cent). LSD use peaked for girls in the junior year at 15 per cent and in the junior year for boys too, at 21 per cent. Alcohol was used mostly by senior boys and girls—84 percent for boys and 79 per cent for girls. In the seventh grade, 18 per cent of the boys and 13 per cent of the girls had tried marijuana; 3 per cent of the boys and 2 per cent of the girls had tried LSD; and 5 per cent of the seventh grade boys and 6 per cent of the girls had used amphetamines. Sixteen per cent of the seventh-grade boys and 11 per cent of the seventh-grade girls had used alcohol ten times or more; and 16 per cent of the boys and 14 per cent of the girls had smoked cigarettes. The Monterey County data (Fries, 1969), which included some Mexican-American families, showed that 46 per cent of the twelfth-grade students reported marijuana experimentation, with

> 16 percent reporting regular use. In the seventh grade, 8 per cent of the students reported illicit experimentation, and none reported regular use. By the seventh grade, 66 per cent had tried alcohol, and 39 per cent had used tobacco. The most commonly used illicit, unsanctioned drug in the seventh grade was glue (used by sniffing), with amphetamines being the second most used.
>
> Some data also exist for adult drug use in communities from which our samples were taken. One study (Blum and Associates, 1969a) showed that, for one community, two-thirds of the adults had used conventional social and proprietary drugs, prescribed painkillers, and psychoactive substances (either on prescription or over-the-counter psychoactives). One-sixth of the population had taken these as well as illicit or exotic substances. (Blum, p. 3)

The United States policy on narcotics and marijuana use deserves a chapter in itself. No single cause of youthful arrest and harassment so clearly illustrates the extremity of the conflict between the young and the old. The striking feature exhibited in the concern with marijuana and narcotic use is not that such use clashes with a Puritanical philosophy of self-restraint, but that it so closely parallels in all essentials the habits of middle America that have long since been *de*criminalized.

The Secretary of HEW has termed alcohol the most abused drug in the United States today, adding the conservative estimate that nine million citizens, making up ten percent of the U.S. labor force, are compulsive and chronic alcoholic drinkers. The same news release reported that alcohol is cited in half of the violent deaths in highway accidents annually, that public drunkenness is the cause of one third of all arrests by police, and that hospitalization for alcoholism and alcohol-caused physical conditions is a major item in medical care. Then comes a statement that is so restrained and reasonable as to be astonishing to millions of young persons. The report concludes that "the criminal law is *not* an appropriate device for preventing or controlling health problems. To deal with alcoholic persons as criminals because they appear in public when intoxicated is unproductive and wasteful of human resources" (HEW, 1972).

The examples of marijuana and narcotic use provide a striking contrast in policy. Far less frequently used than alcohol, and with even the Federal estimates of its contribution to arrests, fatalities, or illness running much lower than alcohol, drug use is punished by uniquely punitive national and state laws which for half a century have functioned to define drug use as an offense following close upon the heels of murder and kidnapping. And a very substantial portion of the persons affected by drug law enforcement are youthful.

The figures released for 1970 by the FBI in their Uniform Crime Reports show 53 percent of persons arrested for drug use were under 21 years of age, and 25 percent of such persons were under the age of 18.

It has not always been so. Some research on drug use calls attention to the correlation between the shift of drug use to despised groups in the nation—the young, the poor, the nonwhite—and the severity with which drug use laws were formulated and enforced. Troy Duster writes:

> Certain social categories lend themselves more to moral condemnation than others. Whereas the lower and working classes had the smallest proportion of addicts in 1900, in 1969 they constituted the overwhelming majority of known addicts. Whereas Blacks were less than 10% of addict population in 1900, they are now more than half of the addicts known to law enforcement agencies. Whereas there were formerly more women than men addicted, the ratio is now at least seven to one for men. Whereas the middle aged predominated in 1900, youth is now far and away the most likely of known offenders. The list could go on, but the point is simply that middle America's moral hostility comes faster and easier when directed toward a young, lower class Negro male than toward a middle aged, middle class white female. (Duster, p. 21)

The intensity of reaction of law enforcement to marijuana use is related to its symbolic association with youth, particularly with a youthful put-down of conventional social patterns in favor of a nonconventional life style. Like shoulder-length hair or chopped motorcycles, it is the life style symbolized that arouses anxiety and attempts to eliminate the practice. The "hippie" life pattern embodies fundamental moral and material challenges to the American middle-class ethos, and criminal penalties on marijuana smoking are a potent weapon with which to chastise those who would live in this manner. Hips, political radicals, war protestors, draft resistors, blacks, Chicanos, and other noncriminals, as well as persons suspected of violations of criminal law, can be arrested or at least harassed by the selective use of marijuana laws.

The deescalation of conflict over youth requires the repeal of primary criminal legislation on marijuana use and sale.

> Marijuana should be legal to grow for self use, much as the liquor law permits manufacture of wine for home use; marijuana should be feasibly regulated by the liquor control commissions in the states. Marijuana use should only be penalized when intoxication leads to risk to public, as alcohol does in drunk driving. Marijuana use in short, should be as legal and simple as a martini or a bottle of beer. (Kaplan, 1971)

8.4 Community Corrections: The Danger of Treatment Sprawl

In adult and juvenile justice and corrections, evaluations of effects of confinement on post-release crime have been a cause of despair. States have begun to attempt to divest themselves of jails and prisons and invest in "community based" systems.

> In the literature on alternatives to institutionalization, the descriptive term "community treatment" has been applied to probation and parole (these being the traditional noninstitutional correction measures); probation alone (parole in this case considered an extension in the community of institutional treatment); aftercare (juvenile parole) and halfway house "bridges" between the institution and free society; community-based institutions (located in the community, with perhaps some use of community resources for health, education or recreation purposes); noninstitutional boarding arrangements such as foster care, small group homes, semi-institutional or "open" cottage living; forestry, work, or outdoor probation camps; and a number of daycare programs, outpatient clinics, and nonresidential work/group-therapy programs. Occasionally, community treatment is viewed as encompassing efforts which are essentially preventive, such as street work with antisocial gangs or early identification and treatment of "predelinquents." The latter are of necessity community-based because in most cases the formal processes of criminal justice have not been invoked. (NIMH, 1971c, p. 1)

The move away from incarceration, on almost any grounds, pragmatic, constitutional or moral, can be endorsed enthusiastically, without the assumption that community programs are at present anymore effective. However, given the newness of some of the community programs, and recalling some of the now embarrassing optimism about prison treatment programs that had been bruited about in the 1950's, there is at present the danger that *community treatment could be the means where by increased control will be imposed on youth who are now subject to the lighter hand of probation, without any compensating gains to the community at large or the youth themselves.*

Sometimes the evidence is ambiguous. One form of program that would be termed community corrections is *graduated release,* permitting a prison or reformatory inmate daytime excursions into the free community (usually for work) while retaining custody over him at night. A study of "work release" by Waldo, Chiricos, and Dobrin reported at the 1972 meetings of the American Sociological Association tested attitudinal effects of a prison work-release program for adults in Florida. Their study does not deal with recidivism, but with perception of opportunity, achievement motivation, self-esteem, legalism, and ideology. The authors call the last "focal concerns" and hypothesize for work-release inmates: "A shift in focal concerns away from predominantly lower class and towards predominantly middle class." They administered questionnaires to inmates at the beginning and end of work-release program. The work-release inmates were compared with a random sample of inmates eligible for work release but who in accordance with the study design were not assigned to it. There were *no discernible differences* between work release and controls except paradoxically that work-release inmates scored lower on self-esteem. Work-release subjects did not show significant change in scores on legitimate opportunities, achievement-motivation, legalism, and self-esteem. It is speculated that the failure of the program to produce hypothesized attitude change may be due to the perception of fear and contempt felt for prison inmates in the outside community, the disenchantment felt in entering the labor market (Florida law defined many occupations as illegal for convicted felons), or other experiences of social rejection. The authors suggest that the stigma of the ex-convict may arouse as much community hostility as the crime did. The authors do not report data on this speculation however. The effects of this work release on parole survival have not yet been reported. The mere increase of surveillance, to say nothing of getting restriction, might increase the violation rate on probationers and parolees. Moreover, there is a lesson from case load size studies that suggests that more intensive contact may not necessarily show a profit when evaluated.

For many years probation and parole authorities decried high case loads as the cause of problems in community supervision of juveniles. How could agents do a good job with case loads of 75–150? But it has been shown that reduction of case load size in itself does not bring about a reduction in recidivism. Studies in Alameda County, California, in 1965, San Francisco in 1965, and throughout the State of California from 1953 to 1964, have effectively demonstrated that small case loads may lead to more revocations, or no difference in number of revocations, depending on the "risk" level of the parolees, and the revocation policy of the youth authority. (See the article by Stuart Adams in Carter and Wilkins, 1970, pp. 364–380, and see also NIMH, 1971, p. 6.) Adams reviews a series of studies of the Special Intensive Parole Unit, the Narcotic Treatment and Control Project, the Parole Work Unit Program, an L.A. County program, and the Intensive Supervision Caseload Project for girls. The factor of case load size was usually found to be *unrelated* to differences in rates of parole success or failure. It is possible to calculate the risk level or probability of parole failure from predictor items known at the time of release (such as age at first arrest, offense, drug history, etc.). High risk (poor prognosis) boys showed a high rate of parole revocation and return to custody whether on large or small case loads; low risk (favorable prognosis) showed a low rate of revocation whether on large case loads, or small; youth classed as middle-risk level did better on small case loads than on large case loads.

8.5 Street Work with Gangs

The unanticipated consequences of intervention may be seen in the experience of "detached worker" programs dealing with urban gangs. Malcolm Klein, in an unusually useful volume assessing the tactics and results of detached worker programs for youthful gangs in Los Angeles, reviews several studies of such programs in other cities. He begins by stating that great importance has been attached to gangs, together with an abiding popular faith that by working with gangs they can function positively in the community. He notes that gang delinquency is a symbol of youthful lawlessness and threats to public safety and security. The significance of gangs has been much affected by the practice of inferring that all offenses in which more than one youthful perpetrator is charged (where two or more persons are alleged to have been involved in a violation) are evidence of gang delinquency.

> Gang delinquency constitutes a minor portion of even big city delinquency . . . which in turn is only one of many serious problems of urban America. The place of the gang in professional literature in the mass media is exaggerated way out of proportion to its contribution to our social ills. (Klein, 1971, p. 125)

He notes that juvenile status offenses (actions that are neither assault nor property offenses and that are not illegal for adults (e.g., curfew violation) are by far the most common of juvenile gang arrests in Los Angeles; that theft is much higher than assault among gang members; that assault and carrying weapons accounts for 10 percent of charges leveled against gang members by police. He concludes that gangs are not primarily assaultive, and that most of their collective behavior is not illegal in any form (See Klein, 1971, Chapter 4). He also cites Thrasher's classic study of over 1300 gangs in Chicago, in which theft, burglary, and robbery were the most frequent criminal charges; a Philadelphia study in which only 23 percent of all gang member charges were against persons; and Miller's Boston data, which show low assault rates in relation to impersonal property crimes (see Thrasher, 1963; Robin, in Klein, 1967, p. 15; Miller, in Klein, 1967, p. 25).

Despite the popularity of the idea of detached gang worker programs, only a few have been systematically evaluated with proper statistical designs. A project studied by Miller in the Roxbury section of Boston from 1954 to 1957 drew on local citizen's groups, family casework, interagency cooperation, and detached workers in touch with street gangs. The findings did not demonstrate the effectiveness of this program on reduction of delinquency when treatment gangs were compared with a control sample of gangs who did not receive detached worker services. In fact, there was some increase in the seriousness of offenses in the gangs that did have a detached worker contact. The Chicago Youth Development Project in 1960 to 1966 likewise is listed by Klein as having failed in delinquency reduction (Klein, 1971, p. 50). Two other projects with which Klein was associated in Los Angeles provided most of the material for his book. The Group Guidance Project showed an increase rather than a decrease in offenses among gang members, and another project (The Ladeno Hills project) showed a reduction in the number of offenses but not a reduction in the rate per gang member (Klein, p. 51).

Klein satisfies himself that the four gang projects evaluated were energetically implemented, and that failure of any of them to produce dramatic results can hardly be attributed to indifferent administration of the program. He argues that "detached work programs, as constituted in the recent past, are *not* effective in the reduction of gangs or the 'violent' activities associated with gangs. They may inadvertently *contribute* to gang violence" (Klein, p. 51).

How can the detached worker program bring about so perverse a result as the *increase* of gang-connected offenses? By group programming, arranging activities for gang participation (dances and outings for example), mediating gang disputes, arranging or supervising truces between warring gangs, conferring status on a gang by the presence of a youth worker in its hangout, and a number of similar activities, the program recognizes the gang as an important neighborhood or municipal entity; it increases the basis of group interaction, providing both occasion and motivation for individuals to orient their conduct in terms of the gang. In so doing the programs are increasing the cohesiveness of the gang, which, in turn, exerts greater group influence toward conformity. With gang cohesiveness increasing, the likelihood of both intergang violence and collective predatory activities increases, as well as the likelihood that police surveillance, often suspicious of the detached worker program, will increase; this situation in turn drives up the arrest rate for gang members who are being reached by the program.

Klein comments:

> The Group Guidance Project was first and foremost an experiment; its ultimate value, as with any experiment, resides in what it tells us about possible future operations.... If we take the data as suggestive rather than demonstrative, we can hypothesize that (a) group programming, especially in the absence of activities designed to wean away gang members, leads to greater levels of gang delinquency; (b) group programming leads to recruitment (of new gang members); (c) detached workers inadvertently become sources or foci of gang cohesiveness, and their removal following achievement of this focal status will lead to a reduction in gang cohesiveness; (d) these effects apply in particular to gangs of lower initial cohesiveness; (e) the effects on offense behavior will be particularly manifest among high companionship offenses and among young boys." (Klein, 1971, p. 139)

One could array various community supervision or control arrangements on a continuum ranging from essentially doing nothing to a highly conditional liberty status after a sentence in prison. Counsel and release at the police station level is the most frequently employed diversion technique and is responsible for tens of thousands of youth being shunted from further contact with the justice machinery. Settling "out of court," dismissing charges at juvenile court, or suspending sentence are means by which the juvenile court has moved accused persons out into the community without further ado.

Probation is another level of supervision in lieu of confinement but one in which intervention is often minimal.

If there is to be any gain from a new wave of community treatment, it would be important to preserve the foregoing strategies. Intensive supervision or clinical counselling, aid or assistance, or special educational, training, or group activities, in lieu of confinement, probation, and police warnings presumably require justification beyond that now deemed appropriate for sentencing a youth to probation.

Klein's findings and their extension to a hypothesis about possible deleterious effects of other "programming" for juveniles confirm the prudence of what Edwin Schur has recently advocated as a policy of "radical non intervention" (Schur 1973). It is even reasonable to consider exploring an extension of this thinking to other community correctional programs. We may inquire whether probational or post-release supervision, particularly group implemented treatment or counseling, may not inadvertently contribute to recidivism of youth rather than reducing it. Comparisons should be made between flat release and programs such as half-way houses, parole, outpatient clinics, and other parole and post-parole arrangements.

Ralph England's review of evaluation studies of probation suggests that the most important component in the success rate on probation is the self-correcting propensity of many probationers to avoid further law violation. Thus, nothing more burdensome need be or should be imposed. Consequently intensive community supervision should be thought of not as something new to do to probationers or as something occurring after prison but as something to do *instead of* commitment to prison.

It is here that some of the studies to date offer supporting evidence. The Community Delinquency Control Project was begun in 1964 in response to overcrowding in California youth institutions. Intensive small case loads and the use of foster or group home placement, activity groups, and counseling services constituted the program. Commitments to confinement went down, and a slightly lower parole violation rate has been reported. Commenting on this program, the NIMH team write:

> The Community Delinquency Control Project, like the Community Treatment Project, has not yet provided unqualified support for the thesis that management of offenders in the community is significantly more successful in preventing further crime than is institutionalization. However, both programs have demonstrated a more important fact: offenders normally

not released to community supervision can be as safely and at least as effectively handled in intensive supervision programs without institutionalization. (NIMH, 1973c., p. 10)

8.6 School as a Custodial Institution

A child born into a society such as the United States faces nearly 12 years of a compulsory benefit: organized schooling. The laws of the various states require that the child be enrolled in some school, public or private, until he is legally free to leave and enter the labor force, or, until quite recently, was subject to being drafted into involuntary service in the military.

The school, being nearly inescapable, becomes an institutional setting for not only education but for the struggles waged by youth against what they often experience as the heavy hand of adult control. The school, being required by law, must exert whatever control is necessary to maintain order and continuity from one day to the next, one year to the next.

The contribution of the school itself to delinquent behavior is hard to separate from other influences in the lives of youth, simply because the school is so pervasive. A number of likely specific influences may be cited from various studies:

1. Failure of a child to succeed in school work decreases rewards for that child while in school; it may also lead to attempts to withdraw or rebel.
2. Misconduct according to school regulations also decreases rewards, and increases penalties for staying in school.
3. The experience of irrelevance of curriculum content and indifference or incompetence of teachers increases felt need to leave school.
4. Lower competence, poorer resources, and decreased amenities of lower-class area schools decrease rewards of school attendance for children who attend these schools.
5. Truancy, school misbehavior, and school-related (or school-referred) offenses may directly lead to a delinquency record.

Many feel that the school itself may be an avenue of upward mobility, or at least, a passage to the adult labor force and adult way of life; failure in school places children in serious and early conflict with the established power in the society.

> The fact that adolescents mostly go to school and adults mostly go to work helps to explain the phenomenon of "teenage culture." It is not the whole explanation. The affluence of industrial societies creates the material basis for cultural differentiation. That is to say, industrial societies allocate to adolescents substantial discretionary purchasing power, and this enables adolescents to demand (and obtain) distinctive clothing, motion pictures, phonograph records, recreational facilities, and eating and drink-

ing establishments. From the viewpoint of understanding delinquency, however, the extension of formal education is probably more important than the development of the adolescent market. The reason for this is that mass formal education has created serious problems of life goals for adolescents with educational disabilities. For academically successful adolescents, school is a bridge between the world of childhood and the world of adulthood. For children unwilling or unable to learn, school is a place where the battle against society is likely to begin. (*Delinquency and Youth Crime*, 1967, p. 143)

Others have severely criticized the schools themselves for failure to educate children who are labeled "unlikely to respond."

> . . . it has become fashionable to attempt to explain the persistent fact of the academic retardation of Negro children in terms of general environmental disabilities. . . . These explanations tend to emphasize the pattern of environmental conditions as the cause which depresses the ability of these children to learn [such as]: culturally disadvantaged, minority groups socially neglected, socially deprived, school retarded, educationally disadvantaged, lower socio economic groups, socio economically deprived, culturally impoverished, culturally different, rural disadvantaged, deprived slum children. . . . [But] to what extent are these contemporary social deprivation theories . . . alibis for the educational default: the fact that these children by and large do not learn because they are not being taught effectively and they are not being taught because those who are charged with the responsibility of teaching them do not believe they can learn, do not expect that they can learn and do not act toward them in ways which help them to learn. (Clark, pp. 130–31)

The President's Commission has reviewed an extraordinary amount of material on the public school in relation to delinquency. It has commented on the dual possibilities of social control of behavior in the schools: on the one hand, the schools are obliged to provide direction and maintain sufficient order that instruction and learning can take place; on the other hand, the application of controls can transform the schoolroom into a battleground of clashing age-sets, cultures, and classes, pushing the nonconforming child further and further from rewarding learning and personal development, and creating the conditions for being officially labeled "underachiever," "problem pupil," emotionally disturbed, truant, or dropout.

The possibility then exists for school to be a compulsory custodial institution for many children. Some studies for urban schools have recorded the almost Dickensian tactics employed by harried staff to maintain conformity to the daily routines imposed. Such tactics include the location of leaders among rebellious pupils and publicly challenging and decisively humiliating them in class.

School under such conditions is an adversary process rather than a learning experience. (For an account of one school see Levy, 1970.)

The same study presents many instances of individual teachers making a transition from a personal approach to pupils to an impersonal and categorical disciplinary approach for personal survival in a conflictful situation.

> Midway's (pseudonym for high school) teachers act individually with the intention of preventing their own destruction and not of maintaining general control. But in taking those measures which make their life bearable in Midway, they also do a job for the school. As each teacher evolves those tactics that allow him to survive, he unwittingly contributes to the unavoidable process of general control. (Levy, 1970, p. 57)

There is some empirical indication for a paradox: the stress of compulsory school for the unsuccessful pupil can be productive of delinquent behavior, and this stress can actually be relieved by the premature withdrawal of the child from school. In some cases, the function of dropping out is to reduce delinquency. A study by Elliott reports data on 743 tenth-grade boys who entered high school in September, 1959. Taking school records covering a three-year period ending with class graduation in June, 1962, a comparison was made of delinquency rates of boys while in and out of school. Each boy was classified as *graduate* or *dropout* (those who moved to another district were excluded). Of the 743 boys, 182 were dropouts and 561 were graduates. Official contact reports by police, sheriff, and other law enforcement agencies constituted the measure of delinquency. Rates were computed on the basis of number of days graduates were in school or dropouts were in and out of school. The analysis was done separately for high and lower socioeconomic status families. Data are displayed in Table 8.1.

Data suggest that among boys from lower SES areas, the delinquency rate for eventual school dropouts is higher than for lower-class boys who

TABLE 8.1

Delinquent Referral Rate per 10,000 School Days for Boys In and Out of School

Socioeconomic Status	*In School*			
	Subsequent Graduates	*Subsequent *Dropouts*	*School*	*Out of School *Dropouts*
Lower	4.13	8.70	4.96	2.42
Higher	4.92	4.95	4.92	2.63
Total	4.34	8.03	4.95	2.75

*Same boys at two different times.
Source: Adapted from Elliott, 1968, p. 197.

eventually drop out; that it is not appreciably different for higher SES graduates and dropouts; that leaving school reduces the delinquency rate for boys who are delinquent while in school. It is to be regretted that severity of offense, type of disposition, and age of boy are not investigated or reported, since the post-school decrease in rate could partly be accounted for by the boy going out of circulation in the court, either because he is confined or because he has attained the age of majority. Nonetheless, the data are suggestive that the stress imposed by school, particularly by poor or unsuccessful school performance, is associated with a higher offense rate than are the vicissitudes of premature departure from high school. The school is viewed by some, however, not as an exacerbating factor in the genesis of delinquent clashes with adult authority but as a potential instrument for the detection and treatment of "potentially delinquent" youngsters. Prominent among a long list of proponents of early detection programs is Senator Abraham Ribicoff, who in the mid-1960's proposed that

> What is needed, it seems to me, is an all out effort to make sure that potentially dangerous youngsters are identified early, effectively brought into treatment and continuously treated as long as necessary to assure decent lives for themselves and safety for society. (Ribicoff, cited in Szasz, 1970, p. 147)

Szasz also reviews a plan proposed by S. Radin for diagnosis and the monitoring of school children by mental health programs. He quotes Radin as urging:

> the clinical team . . . acquire detailed information about the child and his *family* through social casework, psychological interviews, home visits and psychiatric observations—all in an endeavor to understand not only the individual personality of the varied constituents of the family but also the manner in which members interact with one another in both healthy and neurotic fashions. *After an investigation and subsequent understanding of the family has been completed a total plan for the child and his family is formulated* (Szasz, 1970, p. 152)

When it is recalled that community psychiatry specialists were estimating that "about 7.5 to 12% of grade school children are sufficiently emotionally disturbed to require treatment" (quoted by Szasz, 1970, p. 145) the scope of such a program, *were* it ever to be implemented, is to be counted in the millions of children.

8.7 The Politics of Deescalation

It must be left to the reader to develop the policy implications of data on delinquent behavior and delinquency control programs.

The following have been advocated recently and are suggestive of the issues that must be confronted in the intelligent appraisal of policies of delinquency control.

Many critics have noted that the sheer magnitude of the operations of delinquency adjudicating and control operations is a factor in the difficulty of developing effective and nonabusive policies. The scope could be reduced by a more restrictive definition of the authority of agencies to intervene in the lives of young persons. Deescalation of the conflict could be approached by a sharper and more restricted focus of juvenile justice.

It is the responsibility of juvenile justice, law enforcement, and corrections to deter, control, and adjudicate criminal offenses committed by young persons. Excursions into more diffusely defined categories, including obedience to family, sexual precocity, and attendance at school, are beyond the reach of the court. The business of the court should be focused on and restricted to actions, which if committed by adults, would constitute indictable behavior (misdemeanors, felonies, ordinance violation). The juvenile court is no more likely to succeed in articulating and upholding moral or aesthetic standards of proper child conduct than the adult courts have been.

Edwin Lemert has sharply called this to attention in a statement prepared for the President's Commission:

> Truancy, runaways, and incorrigibility already have been shown to be diffuse categories whose conversation into statutory foundation for jurisdiction by the juvenile court is made superficially plausible by unexamined assumptions that they are precursors to delinquency. If the juvenile court is to proceed with approximate uniformity which is a central attribute of law, the weakness of such statutes either as substantive law or as legislative directives for the development of administrative rules is patent. The reasons may be summarized as follows: (1) They lack common meaning from one jurisdiction to another, or between different judge's rulings in the same jurisdiction, (2) they are not derived from any fixed criteria, (3) they assign criminal responsibility to children in many instances where blame or responsibility cannot be determined or where closer investigation would reveal their actions to have been reasonable normal responses to highly provocative or intolerable situations.
>
> If the image of the juvenile court is to be changed from that of a multifarious problem-solving agency, and its function circumscribed to be more consistent with available means, when *its statutory jurisdiction cannot be allowed to rest upon subjective definitions.* Furthermore, if it is *to avoid the risk of making delinquents by a labeling process,* statutes *whose vagueness in some localities allow almost any child, give compromising circumstances, to be caught up in the judisdictional net of the court, must be* altered. (President's Commission: Juvenile Delinquency and Youth Crime, 1967, p. 153)

The most straightforward argument for this proposal is that by so doing a considerable burden would be lifted from youth who, even if exonerated, are handicapped by a juvenile court record. An honest affirmative reply to a question about ever having been arrested, or disclosure of an arrest record, may be cause for an applicant for employment not to be considered. It is reported in one major metropolitan area that 75 percent of the city's employment agencies do *not* make a referral when the applicant has an arrest record, regardless of whether the person was acquitted (see Lerman, 1970, p. 139). The same article discusses numerous abuses of juvenile arrest and adjudication records. By the reduction in the number of juvenile court actions, there would be a corresponding reduction in the stigmatizing of these youths years later.

The policies of the juvenile justice system reflect the most profound and wide-ranging ambivalences and anxieties concerning interpersonal relations between the sexes. Everywhere until very recently, and in many jurisdictions at present, the law and the workings of the agencies of juvenile justice and correction sharply distinguished between male and female. The prevailing cultural assumption of the inferiority of females is reflected in many jurisdictions, in males being beyond the reach of the juvenile court by age 16 while females remain under their authority until age 18. For example, the State of New York in its Family Court Act defined a person in need of supervision as a male under 16 or a female under 18 who is incorrigible, ungovernable, habitually disobedient, or beyond lawful control.

Strouse quotes cases illustrating the effect of differential treatment by gender:

> Jane M., 16½, is brought to court by her parents because she stays out too late at night, hangs around with a boy her parents have forbidden her to see, and has contracted a venereal disease. She is, claim the parents, "incorrigible, ungovernable, and habitually disobedient." She is declared by the court to be a "Person in Need of Supervision," and sent to a state training school for "rehabilitation."
>
> John M., 16½, is brought to court by his family because he stays out too late at night, hangs around with a "wild" group, and has contracted a venereal disease. He is, claim his parents, "incorrigible, ungovernable, and habitually disobedient." "Boys will be boys," the judge admonishes, as he informs John's parents that John is past the age (16) for non-criminal treatment of boys in Family Court. As long as he has not committed a crime, no court action may be taken against him.
>
> Cheryl P. and David B., both 15, have run away from home to live together in a friend's loft. Neither has been to school for six months. They are found by a truant officer and taken to Family Court, where the judge finds them both to be "Person in Need of Supervision." He sends David to the Warwick School for Boys, and Cheryl to the Brookwood Center for Girls. Both have problems in training school, and each time their respective commitments come up for review, they are renewed and extended. David remains at Warwick for three years, until he is 18 and must be

> released because he is no longer under the jurisdiction of the Family Court. Cheryl stays in Brookwood for five years, until she is 20, at which age girls are no longer under the jurisdiction of the Family Court. (Strouse 1970)

Sheridan, writing in 1967, notes Children's Bureau national data, which shows 52 percent of female delinquency allegations were for conduct that is not criminal for adults, while in the same years only 21 percent of male juvenile delinquency cases were for such actions (see W. Sheridan, 1967).

Time, in an article in May, 1972, provides "three typical cases" of the operation of New York's Wayward Minor statute, which dates back to 1923.

> Esther Gesicki, now 20, had been placed in a foster home after her mother entered a state mental institution. When her mother was released, Esther wanted to rejoin her, but a social worker forbade it. Esther ran away and was later locked up.
>
> Marion Johnson, 20, who had lived in foster homes since the age of 5, bore an illegitimate child at 17. A social worker tried to persuade her to give up the child, but she refused and was adjudged "wayward."
>
> Dominica Morelli, 17, had been sexually assaulted by one of her alcoholic mother's four husbands. Moved to a foster home, she ran away and returned to her mother. Placed under a curfew, she made a trip without her mother's permission and was promptly charged with violating probation. (*Time,* May 1972, p. 59)

Although the statute had gradually fallen into only infrequent use in the spring of 1972, there were 236 youths who were under sentence to parole or probation on the charge of being wayward. The court in New York has recently overturned the law and has ordered the State to find other ways of dealing with this "problem."

Such regulations and laws are properly challenged at present since they impose or assume distinctions and liabilities associated with sex roles that are being repudiated by adults and prohibited by law or constitutional amendment. The juvenile court should cease attempting to force females into one or another version of a sex role, and in particular should cease differential enforcement of sex conduct laws.

The schools must be relieved of many of the social control functions that they now, in many cases, exercise. This is particularly the case in the high delinquency areas of central cities. The sociologist Kenneth Clark has commented on the social class conflict as mediated in the school.

> The clash of cultures in the classroom is essentially a [social] class war, a socio-economic and racial warfare being waged on the battleground of our schools, with middle-class and middle-class aspiring teachers provided with a powerful arsenal of half truths, prejudices and rationalizations, arrayed against . . . working class youngsters. This is an uneven balance, particu-

> uarly since, like most battles it comes under the guise of righteousness. (Clark, p. 129)

Finally, it may be wisdom as much as disenchantment to regard modern society as containing structured sources of conflict. Juvenile delinquency frequently develops along the fissures and cleavages of the conflict. To the extent that delinquency represents a clash between the affluent and the poor, the favored and the despised, the strong and the weak, it is exceedingly unlikely that any program could in and of itself rehabilitate, pacify, constrain, intimidate, or isolate troublesome youth.

Are clashes between white police and nonwhite central city youth violations of the criminal law or manifestations of basic social conflict? On both sides of the issue we may resolve the doubt by label and by announced ideology, but both may be rejected by the other side or the inert public. Lunch counter sit-ins by civil rights activists a decade ago seem clear politics to most views today; the Young Lords, Panthers, and other city groups assume a quasi-political stance that is accepted by some of the community and rejected as a mask for criminality by others. Critics assert that police and prison tactics toward blacks are political rather than criminalistic in their orientation. It is deemed improper and bordering on the unconstitutional when a parole board questions a black prisoner about his attitude toward the Panthers before deciding his release date and fitness for parole. As movements like Gay Liberation organize to disavow the pathology label and gain support and tolerance for a deviant status, as the pressure mounts for the legalization of marijuana, and as the repeal of laws decriminalize the former crime of abortion, we move increasingly away from the consideration of delinquent and criminal behavior and toward the consideration of a political process. And in politics it is merely a ruse to label one's opponents criminal.

Ultimately crime and delinquency are, in some degree, indicators of basic conflicts in a society and are in this respect likely to remain resistant to even highly effective specific controls.

REFERENCES

ADAMS, P., LEILA BERGE, NAN BERGER, MICHAEL DUANA, A. S. NEILL, AND ROBERT OLLENDORF

1971 *Children's Rights.* Wellingborough, England: Elek Books.

ADAMS, STUART

1971 "Some Findings from Correctional Case Load Research," in Robert Carter and Leslie Wilkins (eds.), *Probation and Parole,* pp. 364–379. New York: John Wiley & Sons, Inc.

ALLEN, FRANCIS

1965 "Juvenile Court and the Limits of Juvenile Justice," in Francis Allen, *Borderland of Criminal Justice,* pp. 43–64. Chicago: University of Chicago Press.

AMERICAN FRIENDS SERVICE COMMITTEE

1971 *Struggle for Justice: A Report on Crime and Punishment in America.* New York: Hill and Wang.

ARNOLD, WILLIAM

1970 *Juveniles on Parole.* New York: Random House, Inc.

ASCH, SOLOMON

1953 "Effects of Group Pressure Upon the Modification and Distortion of Judgments," in Dorwin Cartwright and Alvin Zander, *Group Dynamics.* Evanston, Illinois: Row Peterson & Co.

BARKAN, ROBERT

1971 "Bringing the Toys Home." *Pacific Research and World Empire Telegram* (November-December).

BAYLEY, DAVID, AND HAROLD MENDELSOHN

1969 *Minorities and the Police: Confrontation in America.* New York: The Macmillan Company.

BEAUMONT, GUSTAVE DE, AND ALEXIS DE TOCQUEVILLE

1833 *On the Penitentiary System in the United States.* Reprint, Philadelphia: University of Pennsylvania Press.

BECKER, HOWARD

1963 *Outsiders: Studies in the Sociology of Deviance.* Glencoe, Illinois: The Free Press.

BEGANSKY, JAMES P.

1972 "An Inmate Family System in a Juvenile Correctional Institution," Second Paper (Spring) Department of Sociology, University of Hawaii (mimeographed).

BEKER, JEROME, AND DORIS HEYMAN

1972 "A Critical Appraisal of the California Differential Treatment Typology of Adolescent Offenders," *Criminology* 10:1 (May): 3–59.

BENSMAN, JOSEPH, AND ISRAEL GERVER

1963 "Crime and Punishment in the Factory: The Function of Deviancy in Maintaining the Social System," *American Sociological Review* 28 (August): 588–98.

BENTHAM, JEREMY

1939 "Principles of Morals and Legislation," in Edwin Burtt (ed.), *The English Philosophers from Bacon to Mill.* New York: The Modern Library.

BERGER, NAN

1971 "The Child, the Law and the State," in Paul Adams, *et al., Children's Rights.* Wellingborough, England: Elek Books.

BERGIN, ALLEN

1971 "Evaluation of Therapeutic Outcomes," in Allen Bergin and Sol Garfield (eds.), *Handbook of Psychotherapy and Behavior Change,* pp. 217–270. New York: John Wiley & Sons, Inc.

BIRD, CAROLINE

1972 "Welcome, Class of '72 to the Female Job Ghetto," *New York* 29 (May): 31–34.

BLOCH, HERBERT

1968 "Juvenile Delinquency: Myth or Threat," in John R. Shatton and Robert Terry *Prevention of Delinquency,* pp. 8–18. New York: The Macmillan Company.

BLUM, RICHARD H. AND ASSOCIATES

1972 *Horatio Alger's Children.* San Francisco, California: Jossey Bass, Inc.

BLUMBERG, ABRAHAM

1967 *Criminal Justice.* Chicago, Illinois: Quadrangle Books, Inc.

BLUMER, HERBERT

1971 "Social Problems as Collective Behavior," *Social Problems* 18:3 (Winter): 298–306.

BREDEMEIR, HARRY, AND RICHARD STEPHENSON

1965 *The Analysis of Social Systems.* New York: Holt, Rinehart & Winston, Inc.

CAYTON, CHARLES

1971 "Emerging Patterns in the Administration of Juvenile Justice, *Journal of Urban Law* 49: 377–398.

CHAMBLISS, W.

1967 "Types of Deviance and the Effectiveness of Legal Sanctions," *Wisconsin Law Review* 3 (Summer): 704–713.

CHAPIN, WILLIAM

1972 *Wasted: The Story of My Son's Drug Addiction.* New York: McGraw-Hill, Inc.

CHILTON, ROLAND

1964 "Continuity in Delinquency Area Research: A Comparison of Studies for Baltimore, Detroit and Indianapolis," *American Sociological Review* 29 (February): 71–83.

CHIRICOS, THEODORE, AND GORDON WALDO

1970 "Punishment and Crime: An Examination of Some Empirical Evidence," *Social Problems* 18:2 (Fall): 200–217.

CHRISTEN, T. JONASSEN

1949 "A Reevaluation and Critique of Logic and Some Methods of Shaw and McKay," *American Sociological Review* 14 (October): 608–614.

CLARK, KENNETH

1965 *Dark Ghetto.* New York: Harper and Row, Publishers.

COHEN, ALBERT, ALFRED LINDESMITH, AND KARL SCHUESSLER

1956 *The Sutherland Papers.* Bloomington: University of Indiana Press.

COHEN, ALBERT, AND JAMES SHORT

1966 "Crime and Juvenile Delinquency" in R. K. Merton and R. Nisbet, *Contemporary Social Problems.* New York: Harcourt, Brace, and World.

COHEN, BERNARD

1969 "Internecine Conflict: the Offender" in Thorsten Sellin and Marvin Wolfgang, *Delinquency: Selected Studies.* New York: John Wiley & Sons.

CLOWARD, RICHARD, AND LLOYD OHLIN

1961 *Delinquency and Opportunity.* London: Routledge & Kegan Paul, Ltd.

DAHRENDORF, RALF

1959 *Class and Class Conflict in Industrial Society.* Stanford, Calif.: Stanford University Press.

DEMERATH, N. J., AND R. A. PETERSON

1967 *System, Change and Conflict.* Glencoe, Illinois: The Free Press.

DERSCHOWITZ, ALAN M.
1968 "Psychiatry in the Legal Process: A Knife that Cuts Both Ways." *Judicature* 51 (10): 370–377.

DONNELLY, RICHARD C., JOSEPH GOLDSTEIN, AND RICHARD D. SCHWARTZ
1962 *Criminal Law: Problems for Decision in the Promulgation, Invocation and Administration of a Law of Crimes.* Glencoe, Illinois: The Free Press.

DOUGLAS, JACK
1971 *American Social Order: Social Rules in a Pluralistic Society.* Glencoe, Illinois: The Free Press.

DOUGLAS, JACK
1970 *Youth in Turmoil.* Rockville, Maryland: NIMH, Center for Studies of Crime and Delinquency.

DOWNES, D. M.
1966 *The Delinquent Solution.* Glencoe, Illinois: The Free Press.

DUNHAM, WARREN, AND MARY E. KNAUER
1954 "Juvenile Court and its Relationship to Adult Criminality." *Social Forces* 32: 290–295.

DURKHEIM, EMIL
1947 *The Division of Labor in Society* (tr. George Simpson). Glencoe, Illinois: The Free Press (originally Paris: F. Alcan, 1895).

DURKHEIM, EMIL
1915 *Elementary Forms of Religious Life.* New York: The Macmillan Company (originally Paris: F. Alcan, 1912).

DUSTER, TROY
1971 *The Legislation of Morality.* New York: The Free Press.

ELLIOTT, DELBERT
1968 "Delinquency, School Attendance and Dropout," in John Stratton and Robert Terry, *Prevention of Delinquency,* pp. 191–199. New York: The Macmillan Company.

EMERSON, ROBERT M.
1969 *Judging Delinquents: Context and Process in Juvenile Court.* Chicago, Illinois: Aldine Publishing Company.

EMPEY, LAMAR T.
1967 *Alternatives to Incarceration.* Washington, D. C.: Office of Juvenile Delinquency and Youth Development.

EMPEY, LAMAR T., AND STEVEN LUBECK
1972 *The Provo Experiment: Evaluating Community Control of Delinquency.* Lexington, Mass.: Lexington Books, D. C. Heath and Company.

EMPEY, LAMAR T., AND STEVEN G. LUBECK, WITH RONALD L. LAPORTE
1971 *Explaining Delinquency: Construction, Test, and Reformulation of a Sociological Theory.* Lexington, Mass.: Lexington Books, D. C. Heath and Company.

ENGLAND, RALPH
1957 "What is Responsible for Satisfactory Probation and Post Probation Outcome?" *Journal of Criminal Law Criminality and Police Science* 47 (March-April): 667–677.

EYSENCK, H. J., AND H. R. BEECH
1971 "Counter Conditioning and Related Methods," in Allen Bergin and Sol Garfield, *Handbook of Psychotherapy and Behavior Change,* pp. 543–611. New York: John Wiley & Sons, Inc.

FISHER, SETHARD
1955 "Informal Organization in Correctional Settings." *Social Problems* 13:2 (Fall): 214–223.

FORER, L.
1970 *No One Will Listen: How Our Legal System Brutalizes the Youthful Poor.* New York: The John Day Company, Inc.

GARABEDIAN, PETER, AND DON GIBBONS (eds.)
1970 *Becoming Delinquent: Young Offenders and the Correctional Process.* Chicago, Illinois: Aldine Publishing Company.

GARFINKLE, HAROLD
1956 "Conditions of Successful Degradation Ceremonies." *American Journal of Sociology* 61: 420-424.

GLASER, DANIEL, BERNARD LANDER, AND WILLIAM ABBOTT
1971 "Opiate Addicted and Non Addicted Siblings in a Slum Area." *Social Problems* 18:4 (Spring): 510-521.

GLASER, DANIEL, AND MARY SNOW
1969 "Public Knowledge and Attitudes on Drug Abuse in New York State." Albany, New York: New York State Narcotic Addiction Control Commission.

GLUECK, SHELDON, AND ELEANOR GLUECK
1956 *Physique and Delinquency.* New York: Harper & Row, Publishers.

GOFFMAN, ERVING
1961 *Asylums.* New York: Doubleday & Company, Inc., Anchor Books.

GOFFMAN, ERVING
1963 *Behavior in Public Places.* Glencoe, Illinois: The Free Press.

GOFFMAN, ERVING
1959 *Presentation of Self in Everyday Life.* New York: Doubleday & Company, Inc., Anchor Books.

GOLD, MARTIN
1970 *Delinquent Behavior in an American City.* Belmont, California: Brooks-Col Publishing Co.

GOLDSTEIN, JOSEPH
1960 "Police Discretion Not to Invoke the Criminal Law: Low-Visibility Decision in the Administration of Justice." *Yale Law Journal* 69 (March): 543–588. (Reprinted in Donald R. Cressey and David A. Ward, *Delinquency, Crime and Social Process.* New York: Harper & Row, Publishers, 1969).

GOODE, ERICH
1972 *Drugs in American Society.* New York: Alfred A. Knopf, Inc.

GORDON, MILTON
1958 *Social Class in American Sociology.* Durham, North Carolina: Duke University Press.

GOULDNER, ALVIN
1970 *The Coming Crisis in Western Sociology.* New York: Basic Books.

HAKEEM, MICHAEL
1958 "A Critique of the Psychiatric Approach to Crime and Correction." *Law and Contemporary Problems* XXIII:4 (Autumn): 650–657.

HARTUNG, FRANK
1965 *Crime, Law and Society.* Detroit: Wayne State University Press.

HAWES, JOSEPH
1971 *Children in Urban Society: Juvenile Delinquency in 19th Century America.* New York: Oxford University Press.

HEFFER, RAY E., AND C. HENRY KEMPE
1968 *The Battered Child.* Chicago, Illinois: University of Chicago Press.

HIRSHI, TRAVIS
1969 *Causes of Delinquency.* Berkeley, California: University of California Press.

HOOD, ROGER, AND RICHARD SPARKS
1970 *Key Issues in Criminology.* New York: McGraw-Hill, Inc.

HOOTON, ERNEST
1939 *Crime and the Man.* Cambridge, Massachusetts: Harvard University Press.

HUMPHREYS, LAUD
1969 *Tearoom Trade.* Chicago, Illinois: Aldine Publishing Company.

ILLINOIS
1880 Biennial Report of Board of State Commissioners of Public Charities, State of Illinois, Springfield, Ill.: H. W. Rokkor (quoted in Platt p. 107).

REPORT OF THE INDIAN HEMP DRUGS COMMISSION
1893–1894 (7 volumes) London: Irish University Press.

INGRAHAM, B., AND GERALD SMITH
1972 "The Use of Electronics in the Observation and Control of Human Behavior and Its Possible Use in Rehabilitation and Parole." *Issues in Criminology* 7:2 (Fall): 35–53.

INSTITUTE FOR BEHAVIORAL RESEARCH INC.
1966 Contingencies Applicable to Special Education of Delinquents (mimeographed)

IRWIN, JOHN
1970 *The Felon.* Englewood Cliffs, New Jersey: Prentice-Hall, Inc.

JAMAN, D.
1968 "Parole Outcome for First Releases for Selected Commitment Offenses by Time Served Before First Release." Sacramento, California: Research Division Measurement Unit, Department of Corrections.

JEFFERY, CLARENCE RAY
1971 *Crime Prevention Through Environmental Design.* Beverly Hills, California: Sage Publications.

JEHU, DEREK, PAULINE HARDIKER, MARGARET YELLOLY, AND MARTIN SHAW
1972 *Behavior Modification in Social Work.* New York: John Wiley & Sons, Inc.—Interscience Books.

JESNESS, C. F.
1965 *The Fricot Ranch Study.* Research Report No. 47. Sacramento: State of California, Department of the Youth Authority.

JONES, JAMES A.
1964 "The Nature of Compliance in Correctional Institutions for Juvenile Offenders." *Journal of Research in Crime and Delinquency* 1:2 (July): 83–95.

KAHN, ALFRED J.
1967 "From Delinquency Treatment to Community Develop-

ment," in Lazarsfeld *et al.* (eds.), *The Uses of Sociology*. New York: Basic Books, Inc.

KAPLAN, JOHN
1971 *Marijuana: The New Prohibition*. New York: Pocket Books.

KAPLAN, LEONARD V.
1969 "Civil Commitment as You Like It." *Boston University Law Review* 49 (1): 14–45.

KASSEBAUM, GENE
1970 "Strategies for the Sociological Study of Criminal Correctional Systems," in Robert Habenstein (ed.), *Pathways to Data*. Chicago, Illinois: Aldine Publishing Company.

KASSEBAUM, GENE, DAVID A. WARD, AND DANIEL M. WILNER
1971 *Prison Treatment and Parole Survival: An Empirical Assessment*. New York: John Wiley & Sons, Inc.

KATZ, JAY (ed.)
1972 *Experimentation with Human Beings*. New York: Russell Sage Foundation.

KING, RUFUS
1972 *The Drug Hang-up: America's Fifty Year Folly*. New York: W. W. Norton & Company, Inc.

KIRESUK, T., AND R. E. SHERMAN
1968 "Goal Attainment Scaling: A General Method for Evaluating Comprehensive Community Mental Health Programs." *Community Mental Health Journal* (4): 443–453.

KLEIN, MALCOLM
1971 *Street Gangs and Street Workers*. Englewood Cliffs, New Jersey: Prentice-Hall, Inc.

KLEIN, MALCOLM
1972 "Police Disposition and Juvenile Recidivism." Paper at meeting of American Sociological Association.

KOBRIN, SOLOMON
1952 "Conflict of Values in Delinquency Areas." *American Sociological Review* 16 (October): 654–656.

KOBRIN, SOLOMON
1971 "The Formal Logical Properties of the Shaw McKay Delinquency Theory," in Voss and Peterson, *Ecology, Crime and Delinquency*. New York: Appleton-Century-Crofts.

KRAMER, JOHN C.
1970 "The State Versus the Addict: Uncivil Commitment." *Boston University Law Review* 50:1 (Winter): 1–22.

KRASNER, LEONARD
1971 "The Operant Approach in Behavior Therapy," in Allen Bergin and Sol Garfield, *Handbook of Psychotherapy and Behavior Change*. New York: John Wilev & Sons, Inc.

LA FAVE, WAYNE
1965 *Arrest: The Decision to Take a Suspect into Custody*. Boston, Massachusetts: American Bar Association.

LANDER, BERNARD
1954 *Towards an Understanding of Juvenile Delinquency*. New York: Columbia University Press.

LEMERT, EDWIN
1967 *Human Deviance, Social Problems and Social Control*. Englewood Cliffs, New Jersey: Prentice-Hall, Inc.

LERMAN, PAUL
1971 "Child Convicts." *Trans-Action* (July-August).

LEVY, GERALD
1970 *The Ghetto School: Class Warfare in an Elementary School*. New York: Pegasus.

LEVY, MARION
1952 *The Structure of Society*. Princeton, New Jersey: Princeton University Press.

LIAZOS, ALEXANDER
1972 "The Poverty of the Sociology of Deviance: Nuts, Sluts and Perverts." *Social Problems* 20:1 (Summer): 103–120.

MACFADEN, WILLIAM E.
1971 "Changing Concepts of Juvenile Justice." *Crime and Delinquency* 17:2 (April): 131–141.

MATZA, DAVID
1969 *Becoming Deviant*. New York: John Wiley & Sons, Inc.

MATZA, DAVID
1964 *Delinquency and Drift*. New York: John Wiley & Sons, Inc.

MCCORD, JOAN, WILLIAM MCCORD, AND EMILY THURBER
1968 "The Effect of Foster Home Placement in the Prevention of Adult Antisocial Behavior," in John R. Stratton and Robert Terry, *Prevention of Delinquency*. New York: The Macmillan Company. pp. 178–183.

MCCORD, WILLIAM, JOAN MCCORD, AND IRVING ZOLA
1959 *Origins of Crime: A New Evaluation of the Cambridge-*

Somerville Youth Study. New York: Columbia University Press.

McEachern, Alex, and Riva Bauzer
1967 "Factors Related to Disposition in Juvenile Police Contacts," in Malcolm W. Klein (ed.), *Juvenile Gangs in Context*. Englewood Cliffs, New Jersey: Prentice-Hall, Inc.

Merton, Robert
1957 "Social Structure and Anomie," in *Social Theory and Social Structure*. Glencoe, Illinois: The Free Press.

Meyer, Henry, Edgar Borgotta, and Wyatt Jones
1965 *Girls at Vocational High*. New York: Russell Sage Foundation.

Milgram, Stanley
1964 "Behavioral Study of Obedience," in Warren Bennis Edgar Schein, David Berlew, and Fred Steele (eds.), *Interpersonal Dynamics*. Homewood, Illinois: The Dorsey Press.

Miller, Frank, Robert Dawson, George Dix, and Raymond Parnas
1971 *Criminal Justice Administration and Related Processes*. Mineola, New York: The Foundation Press.

Miller, Walter B.
1962 "The Impact of a Total Community Delinquency Control Project." *Social Problems* 10:2 (Fall): 168–191.

Mills, C. Wright
1942 "The Professional Ideology of Social Pathologists." *American Journal of Sociology* 60: 165–180.

Monahan, Thomas
1957 "Family Status and the Delinquent Child." *Social Forces* 35: 250–258.

Morrison, Arthur
1946 *A Child of the Jago (1896)*. London: Penguin Books, Inc.

Musgrove, F.
1964 *Youth and the Social Order*. Bloomington, Indiana: Indiana University Press.

Nasatir, Michael, *et al.*
1966 "Atascadero." *Issues in Criminology* 2 (1): 29–46.

National Institute of Mental Health
no date *Criminal Statistics*. DHEW Publication HSM-72-9094.

NIMH Center for Studies of Crime and Delinquency
1971 *Civil Commitment of Special Categories of Offenders*. Washington, D. C.: U. S. Government Printing Office.

NIMH Center for Studies of Crime and Delinquency
1971 *Community Based Correctional Programs.* Washington, D. C.: U. S. Government Printing Office.

Neumeyer, Martin
1961 *Juvenile Delinquency in Modern Society.* New York: D. Van Nostrand Company, Inc.

Newman, Donald
1966 *Conviction: The Determination of Guilt or Innocence Without Trial.* Boston: American Bar Association.

New York University Law Review
1968 "Due Process for the Narcotic Addict: The New York Compulsory Commitment Procedures." *New York University Law Review* 43 (December): 1172–1193.

Notch, Frank, and Milton Bloombaum
1968 "A Smallest Space Analysis of Gang Boys Behavior." *Pacific Sociological Review* 11:2 (Fall): 116–122.

Nye, F. Ivan
1958 *Family Relationships and Delinquent Behavior.* New York: John Wiley & Sons, Inc.

O'Donnell, John A.
1965 "The Relapse Rate in Narcotic Addiction: A Critique of Follow Up Studies," in Daniel Wilner and Gene Kassebaum (eds.), *Narcotics.* New York: Blakeston-McGraw-Hill Book Company, Inc.

Packer, Herbert
1968 *The Limits of the Criminal Sanction.* Stanford, California: Stanford University Press.

Parsons, Talcott
1951 *The Social System.* Glencoe, Illinois: The Free Press.

Parsons, Talcott
1937 *Structure of Social Action.* New York: The McGraw-Hill Book Company, Inc.

Pike, L. O.
1873 *A History of Crime in England,* 2 Vols. London, England: Smith, Elder.

Piliaven, I. and S. Briar
1964 "Police Encounters with Juveniles." *American Journal of Sociology* 70: 206.

Platt, Anthony
1969 *The Child Savers: The Invention of Delinquency.* Chicago, Illinois: The University of Chicago Press.

POLK, KENNETH, AND WALTER E. SCHAFER
1972 *Schools and Delinquency*. Englewood Cliffs, New Jersey: Prentice-Hall, Inc.

POWELSON, DAVID, AND REINHARD BENDIX
1951 "Psychiatry in Prison." *Psychiatry* 14: 73–86.

PRESIDENT'S COMMISSION ON LAW ENFORCEMENT AND ADMINISTRATION OF JUSTICE
1967 *Juvenile Delinquency and Youth Crime*. Washington, D. C.: U. S. Government Printing Office.

QUINNEY, RICHARD
1971 "Crime: Phenomenon, Problem and Subject of Study," in Erwin O. Smigel (ed.), *Handbook on the Study of Social Problems* pp. 209–246. New York: Rand McNally & Company.

REASONS, CHARLES, AND JACK KUYKENDALL
1972 *Race, Crime and Justice*. Pacific Palisades, California: Goodyear Publishing Co.

REMINGTON, FRANK, DONALD NEWMAN, EDWARD KIMBALL, MARYGOLD MELLI, AND HERMAN GOLDSTEIN
1969 *Criminal Justice Administration: Materials and Cases*. Indianapolis, Indiana: The Bobbs-Merrill Company, Inc.

RICHETTE LISA AVERSA
1969 *The Throwaway Children*. Philadelphia, Pennsylvania: J. B. Lippincott Company.

ROBISON, JAMES, AND GERALD SMITH
1971 "The Effectiveness of Correctional Programs." *Crime and Delinquency* 17:1 (January): 67–80.

ROBINSON, W. S.
1950 "Ecological Correlations and the Behavior of Individuals." *American Sociological Review* 15 (June): 351–357.

ROEN, SHELDON
1971 "Evaluative Research and Community Mental Health," in Allen Bergin and Sol Garfield, *Handbook of Psychotherapy and Behavior Change*. New York: John Wiley & Sons, Inc.

ROLDE, EDWARD, JOHN MACH, DONALD SCHERL, AND LEE MACHT
1970 "The Maximum Security Institution as a Treatment Facility for Juveniles," in *Juvenile Delinquency*, James Teele (ed.), pp. 437–443. Itasca, Illinois: F. E. Peacock Publishers, Inc.

ROSEN, LAWRENCE, AND STANLEY TURNER
1967 "An Evaluation of the Lander Approach to Ecology of Delinquency." *Social Problems* 15 (Fall): 189–200.

ROTHMAN, DAVID

1971 *The Discovery of the Asylum: Social Order and Disorder in the New Republic.* Boston, Massachusetts: Atlantic-Little, Brown and Company, Inc.

RUBEN, SOL

1949 "The Legal Character of Juvenile Delinquency." *Annals of the American Academy of Political and Social Science* 261 (January) (Reprinted in Teele, 1970, pp. 4–10).

SANDERS, WILEY B.

1970 *Juvenile Offenders for a Thousand Years.* Chapel Hill, North Carolina: University of North Carolina Press.

SCARPITTI, FRANK R., AND RICHARD M. STEPHENSON

1971 "Juvenile Court Dispositions: Factors in the Decision-Making Process." *Crime and Delinquency* 17:1 (April): 142–151.

SCHUESSLER, KARL, AND DONALD CRESSEY

1950 "Personality Characteristics of Criminals." *American Journal of Sociology* (March): 476–484.

SCREIBER, PAUL

1960 "How Effective Are Services for Treatment of Delinquents?" Washington, D. C.: Social Security Administration.

SECRETARY OF HEALTH, EDUCATION AND WELFARE

1972 *Marijuana and Health: Second Annual Report to Congress.* Washington, D. C.: U. S. Government Printing Office.

SELLIN, THORSTEN, AND MARVIN E. WOLFGANG

1969 *Delinquency: Selected Studies.* New York: John Wiley & Sons.

1964 *The Measurement of Delinquency.* New York: John Wiley & Sons, Inc.

SHAW, C., AND H. MCKAY

1969 *Juvenile Delinquency and Urban Areas* (rev. ed.). Chicago, Illinois: University of Chicago Press.

SHELDON, WILLIAM H.

1949 *Varieties of Delinquent Youth.* New York: Harper & Row, Publishers.

SHERIDAN, WILLIAM H.

1967 "Juveniles Who Commit Non-Criminal Acts–Why Treat in a Correctional System." *Federal Probation* 31:1 (March): 26–30.

SHERIF, M.

1935 "A Study of Some Social Factors in Perception." *Archives of Psychology* 187.

SHORT, J. F. JR., AND F. I. NYE
1958 "Extent of Unrecorded Juvenile Delinquency." *Journal of Criminal Law, Criminology and Police Science* 49 296–302.

SHORT, JAMES, AND FRED STRODBECK
1965 *Group Process and Gang Delinquency*. Chicago, Illinois: University of Chicago Press.

SHULMAN, HARRY
1961 *Juvenile Delinquency in American Society*. New York: Harper & Row Publishers, Inc. (esp. pp. 354–375).

SKOLNICK, JEROME
1966 *Justice Without Trial*. New York: John Wiley & Sons, Inc.

SPROTT, W. J. H.
1952 "Principia Sociologica." *British Journal of Sociology* 111:3 (September): 203–221.

STAPLETON, W. V., AND L. E. TEITELBAUM
1972 *In Defense of Youth*. New York: Russell Sage Foundation.

STROUSE, JEAN
1972 "To Be Minor and Female: The Legal Rights of Women Under 21," *Ms. Magazine* (August): pp. 70–75.

SUMNER, HELEN
1971 "Locking Them Up." *Crime and Delinquency* 17:1 (April): 168–179.

SUTTLES, GERALD
1968 *The Social Order of the Slum: Ethnicity and Territory in the Inner City*. Chicago, Illinois: University of Chicago Press.

SZASZ, THOMAS S.
Ideology and Insanity: Essays on the Psychiatric Dehumanization of Man. New York: Doubleday and Company.

TEELE, JAMES
1970 *Juvenile Delinquency*. Itaska, Ill.: F. E. Peacock Publishers, Inc.

TERRY, ROBERT M.
1970 "Discrimination in the Handling of Juvenile Offenders by Social Agencies" in Peter G. Garabedian and Don C. Gibbons (eds.), *Becoming Delinquent: Young Offenders and the Correctional Process*. Chicago: Aldine Publishing Co.

TITTLE, CHARLES R.
1969 "Crime Rates and Legal Sanctions." *Social Problems* 16:4 (Spring): 409–423.

TULCHIN, SIMON H.
1939 *Intelligence and Crime: A Study of Penitentiary and Re-*

formatory Offenders. Chicago, Illinois: University of Chicago Press.

VINTER, ROBERT
1967 "The Juvenile Court as an Institution." President's Commission: *Juvenile Delinquent Youth Crime.*

VOLD, GEORGE
1958 *Theoretical Criminology.* New York: Oxford University Press.

VOLKMAN, ARTHUR
1958–59 "A Matched Group Personality Comparison of Delinquent and Non-Delinquent Juveniles." *Social Problems* (Winter): 238–245.

VOSS, HARWIN L., AND DAVID M. PETERSON
1971 *Ecology, Crime and Delinquency.* New York: Appleton-Century-Crofts.

WALD, PATRICIA, PETER HUTT, *et al.*
1972 *Dealing with Drug Abuse: A Report to the Ford Foundation* (The Drug Abuse Survey Project). New York: Praeger Publishers, Inc.

WALDO, GORDON, AND SIMON DINITZ
1967 "Personality Attributes of the Criminal: An Analysis of Studies 1950–1965." *Journal of Research in Crime and Delinquency* 2 (July): 185–202.

WALLACE, WALTER (ed.)
1972 *Total Institutions.* Chicago: Aldine Publishing Co.

WARD, DAVID A., AND GENE KASSEBAUM
1965 *Women's Prison: Sex and Social Structure.* Chicago, Illinois: Aldine Publishing Company.

WEINER, NORMAN, AND CHARLES WILLIE
1971 "Decisions by Juvenile Officers." *American Journal of Sociology* 77:2 (September): 199–210.

WEISSMAN, HAROLD (ed.)
1969 *Individual and Group Services in the Mobilization for Youth Experience.* New York: Association Press.

WHEELER, GERALD R.
1971 "Children of the Court: A Profile of Poverty." *Crime and Delinquency* 17:1 (April): 152–159.

WILKINS, LESLIE T.
1965 *Social Deviance.* Englewood Cliffs, New Jersey: Prentice-Hall, Inc.

WILSON, JAMES Q.
1973 "Police Work in Two Cities" in Earl Rubington and Martin

S. Weinberg, *Deviance: An Interactionist Perspective.* New York: The Macmillan Company, pp. 161–172.

WINES, ENOCH C.

1880 *The State of Prisons and of Child Saving Institutions in the Civilized World.* Cambridge, Massachusetts: Harvard University Press.

WOLFGANG, MARVIN E., ROBERT M. FIGLIO, AND THORSTEN SELLIN

1972 *Delinquency in a Birth Cohort.* Chicago, Illinois: University of Chicago Press.

ZELENY, LESLIE D.

1933 "Feeblemindedness and Criminal Conduct." *American Journal of Sociology* 38 (January): 564–576.

ZEITLIN, IRVING

1968 *Ideology and the Development of Sociological Theory.* Englewood Cliffs, N.J.: Prentice-Hall, Inc.

ZIMRING, F.

1971 *Perspectives on Deterrence.* U. S. Public Health Service Publication 205b. Washington, D. C.: U. S. Government Printing Office.

ZINBERG, NORMAN, AND JOHN ROBERTSON

1972 *Drugs and the Public.* New York: Simon and Schuster, Inc.

ZWERIN, MICHAEL

1969 *The Silent Sound of Needles.* Englewood Cliffs, New Jersey: Prentice-Hall, Inc.

INDEX